AFRICAN AMERICAN FOLKTALES

Stories from Black Traditions in the New World

Selected and Edited by

Roger D. Abrahams

PANTHEON BOOKS
NEW YORK

Since this copyright page cannot accommodate all permissions
acknowledgments, they appear on pages 325-327.

Library of Congress Cataloging in Publication Data

African American folktales : stories from black traditions in the new world /
selected and edited by Roger D. Abrahams.
p. cm.
Originally published: Afro-American folktales. © 1985. (Pantheon fairy tale
and folklore library). Includes bibliographical references.
ISBN 0-375-70539-2
1. Afro-Americans—Folklore. 2. Tales—United States. 3. Blacks—
Caribbean—Folklore. 4. Tales—Caribbean. I. Abrahams, Roger D. II. Title.
III. Series: Pantheon fairy tale and folklore library.
GR111.A47A38 1999 398.2'089'96073—dc21 98-42200 CIP

Book design by Ray Hooper

Printed in the United States of America

['99] 9 8 7 6 5 4 3 2 1

AFRICAN
AMERICAN
FOLKTALES

Also by Roger D. Abrahams

African Folktales

*Singing the Master: The Emergence of African American Culture in the
    Plantation South*

*To the great scholar-warriors in
the Transatlantic campaign,
William A. Bascom and Richard M. Dorson*

Now you are going to hear
lies above suspicion.

—Zora Neale Hurston

CONTENTS

PREFACE

These tales have come from many parts of the New World where Afro-American communities were established during plantation times or after emancipation in the nineteenth century. I have included stories from throughout the huge area where plantations were worked, from coastal South and Central America to the Caribbean and, of course, the American South. Although most of the communities from which the stories were collected are within the English-speaking sphere of influence—where an anglophonic Creole is spoken—I have not resisted dipping into the rich patois of Haiti, Guadaloupe, and Louisiana whenever I found representative materials that had already been translated into English.

A few texts are taken from early travel reports and plantation journals —the oldest is from 1815—but most come from documents produced when the most extensive collecting was carried out, beginning in 1881 with the first of Joel Chandler Harris's Uncle Remus collections and proceeding through the 1920s. For more contemporary texts, I have used mostly materials that I recorded in the United States and the Caribbean. In almost all cases, the titles to the stories are my inventions, my attempt to give the reader a hint about the subject and tone of the story to come.

A number of Afro-Americans have collected these stories, but most collecting has been carried out by whites. In retrospect, this does not seem as important as the fact that, with the exception of Zora Neale Hurston's great book *Mules and Men* and a very few others, tale gathering was carried out by individuals who did not live in the communities in which the tales had been maintained. Today, the major differences in quality seem to arise from whether the tales were collected as they were usually performed, by collectors doing their recording as part of a documentation of group life, or by those who were just passing through, trying to get as many stories and songs and riddles as possible in whatever time they had been able to give to their fieldwork.

Following the Harris tradition of rendering tales in dialect, not only through the use of vernacular forms of speech but also by making orthographic modifications of standard English spellings and diacritical markings, most of the collections culled from were originally printed in a style that the contemporary reader would find difficult to read. Moreover, such texts are replete with reminders of the ugliest side of stereotyping. There are thus two very good reasons for making the changes in language and tone that the reader will encounter herein.

In the hands of some collectors, including Harris, the spelling and the cadences of the vernacular used in these early gatherings add up to an honest and reasonable attempt to record local speech variations. But the retellings of the tales by Harris and his followers gave them a kind of literary shape and finish that are never found in actual oral renditions. This serves up to us stories told from beginning to end, and without the repetitions, mistakes, and hesitations that characterize oral tellings; it does not record the performance as accurately as one finds in most collections that come from folklorists who have had the benefit of tape-recorded and transcribed "texts." Moreover, we simply cannot get beyond the racist resonances that the Uncle Remus-style tellings continue to carry, precisely because the stories are rendered in the dialects of slavery times. I have attempted to take some of this stigma away by using contemporary spellings, and by changing some of the vernacular turns of phrase that would have been familiar to the nineteenth-century reader but that have lost their currency—and thus their pungency—today.

In one regard, however, the Harris style does reflect the storytelling context nicely. He presents the stories as told to a group of young children, thus providing a setting for the tales and personalizing them. He puts them in the mouths of storytellers who may be interrupted, questioned, asked to apply the tales to local situations and happenings. In such reminiscences we still do not have versions of the tales as told by blacks to one another in a regular and familiar setting. This point is significant, for in such situations the narrator can assume that nearly everybody knows the stories and therefore need not follow the rule that they must be told from beginning to end. The version we are given always assumes that the fictional hearer has not heard the story before.

The "dialect" itself commonly draws, willy-nilly, from a lingua franca that had developed along coastal Africa; it had a Portuguese as well as local African vocabulary, and with a sound system and grammar developed in this Old World trade setting. Thus, when they came to the New World, the slaves already had a means of communication that transcended the problems of forging a community from so many different cultural and linguistic groups in the Old World. Once in the New World, the speakers of this West African Creole began to draw strongly on the vocabulary of the Europeans who had brought them to the New World, and even more, on the language of the plantocrats. Thus we find in areas colonized by France a francophonic Creole or patois, such as that spoken in Haiti, Martinique, and some places in Louisiana; Papiamentu, spoken in Curacao and Aruba and other Dutch possessions and using vocabulary from Spanish, Portuguese, and English as well as Dutch; and English Creole of various sorts, the best known being Gullah in the Sea Islands off South Carolina and Georgia and Jamaican Creole. Most of the stories in this book were recorded in one or another Creole. To most non-Creole-speaking readers, these renderings in their original form are at best extremely difficult to understand.

Making it even more difficult for readers, jocular storytelling may be judged by how quickly and fluently the talk of the characters can be rendered and how many ranges of voice the taleteller can draw upon. The trickster himself is often portrayed as having a lisp; other animal characters have their own characteristic way of producing their talk, so that a master storyteller may scream, laugh, shout, rasp, whisper, and imitate in some equally stretched manner the way an animal, devil, witch, or ghost might talk.

I have recast these stories in the standard vernacular of the American "common reader" while attempting to maintain the cadences of the personal style of the storyteller and its local tradition of telling. A number of reporters, like Harris and Zora Neale Hurston, developed literary storytelling styles that were very much their own yet that developed directly out of the vernacular. Where I draw on the work of such literary figures, I stay as close as possible to the style in which they couched their tales, recognizing that I cannot also include the surrounding details that they provided, which gave the relationships between the storyteller as a character and his hearers. Other collectors, such as Arthur Huff Fauset, Elsie Clews Parsons, and J. Mason Brewer, simply wrote down tales as close as possible to what they heard. I have tried to maintain the spirit of the storytelling.

The process of transcribing and translating tales from their oral form to a readable written one inevitably reshapes the material; I have employed many changes to convey better an oral style in a literate format. As a folklorist, I am conscious of the impact of some of these changes, simply because the professional idea is to "transcribe faithfully" what our "informants" performed. In traditional cultures the entertainment and instruction of the community are carried out face to face. This seems a simple fact, but its implications are so subtle—and the process itself has been so imperfectly understood—that it seems useful to survey briefly the characteristics of oral storytelling as a way of highlighting some of the changes that I have made.

In oral renderings, the actions being described are usually simply chained together with the use of *and* or *well*, markers of addition rather than causation. I constantly found myself wanting to substitute a *then*, a *thus*, a *meanwhile*, thus introducing a kind of cause-effect language that the oral performer does not seem to use nearly as much. Similarly, a storyteller tends to be much more repetitive than his literary counterpart; repeating something reminds the hearer of where the story is and where it is going, for, unlike the reader, the listener can hardly go back to a previous page. Conventional phrases are used, over and over again, to describe the same characters and situations, and the storyteller does not hesitate to repeat phrases, sentences, and even whole scenes both as signposts for the audience and as devices that call attention to the abilities of the storyteller. In my revisions I eliminated much redundancy and repetition, since this is precisely what a reader neither expects nor appreciates. Where such a stylistic device is used to build dramatic interest in the progress of the story, I have left in most of the repeated material.

Almost impossible to capture on the written page is the importance of the audience in the creation and re-creation of the story. Those in the audience expect to be both surprised and delighted by the doings described in the story, but they do not commonly expect to encounter new ways of telling the story, nor do they want novel and unconventional situations brought into the act. Thus the reader often finds that the tales adhere to conventional story patterns. In this regard, aesthetic delight arises in the deployment of a variety of stylistic effects in the *telling*, such as in the sound effects employed, the change of pace of the delivery, the use of different cadences and sound levels, and so on. One device that is available to the local storyteller and that generally falls flat for the distant reader is the use of topical references within the story, especially those that note, explicitly or by allusion, how the details of the story reflect the idiosyncrasies of someone in the community. Sometimes, in fact, the story parallels a real situation so fully that the story, whenever it is told, is associated with a person whether or not he or she is present at the telling. The performer may also suddenly see a new relationship between the story and someone in the audience, and will draw on this parallel as a means of making the story more interesting to the audience. As stories are told face to face, there is a strong sense of participation in the telling by those in the audience even when, as in some traditions, they remain attentive during the telling. Again, this dimension of the stories is of little interest to readers removed from the scene.

In traditional communities, one seldom encounters just one story told at a time. Instead, tales are told in sessions, and often on an occasion that marks the passage of the month, the year, even a life. One story follows another, generally because in some way it has been suggested by the first. And, just as we often find in joke telling, there is a kind of competition, leading not to winning or losing but to a constant building of energies and a refinement of presentational techniques. This competitive interaction is important in Afro-American performances of all sorts (I think of *jamming* in jazz, *cutting* in tap dancing, and *rapping and capping* in street-corner speech), and it is occasionally to be observed within the action of the story, as in "The Signifying Monkey." But where the competitive element arises between storytellers, it seldom finds its way into the text of the tale.

Even when the lore records the way things were at the beginning or in some definable period (for instance, during slavery times), it is important that the storyteller convey a sense that the events within the story are dynamic and ongoing, that they describe and comment on life as it is lived today. Indeed, with Afro-American tales, this sense of immediacy is often conveyed by Creole language forms. Creole verbs do not carry the same kind of time markers that, say, English or French tenses do; rather, the verbs have a continuing-present feeling to them. Thus, characters often are reported to speak, not with the form "he said" or "she asked," but in verbs that have a sense of ongoingness, such as "he say" or "she ax"—a problem made even more complicated by the use of one pronoun, *e*, meaning "he," "she," or "it." In my recastings of the stories, I have translated all action into the past tense because that is our conventional storytelling verb form, trusting that the vigor of the action and vitality of the expression will carry the essential message of ongoingness.

Finally, oral performances tend to focus on the concrete qualities of the here and now, and on the practicalities and problems faced daily in the village or small-community context in which most of these stories were collected. Personal problems and eccentricities are seldom faced head-on. Instead, those used to operating in an oral manner learn from experience how direct and personal talk about one another's doings can adversely affect the harmony of the community. To them, then, the most effective and artful forms of speech are those that contain indirect arguments, that "go round for long," as some some Africans put it, that couch personal suggestions in impersonal terms. The verbal arts, including storytelling, gravitate toward arresting images and concrete figures of speech. In our more literate and impersonal world, ironically, we tend to address our relationships and their problems more directly, with a greater number of rules of thumb whose formulation draws upon *I* and *you* more readily. The "hidden" and allusive characteristics of the older proverbs and parables seem strangely old-fashioned and even inauthentic because they seem to indicate that we are not speaking our minds. But people who live in one another's laps all the time cannot afford to be so direct or so *openly* confrontative in their rhetoric.

The taletelling tradition of blacks in the New World came, directly or indirectly, from the places where the slaves' ancestors lived in the sub-Saharan area of the Old World. The major evidence for this is the relative consistency of the repertoire wherever Africans found themselves transported in the New World. The notes to sources in the Appendix will direct you to the relevant scholarship in the subject. Perhaps it may seem that I have skewed the argument to some degree by giving many examples of stories that have been more or less established as African in origin in a New World telling; if this is so, it was serendipitous, for I had picked the stories before I began the annotation. And as the reader interested in the subject will recognize, there *are* a number of stories included here that have come into the Afro-American repertoire from Europe or that have been reported from many places throughout the world—for example, the tar-baby stories, here represented by ''Tricking All the Kings.''

I have not included many examples of the jokes that make up a large part of the black repertoire throughout the New World; although they are traditional and certainly very interesting, jokes are a somewhat separate folkloric form, focusing on the ''setup'' and ''punch line.'' I have included only a small selection of jokes, ones that continue and expand the themes, techniques, and concerns of the more leisurely paced folktales.

On the other hand, I have included a good deal of material that is jocular, if not actually in joke form; most of these stories did not appear in print until the twentieth-century collections were published. They report a body of tales specifically focusing on black–white relations under slavery, a subject that was hardly likely to have been brought to the notice of Joel Chandler Harris and his followers. The work of the Afro-American folklorists Arthur Huff Fauset and Zora Neale Hurston—and, later, J. Mason Brewer and Daryl Cumber Dance—really marks the time when the story lore of Afro-Americans in the United States was collected in a manner that might place the lore in the context of the people's everyday lives.

When the Harris books first appeared in the early 1880s, the question of the geographical and cultural origins of at least the Uncle Remus canon was raised; Harris himself, among others, presumed they were mostly African; another group sought to find their origins within the Indo-European complex. As I discuss in the Introduction, the work of recent scholars has pretty well laid to rest the Europeanist position, even for tales from the mainland of the United States. The key documents in tracking down the story behind these stories are Richard M. Dorson's collections, effectively brought together in his *American Negro Folktales*; William Bascom's series of articles ''African Folktales in America,'' in *Research in African Literatures*; Alan Dundes's ''African and Afro-

American Tales," in *African Folklore in the New World*; and Florence Baer, *Sources and Analogues of the Uncle Remus Tales*. I make extensive commentary on these works in the Appendix, and provide full bibliographical references to them (as well as all other cited materials) in the Bibliography.

In great part, these scholars built on the earlier efforts of Elsie Clews Parsons; this indefatigable collector-ethnographer spent much of the 1920s and 1930s collecting, organizing, annotating, and publishing New World Negro stories. My debt to her work is reflected in the tales that I have derived from her books and articles. Moreover, Parsons underwrote the field research and published much of the work of others, most notably that of Melville J. Herskovits and his wife, Frances. I have found their *Suriname Folk-lore* an especially rich resource, unique not only in its subject area but in the felicity of their translations from the Paramaribo Creole tongue, *taki-taki*.

I have also had the pleasure of conversing and corresponding with a number of collector-ethnographers, many of whom have shared texts with me as well as wise words. Daniel Crowley not only has written the most comprehensive work on the performance of tales in this culture area, *I Could Talk Old-Story Good*, but has shared his intimate knowledge of Afro-America without stint; and he has delivered, again and again, the most articulate renderings of the Africanist's perspective on Afro-American lore.

Richard Dorson, the last great and vociferous advocate of the Europeanist perspective, carried out extraordinarily important work among black raconteurs in communities in Arkansas and Michigan in the 1950s, a time when attention to such a subject was out of vogue. His collections reflect the approved professional approach to the transcription and annotation of texts; in addition, his sketches of the performers themselves and his reproduction, *in toto*, of a tale-telling session prefigure recent developments in what we used to call the ''science of folklore,'' and which we call ''folkloristics'' today.

In the wake of interest in the historical condition of Afro-Americans, a number of works have made important contributions to the understanding of the relationship between life and lore, and between studies of lore and the intellectual concerns of specific eras. Compendia of early writings on Afro-American lore emerged as an outgrowth of the Black Studies movement in the United States. Of these, none was more copious and illuminating than Alan Dundes's gathering of a wealth of already printed, diverse materials in his *Mother Wit from the Laughing Barrel*. John Szwed and I attempted to provide a similar service with regard to the *varia* of the West Indian materials in our *After Africa*. The most readily available and reliable resource detailing the complex linguistic story of the Old World origin of the New World Creole languages is J. L. Dillard's argumentative *Black English*. See also Walter Brasch's equally engaging history of the writing of Afro-American talk in his *Black Language and the Mass Media*. The work of the social historians, especially Orlando Patterson and Edward Kamau Brathwaite in the West Indies and Sterling Stuckey, John Blassingame, George Rawick, Eugene Genovese, and Lawrence Levine in the United States, draws heavily on popular and folkloric materials, greatly filling in our understanding of the continuities of black life in one or another part of the New World. Richard and Sally Price's continuing work on Saramakan (Surinam) life allows us to see, again and again, the large-scale similarities as well as the immense differences found in Maroon communities. Moreover, Richard Price's work with Sidney Mintz, commenting on the Herkovitses' position vis-à-vis African retentions and reinterpretations, has substituted reason for wishful thinking as I have developed my perspectives on Afro-American cultures.

Finally, my personal gratitude goes to those who, over the years, have talked through these questions and have led me through the literature: Ken Goldstein, Herbert Halpert, Bob Thompson, Bill Wiggins, Melvin Wade, Jay Edwards, Bill Ferris, Marilyn White, Henry Glassie, Jerry Davis, Rich Price, Karl Riesman, Gene Genovese, Sid Mintz, and more recently, Bill Washabaugh, Skip Gates, Don Brenneis, Debora Kodish, and (always) my co-conspirator, John Szwed.

Wendy Wolf, cherished editor and friend, had the good sense to take the year off while this book gestated and its companion volume, *African Folktales*, went through the rites of publication. Her cheering thus came both from the sidelines and the center of the field, where her play is always superlative (though, by her own admisson, she needs some batting practice).

My wife, Janet, constantly brings me back to the clear and straight, the simple approach, often by asking the hardest questions of my prose in the margins.

AFRICAN
AMERICAN
FOLKTALES

WORDS WITHOUT END

*O*nce upon a time, there was a king who had one only daughter. The king said, "Any man who can give me a story without an end can marry the princess." Many tried but did not succeed. There was one last man who came in after everyone else was done. He was introduced to the king, and right away started into his story. He told the king: "One man had some corn. Some locusts gathered around this corn, and one locust came and took a grain. Another locust came and took a grain of corn. Then another locust came and took a grain of corn. Then another locust came and took a grain of corn." Soon the king grew tired. "I am sleepy. You can go and come back another time."

The man did so. And when he returned the following day, he started in: "And then another locust came and took a grain of corn. Another locust came and took a grain of corn. And then another locust came and took a grain of corn. And another locust came and took another grain of corn."

The king grew tired and he said to the man, "Your story has no end. Take the princess and marry her."

INTRODUCTION

A story that has no end. Surely this is a strange way of introducing the reader to Afro-American folktales. Yet a great many stories in this book are built on similar solutions to a problem that a character has taken on for the sheer fun of trying to solve it, or to get out of the consequences he has brought upon himself. We are given no motivation; instead, we are thrown into the middle of an impulsive action being carried out for its own sake, such as courting the king's beautiful daughter. There is no before and after here, only a clever trick.

In most of the tales, such tricks are constantly being carried out, not in order to better oneself in life, as we find in so many European fairy-tales, but for the sheer joy of taking on the challenge. We expect this when the stories focus, as they commonly do, on the actions of Trickster (Brer Rabbit in the South of the United States and in the Bahamas, the West Indian Compé Anansi, or the Haitian scamp Ti Malice); shenanigans come more naturally to him than to heroes like Jack the Giant-killer. As with tricksters all over the world, even when he seems to win, there is no "living happily ever after" ending to his stories. Instead, there is a "to be continued" feeling at the conclusion; for, as in the adventures of European scamps like Reynard the Fox and Till Eulenspiegel, we know that Trickster will simply go from one predicament of his own making to another.

For over a century, Afro-American folktales have been associated in the minds of readers with the plantation world nostalgically re-created by Joel Chandler Harris; moreover, because most of the stories he reports concern the merry pranks of animals, the tales have been consigned to the category of children's literature even more fully than have the wonder tales of Grimm and Perrault. Consequently, these stories have been neglected by those who wish to celebrate the Black Achievement and have been regarded by observers as predominantly the response of an enslaved and exploited people to conditions imposed upon them. This is certainly an element in the tales that must be dealt with seriously, but the whole repertoire—Harris included—deserves to be looked at more closely and more sympathetically.

Harris's works and those of his followers appear in this collection, but the majority of the stories go far beyond Uncle Remus and his friends in the subjects they deal with, the audience to whom they are directed, and the historical times and geographical places they represent. Their geographical range takes us to Afro-American communities all over the New World—North, South, and Central America and the Caribbean included. Although most of the tales were collected in rural communities, a few texts are included from city settings as far from each other as Paramaribo, Surinam, on the mainland of South America, to Philadelphia. The sources include written accounts that predate the publication of the Uncle Remus tales, later collections carried out by folklorists in the 1920s and 1930s, and still other from the fieldwork that I and my contemporaries have conducted since the invention of the tape recorder.

Like other forms of Afro-American creative inventions—song, dance, and a range of techniques of body adornment—these tales testify not only to the perseverance of an uprooted and enslaved people but to the vitality of the cultural traditions they were able to maintain and build upon. The elements of storytelling were included in the only "baggage" they could carry with them: their traditional styles of personal and social adornment, as well as their ways of performing and celebrating. A great many of the stories included are actually New World versions of ones found throughout sub-Saharan Africa and therefore stand alongside the other great black performance traditions in illustrating the continuing vigor of the African aesthetic. Although many of these performance forms were put together on this side of the Atlantic, they draw upon some of the most profound dimensions of African style. If the importance of the tales in celebrating black creativity has been superseded by more lively and large-scale performances, such as jazz or break dancing, the slower, less-driven rhythms of the stories continue to enchant in their small-scale but equally outrageous way.

These stories are associated throughout the black world with the joyful effusions of nighttime entertainments, especially with the time of the month when the moon shines brightly and old people and young come together to celebrate life's possibilities in the face of the harsh regularities of daytime activity. As Jean Price-Mars rhapsodized three quarters of a century ago about the stories from his Haitian childhood: "They appeal to the mystery of the night as if to soften intentionally the rhythm of the narration and to place the action in the realm of the supernatural. It is . . . on these clear nights at the moment when 'Rabbit is on guard' (as we say . . . to describe the limpid sky studded with stars), it is at that moment that the proud 'storyteller' casts the spell on his audience."[1] The stories also respond to the terrible visitation of death to the community; they are told in their most liberated and outrageous renditions at wakes, after the interment. These tales, then, like the many flowerings of the improvisatory spirit by which the black world has always distinguished itself in the community of nations—through developing forms like jazz and the mambo, the blues and bossa nova, calypso and calinda—are evidence of a great ability to bring meaning to the most seemingly insignificant materials and movements. Like songs and dances, stories live in that part of black life "informed by the flash of the spirit of a certain people specially armed with improvisatory drive and brilliance."[2] It is a spirit with an incandescence that bursts in a shower of sparks and laughter.

Read these stories, then, with this in mind: the outrageous actions they describe and the mirth they elicit are a vital response to the long night of deprivation and to death. Told in dialogue, folded into the overlapping sounds of good company, and locking everyone into the occasion by the interspersed song that animates the tellings, they are not just the frivolous aftershocks of the uprooting and enslaving experience. Instead, they are artful lies that say aloud of life, as the king did in anger and frustration to the storyteller in the tale of the locust and the grain, "Your story has no end!"

I

Make no mistake: this is a book of elaborate fictions told by tale spinners, first and last, for the fun of it, even when the stories are told in the face of a death in the community. They may embody larger truths, but they are called *lies* and *nonsense* nonetheless by those who tell and listen and laugh. For, as Uncle Remus explained to his young white inquisitor who was worried about the morality of some of Brer Rabbit's antics, "Creatures don't know nothing at all about that's good and that's bad. They don't know right from wrong. They see what they want and they get it if they can, by hook or crook." We witness the doings of characters who demand that while we listen to the narrative, we suspend not only disbelief but the kind of moral conscience that asks that we judge such doings on moral grounds. The stories not only entertain but test the limits of the believable, by illustrating situations in which exaggeration, selfishness, and other kinds of reprehensible cutting-up are regarded as normal.

If these tales are such lies, one might reasonably ask, how are they told so that we both laugh at them and take them seriously? The answer is not hard to find. The storyteller presents himself or herself as a masterful liar, through joking openers ("Once upon a time, a monkey shit lime . . ."), endings ("This is what I went out to find out about, and this is what I was able to return, in spite of everything, to tell you, and if you don't believe me go look for yourself . . ."), and the myriad interspersed remarks that remind the hearer that a performance by a master talker is taking place. This running commentary is what Daniel Crowley calls the "double lie" technique; by couching the fictions in such ridiculously exaggerated terms, the wholly fictional character of the tales is underscored, and the storyteller's reputation as an artful liar is enhanced.

Perhaps "liar" seems too strong a term for the teller of these rambunctious doings; in fact, I would not use it if it were not the word that keeps coming up in black discussions of the entertainments they produce. A more pointed and resonant black term for what is happening is *signifying*, playing around by pitting words against each other, characters against each other, just to see what kind of response they will get from being thrown together. In "The Signifying Monkey," the concept simply means stirring things up for their own sake. But the term can mean much more than that, for signifying is one of those bedrock black terms that can be self-contradictory—that is, it comes to mean one thing and its opposite at the same time. (Think of how "bad" came to mean "very good" for a while in "hip" talk.) Signifying can refer, as it does in standard English, to the ability of a word or act to carry deep meanings to the surface. But when used in the black sense of the term, it draws on both the standard definition and the strategy of testing and even casting doubt on the ability to bear the conventional meanings. Signifying, then, becomes a stance toward life itself, in which the significance of a reported action cannot be interpreted as meaning only one thing, for it may convey many messages at the same time, even self-contradictory and self-defeating ones.

To the outside world, such signifying is sometimes regarded as a mark of irresponsible irreverence; it may make serious matters seem playful, the subject of banter. But this is exactly what is intended in the world of *nonsense*, to use the West Indian term for signifying; it provides a context in which the community encourages its wits to test the limits of meaning by exploring the edges of believability, all of this in the service of expressive resilience and improvisational creativity. Nonsense or signifying, then, is not always merely playing around, for the most serious concerns of community life are brought into the discussion, and much is learned about how life ought to be lived, even when the illustrations for the virtuous life are couched negatively and are laughed at as acts of negation.

The strategy of being able to signify is especially useful in dealings with those who have greater power than the good talkers. In the Afro-American world, populated largely by blacks and yet commonly under the political and economic control of whites, the usefulness of learning wariness and counteractive devices of wit is obvious. Again, to paraphrase Uncle Remus in talking about why the animals acted as they did: "In those days the creatures were obliged to look out for themselves, most especially those that didn't have horns or hooves. Br'er Rabbit now, didn't have any horns or hooves so he had to be his own lawyer."

A number of stories presented this point of view in lesson form, lessons that black children needed to learn in their dealings with the "white-folks' world." They were lies that taught important truths, such as the time Sis Goose was caught by Brer Fox while she was swimming around the pond. She got really annoyed about that because she felt that she had every right to swim there; so she took Fox to court. But when they got into court and Sis Goose looked around, the sheriff, he was a fox; and the judge, he was a fox too; and the attorneys, they were all foxes, as were the jurymen. So they tried old Sis Goose, convicted her, and executed her there right on the spot, and soon were picking on her bones. The moral: "When all the folks in the courthouse are foxes and you are just a common goose there ain't gonna be much justice for colored folk."[3]

This kind of mordant message is far from uncommon, even in the jokes of the more urbanized talkers. For instance, a common joke heard often in my first field experience (in South Philadelphia) portrays another lesson—this time between an old dog and his young protégé—and hammers home in even rawer terms its message of wariness. The old dog decided to take his young charge out on the street to learn its ways. They walked from place to place, and at each stop the old dog smelled an object (a garbage can, a fireplug, and so on), and the young one followed suit. Finally, they encountered a "she-dog," which the old dog smelled, nuzzled, and "jumped up on her and knocked himself off a piece." So the young dog did the same. Later, when the old dog was quizzing the young one on what he had learned, the latter admitted he was a little perplexed about things. "What's the idea of being out in the world? I don't see any rhyme or reason to it." To which the old one replied, "Well son, my only advice is anything in this world you can't smell, eat, or make love to, piss on it."[4]

One of the important things to bear in mind when confronting such stories is that signifying is properly carried out on street corners or wherever young men joke with one another when they are out of the house and *sounding* with their friends. Otherwise, they open themselves up to the force of the proverb "Signifying is worse than dying" from those demanding respectful, straightforward talk. However, the subject of men is discussed in similar terms among women, and adults of both sexes often go on at length about the unreliability of children! Tales that tackle, directly or obliquely, how to make the most out of life, especially how to conduct one's relationships with members of the opposite sex, are not only common but distinctively widespread throughout Afro-America, extending from the streets of South Philadelphia, in the story above, to the most remote runaway (or Maroon) communities of Surinam on continental South America. As Richard Price noted in his anthropological survey of one such community: "The Saramakas quite generally operate from a position of mistrust. Proverbs and folktales are loaded with warnings about confiding in anyone. . . . Deception is an expected aspect of all social relations."[5] There is a strong attempt to keep one's doings to oneself and to operate with others as if the phrase "nobody's business but my own," which one hears often in songs (as well as in response to gossip), encapsulates an entire philosophy of life. This does not imply, by any means, that such gossip is forbidden or even looked down on, for no small community would be able to operate effectively unless everyone knew everybody else's story. Moreover, not to be talked about is not to be a member of the community. The key in such village or neighborhood situations is not to prevent being talked about but to control as much as possible what is being said about you, to control your *name* as fully as possible, often by making choices about whom you leak information to and under what conditions you hide it.

The problem of maintaining any kind of privacy in the small community, whether village or neighborhood, is great indeed. The danger is greatest when private events threaten to become public in a way that will bring shame to those involved, especially in those cases where an argument takes place. When a fight begins in a family, it might seem helpful to bring in a go-between to help *judge* the situation. But to do so is to introduce the further complication arising from the distrust one has learned for discussing one's business with anyone else, no matter how trustworthy. Indeed, a great number of proverbs and stories make precisely this point. For instance, in Surinam, they tell of the time when Anansi and Cockroach had a contest to see who could climb highest. What Anansi forgot was that cockroaches can fly when they need to, so when he got to the top, he found himself beaten. They proceeded to argue about whether flying had been included in the original wager, but they couldn't decide the question between themselves. So they had to find a judge; and who did they call but Fowlcock to settle the dispute. He came and looked over the situation and the two friends that had had such a falling out, and he puffed out his chest and began to crow: "Come over here! Come over here!" So they went over to hear his verdict, and just as Cockroach got over near him, he gave one big peck and ate him up. If you can't trust the judge, who can you trust.?[6]

Mistrust pervades these stories as a direct reminder of how careful people should be in life. Perhaps more important, such stories often

serve as roundabout techniques for talking about how one person is acting with others in the community without having to *call out* anyone's
name. They draw on native wisdom for addressing recurring problems,
suggesting how they may be taken care of, and doing so without making
any personal reference to anyone who happens to be facing that problem
at the moment.

It might be argued, then, that stories both reflect and refract reality,
for people who entertain and instruct one another in face-to-face ways
need to hide their words sometimes. Moreover, hiding words by couching
them in impersonal nuggets of wisdom may give the storyteller a greater
sense of power simply because the use of indirection is often the clever
and masterful way by which the oral artist operates. Even a scandal
song or play that reenacts some especially ludicrous or antisocial activity
in the community must be reenacted by making up nicknames for the
miscreants.

II

I might not even have to get into this aspect of storytelling were it not
that, on their face, so many of these tales appear to confirm certain
stereotypical notions about Afro-Americans, some of the very ideas that
I set out to dispel in putting this work together. By bringing together
these tales, I may seem to subscribe to the notion that they are models
of trickery to get around Old Master, or models of directed deceit and
anger to get back at Whitey. In fact, they are models of how *not* to act
in most cases, and they are told under conditions in which the action is
so frenzied and so replete with acts of social disruption that the audience
can only shake its collective head in wonder while laughing at the audac-
ity (or gullibility) of all creatures great and small.

One of the most important dimensions of this deliberate nonsense is
in the language in which the stories are cast. As noted in the Preface,
when the slaves were first brought to the New World, they had a ready-
made lingua franca that some of them had learned in West Africa and
by which they could communicate. Often, it was a matter of survival to
be able to communicate in a language that was only partially understandable to the slaveholder and overseer, and so this Creole tongue began
to take on some of the symbolic properties of a secret language (more
strongly in some areas of the New World than others). Among other
things, changes in the meanings of words—changes that sometimes
amounted to complete transvaluation—were encouraged by the slaves'
underclass situation. Words came to mean the opposite of what they
mean in standard speech. I do not mean to overstress this subversive

capacity of the language because we have only limited examples of this expressive strategy. It is more important for an understanding of the art of storytelling to realize that the slaves themselves recognized that the whites considered this speech system to be a mere imitation of whites (the vocabulary, remember, was predominantly English or French) and a poor one at that—the slaves were "murdering the language." The use of patois, then, confirmed the white stereotype of blacks as uncivilized, a fact that hardly went unnoticed by the blacks.

Clearly, the ability of blacks to speak in the standard European vernaculars was considerably greater than acknowledged by the slaves and their descendants. Every once in a while, a white would overhear a ceremony or some other event of high seriousness and would notice the black speaker's fluency in the elegant turn of phrase and the eloquent quotation. But, given the twists and turns of the plantocrat mentality, this too was regarded as a bad imitation of white oratory and was more or less dismissed from the record. Nevertheless, it is clear from journal accounts that the high value placed on eloquence in Africa had been translated effectively into various Afro-American forms of eloquent and ornate speechmaking. Moreover, such speaking was associated with the orderly and respectable household and church; the broadest Creole was employed with crossroad and street-corner good-timing behavior. A firm distinction is commonly made by the "good talkers" of Afro-American communities between low status, deep Creole (called *talking bad, patois, broken talk, talking country*, among other things), and a respectable way of speaking, often involving hypercorrect forms, and referred to as *talking sweet* (and not in the sense of using language to romance someone!) Thus there is a contrast made between ways of speaking that carries with it the social contrast between public and private worlds, and between respectable behavior and orderliness, and seeking after a reputation.

These stories are self-consciously delivered in the deepest of *broad talk* and thereby represent the most artful deployment of that language. It is therefore extraordinarily difficult for non-Creole-speakers to understand, especially because some of the best storytellers enliven the narration by going more and more quickly, using a lot of sound effects and often giving each of the important characters a special way of talking. These are not stories of language gone out of control, but are entrancingly and energetically delivered examples of talking bad on purpose. They represent a kind of linguistic liberation that contrasts both with the way Old Master talked and with the ornamental speechmaking that takes place in church or at wedding feasts, baptisms, and other formal occasions. In this situation, talking black is the language of action and energy and is strongly associated with males and public places (the street corner, the rum shop, the crossroads, wherever *hanging out*, or as they put it in the Caribbean world, *liming and blagging*, takes place). Talking bad, then, establishes its place in the speech system by contrast with the orderly and formal codes of behavior observable on those occasions that bring together the whole family and community. And talking sweet is strongly associated with good manners, and with paying appropriate respect to those in the community that deserve it, especially older women.

This talking sweet is widely observable as the prestige form of serious speech in Afro-American communities throughout the New World. Speaking in this manner elevates the status of the speakers as they address themselves to the important subject of how to endure with dignity and respect. Being able to master such speech is to startle the audience members into attention and provide them with a sense of the possibility of a different kind of mastery—a dominion over their lives and their souls. Many traveler-observers of black life in the American South overheard such talk but only half understood that something culturally different was taking place. For instance, Joseph Holt Ingraham noted that, on occasion, blacks were to be found "collecting in little knots in the streets, where, imitating the manners, bearing, and language of their masters, they converse with grave faces and in pompous language, selecting high hard-sounding words" to dazzle those auditors who did not have as great a verbal command.[7] Such commentary is one of the staples of observers of Caribbean life as well.[8] In perhaps its broadest (and most insidious) form, this speechmaking and other high-style behaviors made their way into the minstrel show as a major way in which black "pretensions to respectability" could be lampooned.

III

From the early nineteenth century well into the twentieth, the minstrel show was the most popular form of entertainment, not only in the American South, but throughout the United States. In England and the rest of Europe it found very large audiences as well; Americans were assumed to be able to perform "coon songs" wherever they went. Elevated forms of speech, of course, were hardly the most common form of black speech that provided material for parodies on the minstrel stage. Indeed, several of the most dramatically distinctive Afro-American styles of doing things were brought to the attention of Americans through explicit white imitations of blacks onstage. These shows drew much of their dance material, as well as certain other Afro-American styles of walking, dressing, and interacting, and developed a distinctly American entertainment form that included the song and dance and came to symbolize not only the black-face show but the racist southern world out of which the stage form grew. Indeed, Jim Crow originally was simply one of the stock characters in a minstrel show; "Jump, Jim Crow" was the song that gave him his name. This was noticed by W. J. Cash, one of the most insightful southern white commentators on the etiquette of race relations. "With Jim Crow we see manifested the deepest kind of ambivalence of the Southerner toward their black charges who they dominated and intimidated but could not help but imitate and even lean on: thus, they deployed the black-face, the 'broken speech,' the sentimental and satiric songs and dances as a way of exploring their misgivings about their precarious hold on social order and even psychological stability." Cash continues: "What is worth observing also is that the Negro, with his quick, intuitive understanding of what is required of him, and his remarkable talents as a mime" caught these conventional "figures" and their stereotypical styles and "bodied them forth so convincingly that his masters were insulated against all questions of their reality. . . ."[9] What Cash began to glimpse (albeit from the "liberal" perspective that views black culture primarily through the ways it is borrowed from by whites) was the dynamics of an Afro-American expressive system that was considerably wider and deeper than any stereotypical perspective could render. When black speaking could be interpreted as a misunderstanding of white standard talk, then things in black dialect could be (and were) drawn on for comic purposes. But as many concerned whites discovered, as soon as one came to know individual blacks intimately, the stereotype began to dissolve, and the degree and intensity of cultural exchange and respect had to be acknowledged.

On those occasions when the cool, high style of self-presentation was observed, however—blacks displaying themselves to one another in what today might be called "styling-out"—the white reaction was commonly one of amused derision, seeing the effort as simply one more bungled black attempt to imitate white cultural practices. Styling-out was expressed in a wide range of dress and a parading style of public walking (imitated by whites in the famous *cakewalk* of the minstrel show), as well as in oratorical forms of speech. These oratorical forms were mimicked in hypercorrect and ultracorrupted fashion in the "fancy talk" speeches, also found in black-face shows, providing white anecdotalists with a subject for many of their most popular routines, stories in which a character attempts to use jaw-breaking words but manages only to come up with malapropisms. The minstrel show usually imitated a limited range of black traditional display forms and then only for the purpose of depicting plantation life through the playful antics of the singing, dancing, joking happy slave. That this depiction had little to do with real plantation life is almost beside the point; it was the only form in which whites could acknowledge and tolerate black culture. Moreover, after the Civil War, this popular form of entertainment was seized upon by blacks themselves. They formed troupes that found ready audiences wherever they traveled, especially outside the United States.

A by-product of the minstrel show were books of songs and stories delivered in "black dialect," sometimes written by minstrel performers or producers and sometimes by local wags—journalists and parlor raconteurs who developed a repertoire of such pieces primarily for reputation enhancement rather than to make money. In fact, these folios, which were generally produced on local presses, were often put togther by judges, doctors, professors, and other genteel types out of stories to which they had gotten a good response from their friends and acquaintances over the years.

These subliterary productions are strange documents from a folklorist's perspective because they often contain traditional tales that appear in independent sources, clearly tales told *among blacks* for different purposes. For instance, one kind of story that is very often found among both white and black raconteurs turns on a clash of wits between a master and one of his slaves, usually focusing on, and ending with, an amusing turn-off phrase uttered by the slave: the Master-John tales, as they are widely called.

One of these widely reported tales concerns a remarkable hunting experience recounted by the planter. The planter brags to a friend that he has shot a deer in the head and a hoof simultaneously. He then turns to the slave who had been with him to verify this wondrous deed. The slave quickly confirms what his master has reported, cunningly explaining that the deer had been scratching his ear when Old Master got the shot off. As soon as the friend leaves, the slave asks his master not to get his lies so far apart next time: "Please don't scatter them so, because I had mighty hard work to bring them together."[10]

One would readily assume that this story, told in the southern milieu, reflected the ambiguous relationship between master and slave. As with so many such tales, it is reported from white and black raconteurs; when told by whites, it was a joke on themselves. But as William Bascom has shown, this tale of the remarkable shot is given in a number of African collections[11] (but none from Europe), and so we may assume that the story was brought to the United States by the slaves themselves. They adapted it to local circumstances—ones in which lying is countenanced on both sides of the racial line.

An even more commonly collected story in Africa relates the story of the skull who speaks to a hunter one day and then refuses to speak when the hunter brings his king (or master) to hear this amazing feat. This results in the hunter's head being chopped off. When the skull asks the dead one why he is there, the hunter's head replies, "Talking brought me here!" This story has also been widely collected in Afro-American communities in the New World, primarily the United States, and again often as a Master-John story. In one version a snake refuses to talk to Old Master and embarrasses John, and when asked why, is told, "John, you let me down. I spoke only with you, and you had to go and tell a white man!"[12] Both stories, then, are African stories that have been adapted to a format that addresses specifically American conditions.

The ironies that emerge from such stories today place the contemporary reader in a much better position to understand the amount of actual social information stored in the tales. Until now, the relationship between Master and John, or between Massa King and his minions, was neither recognized nor understood by readers outside the black community. What these stories reveal is a tremendously complicated relationship between the blacks who found themselves enslaved and those whites who affected their lives. The frustration and helplessness felt throughout Afro-America by blacks about whites is registered in these stories, but so is a kind of benign resignation that whites are eccentric people who do strange things all the time. Not least of these anomalous actions is the contradictory actions and attitudes of the plantocrat, especially with regard to issues of trust, industry, and civility. Repeatedly, Old Master is shown to be lazy himself, even while he accuses John of contrived inactivity; similarly, these stories are filled with trickery on the part of the whites combined with their encouragement of their slaves to display wiliness or cunning—all of this behavior in the face of the white stereotype of blacks as untrustworthy. These stories, then, are about the strange inconsistency of Old Master as much as anything else.

In the tales about Massa King, another kind of white eccentricity is discussed. Not only do whites do strange things, such as keeping their beautiful daughters locked up in glass cages or creating situations in which arbitrary contests are held for the rights to the kingdom, but the powerful whites allow this anomalous behavior to be made public business. In "The Singing Bones," for instance, the initiating idea of the tale—that a father would ask his son and daughter to compete for his affections by gathering the most beautiful bouquet of flowers—is discussed by those who tell the tale as an example of the really strange things that go on in "white man's yard." Similarly, in "Three Killed Florrie, Florrie Killed Ten," the idea of Massa King's establishing a contest for his beautiful daughter's hand receives no little comment from storytellers or members of their audience about how you just can't account for how people in power like that are going to act.

Though many of these tales are derived in some way from the Old World repertoire, their reinterpretation in the light of the New World social situation is important to bear in mind. For it is both the continuities and the changes that occur in these stories as they are transmitted that allow us to regard them as useful devices for understanding the dynamic of the life of Afro-Americans in this alien environment.

IV

In 1877, in the first journalistic notice of Afro-American tales in the United States, William Owens observed: "Anyone who will take the trouble [to look at the] predominate traits of negro character . . . and the predominate traits of African folk-lore" will discover a kind of "fitness of each to each."[13] In making this observation, Owens was not arguing with any forcefulness that African folklore had been retained by the slaves as much as averring that certain traits of blacks went deeper than any historical disruption could affect. Moreover, by arguing in this fashion, Owens gave the impression that the materials he was presenting were authentic.

It was precisely this question of authenticity that led a fledgling newspaperman, Joel Chandler Harris, to mount a counterattack. Harris saw the Owens piece in an advance copy of *Lippincott's* and found it "remarkable, more for what it omits . . . than what it contains." The problem, as Harris saw it, was that Owens did not demonstrate a true intimacy with the material because he failed to present it in appropriate speech patterns and manner of presentation. Harris seems especially to have been upset by the lack of respect paid to the tellers of the tales, as well as to the tradition they represented. Harris was to verify the authenticity of any story he published, even going to great lengths to distinguish between those that came from pure Afro-American sources and those that came from storytellers who had intermarried with Indians.

The principal means of verification used by Harris was to correspond with other southerners brought up under the scrutiny of tale-telling blacks, rather than conduct interviews with the informants themselves. This we may attribute as much to Harris's enormously shy character and his embarrassment over his inability to talk without a stutter as his unwillingness to interact with blacks. His books, through their enormous success with white readers, publicized the existence of these fascinating Afro-American stories throughout the English-speaking world and led to a great many other collections, some of which provide us with stories as they were performed within the black communities among blacks themselves.

The "signature" of the Harris-style plantation story was, of course, the tale of Brer Rabbit's romantic interaction with the female figure made of tar, and the disastrous consequences that occurred when he felt that he was being spurned by her failure to respond to his sweet words. Ironically, Owens's version of this encounter was closer to the way in which the tale is commonly told in Africa than was Harris's rendition. Owens's account begins with the common African storytelling scene in which members of the community feel the need to dig a well for all to use. The trouble arises when Brer Rabbit refuses to help and then characteristically not only avails himself of the water but muddies it for everybody else's use. The tar-baby is then devised as a technique to snare the culprit—and Brer Rabbit finds himself in his familiar fix.

Both Harris and Owens seem to have realized that the tar-baby provided only one opportunity for this trickster to test his wits in working out an escape from his predicament. Though many think of the story as fixed in sequence, as in the Harris reporting, the trick by which the vexatious and malingering Rabbit is caught is found in many other stories, including some that are quite different in plot development. Consider, for instance, the story included here, ''Tricking All the Kings,'' in which the tar-baby capture is instigated by Master King in his effort to ensnare Anansi the Spider (a trickster found in stories throughout the West Indies and in the coastal areas of South and Central America where Afro-American communities exist) because Spider has been stealing water from his well. Anansi is caught and escapes by being thrown by his captors, not into the briar patch, but into the sea. There he encounters Buh Shark; he convinces him to make a great catch of fish for them to eat on the shore. There Anansi encounters the voracious Lion; Anansi knows that Lion is going to want to share in the feast and will end up eating most of the catch. Through a further trick, then, Anansi tricks Lion into allowing himself to be tied to a tree. Anansi consumes the fish, while Lion can only look on and pull at the rope that is constraining him.

Strangely enough, the earliest record of such a tale from the New World comes to us from Jamaica. I say ''strangely enough'' because there the slaves and masters came into less contact than in the more family-style agricultural enterprise that typified the southern United States. Unlike most southern planters, the West Indian did not generally regard himself as rooted permanently to his land and its product. He built less stately homes, saving his money for investment back in England. In addition, the ratio of blacks to whites was far greater in the West Indies, and so there was considerably less interaction between them. Not that there was no interest about black ''manners and morals,'' as West Indians phrased it in their journals. Indeed, virtually every account of

West Indian life included some information about how the Africans and their descendants lived. But not many noted the stories that were being told, primarily because of the amount of time and energy it took to sit and record such information.

The earliest record of taletelling in Afro-America is found in the *Journal of a West Indian Proprietor*, written by the gothic novelist Matthew Gregory Lewis, best remembered for his work *The Monk*. Lewis inherited a Jamaican estate in the early nineteenth century and visited it for the better part of 1815–16, keeping a journal that was not published until 1834. He brought to his journal an interest in personal interactions, especially dialogue, as well as the more general European concern with questions of slavery and the culture-bearing capabilities of the Africans. Consequently, he recorded a number of detailed scenes of slave life that went beyond simple master–slave interactions, including the observation: "The negroes are also very fond of what they call Nancy stories, part of which is related and part sung."

Lewis proceeds to relate four stories of the sort that one still finds in the West Indies, alternating between narrating the action in his own style and giving the dialogue in the manner of the slaves. One of these concerns the fortunes of a young girl, Sarah Winyan, who is lured away to the bush by a black dog named Tiger, a trick easily pulled off as she was feeling rejected and despised by her stepmother to the point that she constantly sang of her despair:

> *Ho-day, poor me, O!*
> *Poor me, Sarah Winyan, O!*
> *They call me neger, neger!*
> *They call me Sarah Winyan, O!*

The dog entices her to follow him because he has the special bewitching powers of obeah. But she has misgivings all the while, and continues to sing her song as she goes ever deeper into the bush; finally, she is heard by her brothers, who rescue her and subdue Tiger.[14]

This story and others given by Lewis are still widely told throughout the black world on both sides of the Atlantic. While the animal differs in the various renderings, as does the age and station of the young girl (often, she is presented as the king's beautiful daughter), the pattern of seduction and rescue has remained remarkably stable. It is represented in this collection by "A Boarhog for a Husband."

Unfortunately for us, not all types of African traditional tales survived the transatlantic passage to the New World with their vigor and moral range intact. While some of the myths of the West Coast cultures, such as Yoruba and Fon, are to be encountered within the vital context of the great syncretic religious system of Vodun, Santería, Shango, and Candomble in Haiti, Brazil, Cuba, and a few other areas, in most of Afro-America neither myths nor other details of African religious practices were maintained in any full and systematic manner. Moreover, the grand bardic forms of epic and other kinds of praise singing, the elaborate recitations of genealogies, and with a few important exceptions, the chants accompanying the casting of cowry shells—all these forms were lost. Of the bardic forms that persist, the elaborate boasts and curses, including many in verse form, are still found in song (for example, the early calypso), and in verse in the elaborate *toasts* told on street corners and saloons in urban areas, in prisons, and in juke joints throughout the American South. The epic accounts of great heroes and leaders of the people have been replaced by hero stories in prose, song, or the jingling verse of the narrative toasts featuring radical individualists, great fighters and outlaws, such as ''Stackolee'' and Shine in ''The Sinking of the *Titanic*.'' Even the dilemma tales, so characteristic of African situations of moral disputation, seldom made their way to this side of the ocean, indicating that most of the political and philosophical dimensions of African story were lost to us in the Middle Passage.

What did survive in this hostile environment? Above all, the importance of storytelling remained in the lives of the slaves and their descendants. Told at night, for entertainment as well as instruction, in the traditional African style in which the entire community might be involved in the telling, these stories as performances provided entertainment by which the community could celebrate its identity as a group simply by singing, dancing, and, most important, laughing together. The stories are filled with action designed, it seems, just to get something stirred up—both in the world described in the stories and in the community of performers. Contrast this with the intent of the usual Indo-European fairytale, where action is initiated by an individual seeking to better herself or himself and advance to the point of happily-ever-aftering. We also fail to find the style of story, so common in Euro-American traditions, that conveys the message that moral violations must be punished. The African and Afro-American stories more commonly chronicle how a trickster or a hero uses his wits to get something he wants—or how he is frustrated by the acts of someone as clever or with as great powers as himself. Together, they demonstrate a wholeness in this folk literature, an integrity of theme, a consistency of style and pattern that owes much to its African origins, even while it breathes with a life of its own. And while we owe the publication of stories with this perspective to the literary initiative and sense of authenticity of Joel Chandler Harris, we can look back from our contemporary perspective and see that he was able to glimpse only a small portion of a cultural record far richer, more varied, and much more uproarious than he recognized.

V

A majority of the tales in the black repertoire depict the antics of Trickster and his foolish behavior, which is to be laughed at and learned from. So dominant are such stories, in fact, that all stories performed in tale-telling sessions tend to be called by the name of the primary trickster of the area: Brer Rabbit tales in the southern United States, Anansi stories in the West Indies. Moreover, as one may see in "Why They Name the Stories for Anansi," there are tales to explain just why this should be, stories that turn on the superior ability of Trickster in improvising actions, in reacting quickly, and in prevaricating.

Taletellers treat these characters as familiar members of a family, referring to them by a number of pet names that might change from one moment to the next. This is especially true for Trickster; Spider may, in a single story, be called Anansi, Buh Nansi, and Compé Anansi (meaning something like companion or pal). The name is also written as Nancy, Anancy, and even Aunt Nancy. Moreover, word play brings the name close to "nonsense" and to "nasty," both important themes in Trickster's behavior. Other characters receive similar treatment. The godlike King is variously called Master King. Marsa King, Marster, and Mister King; Old Master, in the Master-John tales, is referred to as Master, Marster, Ol' Marster, and so on.

There is a long history of conjecture about why such stories should have achieved a place of honor—conjecture largely indulged by white scholars who have sought to give at least the dignity of fighting back passively to these exploited people. These observers have tended to interpret the stories simply as records of oppression, or what Lawrence Levine calls "strategies for survival."[15] These strategies focused on learning how to play a number of roles, especially the stereotypical ones assigned by those in power, both before and after emancipation. These roles were all guided by the ironic perspective and tactics discussed above as *signifying*, even if that meant seeming to play the monkey, or to find a way of prevaricating to save your neck, or just to save the trouble of going through explanations that you knew were not going to be believed or trusted.

Though this equation between the wily heroes of the tales and blacks was hardly instigated by him, Joel Chandler Harris's argument that "the negro selects as his hero the weakest and most harmless of all animals and brings him out victorious" seems to have become almost an article of faith among commentators of many political persuasions. This position was taken for granted in spite of the fact that Rabbit gets his come-uppance in a number of stories. And this position was echoed by many who followed Harris in collecting and commenting on these tales. Mrs. Christensen, for instance, in the introduction to her rich collection of Sea Island tales in 1892 opines that "the Rabbit represents the colored man" inasmuch as "the negro, without education or wealth, could only hope to succeed by stratagem." Octave Thanet maintains in the same year: "Brer Rabbit . . . personifies the revolt of his race. His successes are just the kind . . . his race have craved."[16] As Levine notes, the motives and moral attitudes of the protagonists of these tales are just too complex and too ambiguous to argue that the stories provide a simple substitute for the lack of power over their own lives. The slave—and Afro-Americans since Emancipation—could sympathize with, perhaps even identify with, the trickster in some of his stories; but what can we say of those stories in which the trickster is despicable and his dupe somewhat more admirable? Or how would this theory address those tales, such as "The Tug-of-War between Elephant and Whale" and "You Never Know What Trouble Is until It Finds You," that pit one trickster against another? Rather than exhibit deflected power motives, these stories present the world as a contest between wit and strength. If there is any advice for real-life behavior in the stories, it is to remind us to be on guard constantly for others' tricks, and at the same time to admire those who are able to win the contest by their wits. As in Africa, Trickster's vitality and inventiveness are valued for their own sake.

VI

Many of the stories in this collection begin like familiar European fairytales with the beautiful young unmarried lady hidden away in the palace or the poor-but-ambitious young man who finds some reason to go traveling in search of wealth and position. But there the familiarity ends; the action takes off in quite a different direction in Afro-America. We have to pay careful attention to the reasons for this divergence if we are really to understand and interpret these tales seriously—a point that it took me some little time living and working in black communities to come to terms with.

My first career in folklore was as a folksinger and song collector, and I was fascinated on reaching the West Indies to find that so many of the older British ballads were performed as tales, in the West Indian style, of course, with a song introduced regularly into the narration. Thus, I encountered such standbys of the Anglo-American repertoire as "Little Mattie Groves," "The Maid Freed from the Gallows," and "The Two Sisters" (often called "Binnorie" in ballad anthologies). This last song is a ballad rendering of the international tale in which a murdered person's bones are fashioned into a musical instrument, which then sings a song that reveals the details of the killing and the identity of the murderer.[17]

The story, as I first heard it sung in the southern Appalachians, describes how two sisters are courted by the same knight, who picks "the young and the fair." The darker sister then entices the other to the riverside, and pushes her in. She floats down to the milldam where a harper or fiddler takes the body and makes an instrument of its parts. The song of revelation ensues, leading to the hanging of the sister.

In the West Indies, the same story is widely told as a brother-sister rivalry, as in "The Singing Bones" in this volume. Massa King has a son and a daughter; he sets a contest for them to see which will gather the more beautiful bouquet. The girl, with her better eye for flowers, is obviously going to win. But she is struck over the head and killed by her brother, who then buries her beneath a willow tree and steals her flowers. A shepherd boy and his dog discover a bone from her skeleton. It looks like a flute to him, so he plays on it, and it sings the song that reveals the brother's wrongdoings.

I came to the story through the ballad. When I first heard it, I interpreted it as a beautiful rendition of a conventional morality tale: envy leading to wrongdoing leading to punishment. Yet the discussion of the tale that took place in the communities in which I lived did not dwell on this dimension of the story; instead, they were amused by this strange and silly thing the king did—setting such a task for his children—for any sensible person would be able to tell that it would lead to a destructive fight. Moreover, it was regarded as one of those stories about Massa King and his doings and undoings that are, by their very character, strange because he is identified as white. Therefore, his family affairs are in many ways incomprehensible—but always interesting.

The "Singing Bones" story then seemed more and more nonsensical to me, closer to what is widely called "nigger business" in the anglophonic Caribbean—the playing out of family affairs that have gotten out of control, for they can no longer be kept at home or "within the yard." Call it West Indian high gossip if you wish, but hardly illustrative of the simple message that villainy will be punished. The major change within the tale is the addition of the shepherd boy. Depicted as a black servant who unwittingly uncovers the foul deeds, he serves a much more important role than I realized when I first heard the story. In fact, it was only when I re-transcribed my tapes, ten to fifteen years later, that I could hear the ongoing commentary from the performer and audience.

In a great many of the tales found in this book, especially those that concern the doings of Massa King and his family, an almost invisible character enters the action in a similar fashion as the shepherd boy. In his more common rendering he is a "dark" figure: an "Old Witch Boy," a dirty and diseased misfit, a mysterious member of the king's family, someone who must live under the bed or in another cranny within the house. Tucked away like that, this character is all too easily overlooked by nonblack audience members. Like Trickster, he lives at the margins between the family and the wilds, and can be seen as something of a contaminating anomaly, and thus, like Trickster, the upsetter of order. Described variously as "dirty," "smelly," covered with ashes (like Cinderella), he is best known for his ugly foot, which is described, alternatively, as diseased, constantly surrounded by fleas and nits (as are all open sores in the tropics), or as a clubfoot. Like Anansi, he is known by a number of names, the most common being "The Chiggerfoot Boy" (referring to the diseased member) or "The Jiggerfoot Boy" (the local term for a clubfooted person). He is contrasted with the king's beautiful daughter, ostensibly his sister.

In the usual story featuring this strange family, the daughter is courted by many of the best men in the land, but she rejects them all until one man comes riding by with whom she falls madly in love. Their courtship and marriage is therefore quickly achieved, and her new bridegroom carries her off with him to his home in the bush. The boy, through snooping or using one of his witching powers, is able to follow the couple and discover that his sister has married an animal or bush spirit that has been able to transform itself into human form. The boy also discovers how the transformation is brought about—it is commonly a song—and he persuades his father to accompany him to witness what he has discovered. The boy sings the song, the bridegroom is transformed, and the king then does what he must do.[18]

An important variation of this story type involves a transformed bridegroom who has achieved his change by borrowing various parts of the body to pass himself off as an appropriate suitor. After the marriage, as they return to his home, he must return what he has borrowed, whereby his new wife discovers his identity slowly and agonizingly.[19]

This pattern is especially notable in that it is so very different from the way in which European fairytales use the animal-human bridegroom theme. In the latter, the apparent animal, like the Frog Prince, is revealed in the end to be human—the very opposite of stories from the black world. Clearly the two traditions share motives and paraphernalia, but employ them to widely differing effects. If the European princess is rewarded for kissing a frog, are we to regard her Afro-American counterpart as punished for her finickiness in choosing a husband, or for her ill treatment of her diseased brother? Hardly. Instead, these tales betray an aesthetic fascination on the part of Afro-American storytellers with the transformative possibilities that can occur where the bush and human habitation abut, and where figures like Old Witch Boy (to say nothing of Trickster) are able to operate in the margins, playing the role of in-betweener to a fare-thee-well. The Chiggerfoot Boy, the shepherd, and their equivalents live between nature and culture and thus are able to see through the mask and costume of others. These figures break down all boundaries by roaming between the various worlds. There is no privacy, no family business to which they are not privy. And the moment of triumph for such a character is at that point when he can reveal the nefarious doings of others, though we seldom hear of his raising his status by pulling off such a trick.

The delight of these stories, then, lies in their dramatization of a disordering of society that opens us up to life itself. Though Massa King and his daughter are associated in the minds of many blacks with being both white and powerful, it would be difficult to argue that these stories embody any wish for the disintegration of the king's family, any more than Trickster's outrageous activities can be regarded as protorevolutionary. For in these stirred-up conflicts, no one wins and no one loses; in fact, winning and losing seem quite beside the point. Instead, such patterned disordering displays the sheer pleasure of getting the action going through some kind of boundary-breaking revelation. These tales recognize that actions have consequences; but, for the moment of storytelling, the principle of vitality seems more important than that of right and wrong.

This figure of the little, rejected boy with strange powers clearly places him in the same category as the classic tricksters of the Afro-American tradition: John the Slave and John the Fool, Brer Rabbit and Compé Anansi (the shape-shifting Spider), Bouki, Pigeon, Terrapin, and the many others who animate this collection. The centrality of such little creatures, who inhabit the nooks and crannies of the human community but who also maintain a kind of natural wildness, helps us both see the narrative patterns and figure out why these patterns seem so alien to the rest of the folktale literature. Their roles point up what seems a kind of plotlessness to the plotting, for the motives of Trickster and the other in-betweeners are never morally clear. Initiating action and keeping it moving is all one looks for in many of these stories.

Even when he is a principal actor, Trickster does not necessarily initiate the action; other animals may set up the trap to put an end to his rapacious ways with varying degrees of success. For instance, one of the more powerful animals lures Trickster into his house by clever means (or so it seems to him), thinking by this that he has captured him. Trickster, in response, figures out what has happened and devises an appropriate ruse to escape, sometimes also luring the instigator to his capture and demise. Indeed, the first published Uncle Remus story, called by Harris "Uncle Remus Initiates the Little Boy" (and included here as "No Chicken Tonight"), fits this pattern.

It is in the area of the repeated and overrepeated action that we can see how much variation is possible, even in portraying how successful Trickster is in his machinations. A great many stories tell of the thieving and sometimes even murderous activities that Anansi brings about, but because he tries a trick once too often, he is captured and usually flogged or executed. Typical here is "He Pays for the Provisions," in which, during a famine, Anansi agrees to let Blacksnake give him a lash with his tail in exchange for every bag of food that he takes from Blacksnake, who has planned for just such an opportunity. Anansi devises a way to get another animal to substitute for himself. The lash kills the other animal, and so Anansi is able to provide meat for himself as well as potatoes. But he pulls the trick once too often; he finds one animal who has figured out why the others are disappearing—thus forcing Anansi to take his own beating. The pattern holds in an even wider range of stories, for it is not always the greedy trickster who is caught by repeating an action once too often. Even more often, Trickster finds a dupe who will imitate *him* and who winds up being held responsible not only for his own actions but for what Trickster has done before him.

VII

Daniel Crowley's sturdy account of storytelling relates that "in the Bahamas tradition provides the narrator with a stock of theatrical devices with which to recreate a fresh story at every telling." These devices include pointing at someone in the audience, making sudden turns and changes of pace in the telling, beating on a table for effect, or going into a dance or some other stylized movement. Of one narrator, Crowley notes: "He danced, changed his facial expressions, leered, sobbed, rubbed his eyes, expressed surprise, stabbed imaginary enemies," all while keeping up "a barrage of talk."[20]

One major way in which a good storyteller is judged in many groups in Africa is through his or her command of ideophones and other vocal effects. The older collections of Afro-American materials do not take such effects into account very often, given the difficulties in on-the-spot transcription, but they have been increasingly incorporated in tales collected since the wide-scale use of the tape recorder. (Wherever they occur in this book, I have put them in italics.) Similarly, many animals are given dialogue delivered in the "voice" of that animal.

The tradition of imitating animal speech is, in fact, so strong that collections from the earliest to the most recent have virtuoso pieces in which the story is almost totally told in sound effects. For instance, most Afro-American versions of the race between the tortoise and the hare (here given as "The Race between Toad and Donkey") are moved along at each stop by songs that are imitations of the animal sound. In fact, the storytellers of repute in the West Indies have a little display "story" in which the animals converse with each other in their various voices:

> Fowl cock say, "*Marster, t'ief come.*" Sheep say, "*Nevah!*" Guinea Fowl say, "*You did it, you did it.*" Duck say, "*A-wa, a-wa, a-wa.*" Turkey say, "*It's your habitual practice, it's your habitual practice.*" Hog say, "*Good, good.*"

For the less adept teller, these voice modifications and imitations become comic devices to build up dramatic interest in a traditional tale. Arthur Huff Fauset reports such a story from Alabama: A crow and a buzzard see an old mule lying in a field. Each regards the mule as a possible meal, but they are both too scared to find out whether he is dead or just asleep. The old buzzard begins to walk around and around the mule, and the crow, sitting in the tree above him, starts in on him: "*Try him! Try him!*" he crows forth. Buzzard gets annoyed at all this and starts to walk away, and then Crow starts, "*Don't! Don't!*" So when Buzzard gets away around by the mule's tail, Crow starts in with this "*Try Him!*" stuff again, so Buzzard bites into the tail. And that's when the mule gets up and really takes off. Now Crow starts in all over again: "*Pull! Pull! Pull!*" All that Buzzard can do is yell back, "How the devil can I pull when there's more than *my* feet touching the ground?"[21]

I have not included many stories of this sort simply because they seem to "tell" better than they "read." But the humorous device emerges again in contemporary joking. A number of recent collections contain routines that are directly in this tradition of building stories out of comic sound effects. For instance, in Daryl Dance's recent collection,

Shuckin' and Jivin', there are several such routines, including one called "Crap Game in the Barnyard" that has Rooster asking *"What did they throw?"* Duck quacking *"Crapcrapcrapcrapcrapcrap!"* and Old Gander honking *"He'll never make it, he'll never make it."*[22]

Such sound effects certainly add to the theatrical qualities of tale-telling. But do not mistake this expressive range of vocal and gestural effects (especially sermonizing, speechmaking, and ritual activities) for the stereotypical artificial performance filled with overemotion and frenzy. Suffice it to say that black vocal style demands that, on occasion, the voice be used not so much for informational as deliberate textural purposes; one may hear growls, squeaks, screams, rasp, falsetto (and false-bass) effects, among many others, and often in the same story.

Black style in both Old and New Worlds, in fact, encourages an overlap of voices and voice textures, an effect that to Westerners can seem over-emotional and even chaotic. This is as true of story performances as religious services. To the observer from another culture, the storytelling might seem to be as much a singing, dancing, and joking occasion as a recounting of a tale. This effect is all the more heightened when the story is "told" only in part, for the narrator relies on the audience members' familiarity with the plot and draws them into the very telling of the tale. A song is often associated with a specific tale, and simply leading the group into that song may make it unnecessary to give any further plot details, freeing the narrator to concentrate on what he or she thinks more important or on additional textures.

Consider this example: As I discussed earlier, one of the most common story patterns calls for the planned concealment of a lovely young girl from the world. The "story" then focuses on how this situation is discovered and revealed, which then leads to the girl's being spirited away by an animal in human form or some other "scary" figure. One episode often describes a conversation between a mother and daughter where the girl is told to lock the door when no one else is there, and not to let anyone into the house unless she hears a password or a special song. Even with such a conventional narrative situation, I heard a number of renderings of this story situation that I simply could not follow in terms of plot development. In one case, the story was begun with a song that I did not recognize, and the storyteller entered the telling (insofar as she told it at all) somewhere in the middle, knowing the rest of her audience was adequately clued in by the song.

A number of stories had been performed at a wake that I was attending in Richland Park, St. Vincent, when an old lady, Nora Bristol, broke into the already tumultuous proceedings, yelling out, "See-ah" (meaning "look here" or "look there" or even "watch out"). A number of people looked her way but gave no vocal response. Again she shouted in her ancient growl, "See-ah." This time, two or three people responded, "See-ah," almost intoning the words. She then growl-sang, "See-ah, Nanny," to which everyone in the room responded, now singing:

> *See-ah, Nanny, see-ah.*

She took the audience one step further, singing in ringing tones:

> *See-ah, Nanny, see-ah.*

Knowing by now that the others would repeat what she had sung, at this point she got up and began to do a little shuffle-dance, knees slightly bent and body turning slightly to the left as the singing began in earnest:

> *See-ah, Nanny, see-ah*
> *See-ah, Nanny, see-ah*
> *Me Mammy Nanny coming (for to)*
> *See-ah, Nanny, see-ah.*

This song and dance lasted at least five minutes and managed to involve, in one way or the other, most of the people in the room and many of those right outside the windows, in the yard of the recently deceased man. Then she suddenly yelled out, "Oh no, that is not my mother's voice up in the cotton on the mountain." Again, the insistently repetitive song and dance started up, and lasted for another few minutes. At some point in the middle of a line, someone else called out, "Crick!" This is the common West Indian way of calling attention to the story. "Well then," Nora now said, "this woman had this only daughter, and whenever she left the house to go to the fields, she always told her daughter, if anyone came and called out to her, that she should tell them that she [her mother] had gone to the mountain [and therefore she could not open the door.]"

But the force of the singing and dancing was still coursing through the group, and they broke into the story, singing over and over:

> *See-ah, Nanny, see-ah*
> *See-ah, Nanny, see-ah*
> *See me, Mammy Nanny coming (for to)*
> *See-ah, Nanny, see-ah.*

Again, after a minute or so, she yelled, "Crick-crack!" now getting the traditional response from the others: "Rockland come." And she went on: "Then Nanny [the little girl's name] was surprised [by the witch-woman who had successfully imitated her mother's voice]. She went into the first bedroom, Nanny wasn't there. She went past the stairs and into the second bedroom, she couldn't find Nanny. She went downstairs, no Nanny. [Clearly Nanny had seen her mistake and run away.] She went back onto the mountain, and called out:

> *See-ah, Nanny, see-ah*
> *See-ah, Nanny, see-ah."*

Naturally, the song was again picked up by the entire group and carried on in three repetitions. This time, the singing came to a halt of its own, for the group was waiting for an indication of where the story was being taken. "No Nanny," she called to the mountain and she called to the cotton field:

> *See-ah, Nanny, see-ah*
> *See-ah, Nanny, see-ah.*

Clearly, Nora and her audience were more interested in singing and dancing than telling the story. Though I knew the language fairly well, I could not understand how the plot was being developed, for she had provided none of the clues to which I was accustomed. She proceeded to give a bit more dialogue, and to act out some more of the chase. But the tale was brought to a close, not through a profound ending to the action, but almost without warning, by a *deus ex machina* trick: "Her husband came down with his cutlass and ax and all and cut down all the trees, and gave that old lady a *whoppu!* and I came right here to tell all of you this story!"

Throughout the telling, this immensely animated lady leaped about as if she were wound up like a spring, pointing her crooked finger in the face of all the little girls listening, chuckling to herself about these ridiculous doings even while she sang at the top of her lungs, danced around, and brought other people onto the floor with her. Her performance was roundly enjoyed, not least because of her age and reputation, and because she was breaking the usual rules of decorum and obviously enjoying doing so. To be sure, such singing and dancing and other animating acts are the norm in West Indian performances at wakes, but few women—and especially, few older women—are willing to so perform.

Far from being judged harshly for garbling the plot, she was applauded for her abundant energies and her ability to bring everyone into the performance.

Many storytellers attempt to gain everyone's attention by starting a song with which everyone will begin to sing; or by shouting out the conventional opening, "Crick-crack!" Often, of course, this ploy will not work, as more than one person will attempt to grab the audience's attention. There may also simply be too many other things going on at that moment for even the best of the storytellers to gain center stage.

A number of other features of storytelling in such communities underscore how narration is open to interruption and digression, preventing tales from being told beginning to end. Scenes are not necessarily recalled in chronological sequence; I have recorded a great many stories that seem to begin in the middle or even at the end, only to go back to some scene that occurs earlier in the string of actions that make up the "plot," as we think of it conventionally. The tales, after all, are made up of commonplace episodes and characters, recognizable to the audience, and can therefore be played around with. The story may be stopped at any time, and on occasion, may be started again some time later, even after another story or two has been told, or after some other songs have been launched. In some cases, the sequence of episodes is fixed, and the effect of the story relies on a building of drama in a specific way. Naturally enough, these are the stories that have tended to be written down and put into folktale collections. But, equally often, the stories are picked up and put down almost serendipitously, and the narrator may string together conventional episodes in any of a number of combinations, a practice that led one early observer to regard them as "pointless, disjointed, mutilated fragments . . . [which often] break off just when the interest has reached its highest point."[23]

Nothing demonstrates the string-of-beads effect more than those stories, reported from a number of places in Afro-America, that begin or end with a song that seems to have little to connect it to the plot. For instance, the story "Assaulting All the Senses," from Surinam, concerns killing a tiger by getting him to drink monkey urine, yet ends with a song that apparently bears no relation to the story's action.

The use of such non sequiturs has been reported from one end of the sphere of Afro-American culture to the other. Daniel Crowley, for instance, in his many intimate descriptions of tellings, tales, and tellers, includes interruptions to the narrative flow caused by audience questions and comments, parenthetical remarks (including jokes and elaborate "I was there"-type exaggerations by the narrator), and the inevitable breaking out in song.

In an even more radically punctuated tale tradition, described and summarized by Richard and Sally Price among the Saramaka of Surinam, speakers introduce whole stories, little comic testimonial speeches about the truth of the story and veracity of its teller, and songs that are by convention attached to another story, in addition to the usual running commentary on the effectiveness of the tale or the truths implied in its message.

To the uninstructed ear or eye the usual tale from this tradition often seems formless and directionless, wittily or eerily animated but without the strong sense of whole-plottedness to which we are accustomed. I am sure that if we were able to go back to the original oral versions of many of our most common literary folktales, we would be surprised at their rambling character, their repetitiveness, and the number of parenthetical remarks introduced that sometimes develop into large-scale digressions. Storytelling, especially when it occurs at a wake (or some other celebration of life-transition), provides a context within which a number of other types of performance are encouraged, including riddles, games, and singing and dancing. When we read it, the song can also serve, as we have seen, as one character's "signature" or as a way of moving the story along. Listen to "The Old Bull and the Young One" and hear a father and son, locked in mortal combat over the control of the herd, sing of their powers to each other. The song can convey vital information, as in "My Mother Killed Me, My Father Ate Me" and "The Singing Bones," the verses revealing murderous wrongdoing. The song provides a comic point or even the punch line in stories like "The Latest Song" or "Poppa Stole the Deacon's Bull," which turn on self-incrimination. Similarly, in stories in which an animal transforms himself to human form to court and carry away the king's beautiful daughter, the change is sometimes accomplished through singing a magical song. When it is heard by the observing Old Witch Boy, the song becomes the key to the boy's ability to unmask the animal's disguise.

Since Trickster is often a marvelous fiddler, singer, or dancer in tales like "Making the Stone Smoke" or "Dancing to the River," the song and dance become a way of pulling off the trick around which the story revolves. In "Brer Rabbit's Riddle," Rabbit's singing and dancing abilities themselves become a matter of comment by both the narrator and the other characters.

Finally, a number of stories are told almost totally in song, such as "Don't Shoot Me, Dyer, Don't Shoot Me"; each development in the story is paralleled by a change in the song text. Hardly a simple embellishment, the song often determines the way in which the plot is developed.

In such involved performances the narrator becomes almost a character in the action—introducing personal remarks parenthetically (for instance, about how some character in the story is like someone in the audience or the community). The vibrancy of the narrator's role is made all the more interesting by the personalized "I" of conventional openings and endings. The taleteller can not only shout out the song or a characteristic speech ("Please don't throw me in the briar patch!") but can also introduce other first-person remarks, especially in the joking formulaic endings, such as you find in "Golden Breasts, Diamond Navel, Chain of Gold": "And so I myself ate at the wedding feast and they shot me with a cannon, till I sat down here."[24] This is another example of Daniel Crowley's aptly named "double lies"—a *lie* (prevarication) on top of a *lie* (story), which underscores the fictional quality of the tale while sustaining the reality of the speaker. A similar device is the "signature" ending that comes in many of the contemporary stories told in verse, such as "Stackolee":

> *I was born in the backwoods, for my pet my father*
>   *raised a bear,*
> *I got two sets of jawbone teeth, and an extra*
>   *layer of hair. . . .*

Bringing together first- and third-person narrative techniques sometimes animates an entire story, such as the routine, included in this book as "A Chain of Won'ts," or the following comic monologue of interlocking requests that Elsie Clews Parsons reports from Nevis in the West Indies:

I went down to Hilding Gilding, I met an old lady stooping. I asked for a glass of water. She said I must ask her daughter. Her daughter said, "Go to the well!" The well said, "Go to the cistern." The cistern said, "Go to the kettle." The kettle said, "Go to the bucket." The bucket said, "Go to the goblet." The goblet said, "Go to the glass." The glass said, "Drink up and leave me alone."[25]

VIII

One of the special delights of folktales of any sort is seeing how things of this world can be put together and taken apart, constructed and exploded without any need for logical explanation. Perhaps pointing this out verges on the obvious—that folktales operate in their own worlds, ones that depart from the everyday but in predictable directions. We can therefore give ourselves up to these alternative worlds without care— or even in the spirit of celebration and affirmation. Reading traditional tales becomes one of many activities in contemporary American culture that we classify as *play*, a term that encompasses all those encapsulated experiences that have their own rules, boundaries, and sets of expectations that ask us, albeit only for the moments of play, to give the leaders of the revels their due by willingly suspending disbelief in what is going on. Or, to put it more positively, to the extent that we give ourselves up to these experiences we willingly lend our energies to a process that promises us no payoff except the pleasure of the experience: for the fun of it all, or in terms consonant to many of the tales, "for the hell of it!"

A great many of the stories are actually told in the face of death, at wakes. They carry the special burden of taking community life apart and putting it back together again, through reaffirmation, through that special feeling of *communitas*.[26]

The stories represent the spirited voices of the night directed at the surrounding dark, and in the case of those told at wakes, they are expected to fill that void, at least for the first nine nights. If these seem like childish stories, that is not because they are juvenile in theme but because they are so direct and so vital, so essentially useful in the exuberance of their lies.

To introduce the particular worlds of these stories to you, I have chosen sections that describe what seems to be the major thematic development of the tales therein. For instance, the first group of stories dramatize how the world is put together, how well ordered it is, and how egotistical individuals become when they are discovered attempting to alter this order. It is especially concerned with the establishment of power relationships, relating power to one or another capacity given an animal or human; these stories are often concerned with the usefulness of testing this arrangement.

In the succeeding sections, the central conflicts are between respectable and riotous behavior. For instance, how-to-behave stories are balanced by how-not-to-behave stories! A great number of tales center on ingenious tricks that work, balanced by others in which our hero-scamp (or some other reprehensible type) gets caught. One whole section is given over to stories about the actual power confrontations that occur between blacks and whites in situations in which the former are exploited and forced into subordination—and insubordination—by the latter. Clearly, making such distinctions is strictly arbitrary, for the same characters, situations, even the same tricks may be found in many different sections. Moreover, the final segment is given over to little performance routines, fixed-phrase texts of the "for want of a nail the shoe was lost" sort, routines that, though they tell a story, do so with totally nonsensical means. Here too I base the distinction between these and tales in other sections on emphasis, for many of the other sections contain lies just as nonsensical as the ones found in this last grouping.

Just as this introduction began with an illustrative anecdote, let me so end it, with one that encapsulates a great deal of the vitality and the value placed on both wit and resilience in these tales. A story—"Some Are Up and Some Are Down"—widely told among blacks in the American South relates how Brer Rabbit and Brer Terrapin were feeling the drought one summer and complaining about how hard it had become to find water to drink. They decided they would pool their talents and make a search together, but Brer Rabbit just bounded off into the woods. He found an old house, and there was an old cistern at the house that operated on the two-bucket principle—when one bucket was up, the other was down. Rabbit just couldn't resist; he jumped into the empty bucket, and down it went right into the pool. Well, he drank his fill, but then he found that he couldn't get up.

Along came Brer Terrapin looking for his "friend." He heard a big racket going on in the middle of the woods. He ran to where the noise was coming from, and he saw the other bucket and the cistern below it. So he yelled down and asked if that was Brer Rabbit in there making all that commotion. Rabbit was glad to hear his voice, of course, and he yelled back up that, yes, it was him down there and he found all of this cool water. Didn't Brer Terrapin want to have a good long drink and swim? Terrapin thought that sounded like a good idea, so he asked Rabbit how he had gotten down there. Rabbit told him just to jump in that old bucket and it would bring him down. Meanwhile, Rabbit was getting set by getting back into the first bucket. So Brer Terrapin got in the bucket, and it went right to the bottom and brought Brer Rabbit back up to the top. After Terrapin had had his drink and had swum for a while, he yelled up to Rabbit and told him to bring him back up. Brer Rabbit naturally declined this privilege, and told Terrapin so. Terrapin said, "Are you going to go off and leave me down here in this well?" To which Rabbit replied, "You know, that's the way the world is going these days: some are up and some are down, and I don't think that's going to change much!"[27]

Notes

1. Jean Price-Mars, *Thus Spoke the Uncle*, tr. Magdaline W. Shannon (Washington, D.C.: Three Continents Press, 1983), 15–16.

2. Robert Farris Thompson, *The Flash of the Spirit* (New York: Random House, 1983), 18.

3. Henry-Louis Gates's recent survey of the rhetorical strategies of the term is useful here: "On 'The Blackness of Blackness': A Critique of the Sign and Signifying Monkey," *Critical Inquiry* 9 (1983): 685–723.

4. Reported in Langston Hughes and Arna Bontemps, *The Book of Negro Folklore* (New York: Dodd, Mead, 1949), 13.

5. Richard Price, *Saramaka Social Structure* (Rio Piedras: Institute of Caribbean Studies of the University of Puerto Rico, 1975), 18.

6. Melville and Frances Herskovits, *Suriname Folk-Lore* (New York: Columbia University Press, 1936), 195.

7. Walter M. Brasch, *Black English and the Mass Media* (Amherst: University of Massachusetts Press, 1981), 42.

8. See Roger D. Abrahams and John Szwed, eds., *After Africa* (New Haven: Yale University Press, 1983), 40–47, 77–107; Roger D. Abrahams, *The Man-of-Words in the West Indies* (Baltimore: Johns Hopkins University Press, 1983), 21–39.

9. W. J. Cash, *The Mind of the South* (New York: Vintage Books, 1941), 95.

10. Reprinted by Ben A. Botkin in *A Treasury of Southern Folklore* (New York: Crown, 1949), 69–70; from a newspaper report of 1859.

11. William Bascom, "African Folktales in America": VIII Deer's Hoof and Ear," *Research in African Literatures* 2 (1980): 175–78.

12. Also the subject of an article by William Bascom, "African Folktales in America: The Talking Skull Refuses to Talk," *Research in African Literatures* 8 (1977): 226–97. For the snake version, see 282.

13. William A. Owens, "Folklore of Southern Negroes," *Lippincott's Magazine* 20 (1877): 748–55; reprinted in *The Negro and His Folklore in Nineteenth Century Periodicals*, ed. Bruce Jackson (Austin: University of Texas Press, 1967), 144–56.

14. Matthew Gregory Lewis, *Journal of a West Indian Proprietor* (1834; reprint ed., Westport, Conn.: Negro Universities Press, 1974), 290–96.

15. Lawrence W. Levine, *Black Culture and Black Consciousness: Afro-American Folk Thought from Slavery to Freedom* (New York: Oxford University Press, 1977).

16. Ibid., 112–13.

17. The story, under the title "The Singing Bones," is surveyed worldwide in Antti Aarne and Stith Thompson, *The Types of the Folktale* (Helsinki: Finnish Scientific Academy, 1961), where it is given the number-type 780.

18. Such a pattern was discerned by Alice Werner as early as 1907, in her introduction to Walter Jeckyll's *Jamaican Song and Story* (London: David Nutt, 1907), xxxv. She relates this to African forms of story.

19. For a Vincentian localized rendering, see Abrahams, *The Man-of-Words in the West Indies*, 184–86.

20. Daniel C. Crowley, *I Could Talk Old-Story Good* (Berkeley: University of California Press, 1966), 17.

21. Arthur Huff Fauset, "Negro Folktales from the South: Alabama, Mississippi, Louisiana," *Journal of American Folklore* 40 (1927) : 302.

22. Daryl Cumber Dance, *Shuckin' and Jivin': Folklore from Contemporary Black Americans* (Bloomington: Indiana University Press, 1978), 260–61.

23. Charles Rampini, *Letters from Jamaica* (London, 1877), 116.

24. Crowley, *I Could Talk Old Story Good*, 23.

25. Elsie Clews Parsons, *Folklore of the Antilles, French and English* (New York: G. E. Stechert, 1936), 2:35.

26. I use *communitas* in the sense developed by Victor W. Turner in his series of studies of rituals and celebrations; see his *The Ritual Process* (Chicago: Aldine, 1969) and his introduction to *Celebrations* (Washington, D.C.: Smithsonian Press, 1982), 11–30.

27. Roger D. Abrahams, *Positively Black* (Englewood Cliffs, N.J.: Prentice-Hall, 1970), 51–52.

Part I

GETTING THINGS STARTED: HOW THE WORLD GOT PUT TOGETHER THAT WAY

INTRODUCTION

Stories of the earliest times establish how and why matters came to be the way they are today. Afro-American folktales reveal a different vision of just how life is ordered and given value from the "Once upon a time . . . happily ever after" kind. To a certain extent this difference lies in the small part of the repertoire given over to plotted success about villainy or sinfulness and its punishment. Instead, the Afro-American "In the beginning" stories underscore the value of accommodating yourself to the way things are (and always will be). The characters find themselves almost in perpetual opposition; we watch how the antagonists throw themselves, enthusiastically and playfully, into the eternal dramas pitting humans against animals, men against women, master against slave, even God against the Devil.

In a few rare stories, such as "Bringing Men and Women Together," a trick is pulled off by Anansi, to resolve the oppositions at least temporarily. More commonly, a resolution occurs because one or another of the opposed parties is able to persuade God (or some other judge) of the virtue of their position. Even more frequently, the figure making the judgment gets annoyed at what he has done and works out a countermeasure to reinstate the original opposition in different terms. For instance, in "Getting Common Sense," the achievement of Anansi in gathering together all wisdom is balanced against his dropping of the calabash in which he is carrying his collection, thereby allowing others back in on the storehouse of common sense.

The first anecdote, "Never Seen His Equal," suggested by Genesis, demonstrates this point nicely. In it we see, in spite of the statement of the all-powerfulness of God, that the Devil sets himself up in opposition to his Maker, and is able to translate this opposition to the relationship between men and women, work and leisure, and by extension, life and death. This tale, and similar ones, are jocular stories; both God and the Devil (in his many forms) are humanized, indeed given playful personalities. In "The Man Makes and the Woman Takes," for instance, God is portrayed as someone who can be persuaded to do something if you know how to address him effectively through grandiloquent speeches in praise. But he can also be easily angered by bickering or special pleading, and he will renege on a commitment when he sees it is excessive. This is precisely the situation in "Hankering for a Long Tail" and

"Getting Common Sense," where it becomes evident that the animals making the requests have overstepped themselves.

These tales tell us, then, how social and natural phenomena came into being, even to the inclusion of a number of charming "Just So" stories. But the way things *are* involves a good many social inequities, and the storytellers do not hesitate to use the stories of how things came to be that way to underscore the fact that life isn't usually very fair.

1
NEVER SEEN HIS EQUAL

I have seen something that God has never seen. What is it?''

''Now that could never be, for God has seen everything. He made the world and everything that's in it. Now if you call yourself smart, tell me something that God has never seen.''

''Well, I have seen my equal, and *that's* something God has never seen!''

''You're right there. There never has been a man who has seen his equal. But there was this one time when the Devil tried to be equal with God, too. The Devil was a chorister, you know, a leader of angels in Heaven, a pretty angel if there ever was one, and God when he created man made the Devil into his Overlord. But Lucifer tried to give the orders himself and had eaten of the Tree of Knowledge. Then Adam and Eve were so ashamed they were naked that they went and pinned fig leaves on themselves. The Devil came to them in the form of a serpent and told Eve when she asked, 'Oh no, you surely won't die if you eat now. God knows that the day you eat of this you will know good from evil and be his equal in that way.'

''So she ate, and God gave her the curse that she should have childbirth and that man would be her boss ever after. And Adam had to eat by the sweat of his brow and till the earth—until he could die and return to the earth.''

—Michigan

2
THE MAN MAKES
AND THE WOMAN TAKES

Y<small>ou</small> see, in the very first days, God made a man and a woman and put them in a house together to live. Back in those days the women were just as strong as the men, and both of them did the same things. They used to get to fussing about who was going to do this and that; and sometimes they'd fight. But they were even balanced and neither one could get the better of the other.

One day the man said to himself, "I believe I'm going to go see God and ask him for a little more strength so I can make this woman obey me. I'm tired of the way things are." So he went on up to God. "Good morning, Old Father." "Howdy, man. What are you doing around my throne so early this morning?" The man said: "I'm troubled in my mind, and nobody can ease my spirit except you." God said: "Put your plea in the right form and I'll hear it and answer."

"Old Maker, with the morning stars glittering in your shining crown, with the dust from your footsteps making worlds upon worlds, with the blazing bird we call the sun flying out of your right hand in the morning and consuming all day the flesh and blood of stump-black darkness, and flying home every evening to rest on your left hand, and never once in all your eternal years mistook the left hand for the right, I ask you please to give me more strength than that woman you give me, so I can make her obey me. I know you don't want to be coming down way past the moon and stars to be straightening her out all the time. So give me a little more strength, Old Maker, and I'll do it."

"All right, man, I'll give you more strength than the woman."

So the man ran all the way down the stairs from Heaven until he reached home. He was so anxious to try his new strength on the woman that he couldn't take his time. As soon as he got in the house he hollered, "Woman! Here's your boss. God told me to handle you in whatever way I please. So look at me good and listen well, for from now on I'm your boss."

The woman started fighting him right away. She fought him hard, but he beat her. She got her second wind and tried him again, but again he beat her. She got herself together and made the third try on him vigorously, but he beat her every time. He was so proud that he could whip her at last that he just crowed over her and made her do a lot of things she didn't like. He told her, ''As long as you obey me, I'll be good to you, but every time you disobey, I'm going to put plenty of wood on your back and plenty of water in your eyes.''

The woman was so mad she went straight to Heaven and stood before the Lord. She didn't waste any words either. She said, ''Lord, I come before you mighty mad today. I want back the strength and power I used to have.''

''Woman, you got the same power you had since the beginning.''

''Why is it that the man can beat me now and he used to not be able to do it?''

''He's got more strength than he used to have. He came and asked me for it and I gave it to him. I give to them that ask, and you haven't ever asked me for more power.''

''Please, sir, God, I'm asking you for it now. Just give me the same as you gave him.''

God shook his head. ''It's too late now, woman. What I give, I never take back. I gave him more strength than you, and no matter how much I give you, he'll always have more.''

The woman was so mad she wheeled around and went on off straight to the Devil and told him what had happened. He said, ''Don't be discouraged, woman. Just listen to me and take those frowns out of your face. Turn around and go right on back to Heaven and ask God to give you that bunch of keys hanging by the mantelpiece. Then you bring them to me and I'll show you what to do with them.''

So the woman climbed back up to Heaven again. She was mighty tired, but she was more mad than she was tired. So she climbed all night long and got back up to Heaven again. When she got before the throne, butter wouldn't melt in her mouth.

''O Lord and Master of the rainbow. I know your power. You never make two mountains without putting a valley in between. I know you can hit a straight lick with a crooked stick.''

''Ask for what you want, woman,'' God said.

''God, please give me that bunch of keys hanging by your mantelpiece, and I won't ask for anything more.'' He laughed and said, ''Take them.''

So the woman took the keys and hurried on back to the Devil with them. There were three keys. The Devil said, ''You see these three keys? They have more power in them than all the strength the man can ever get if you handle them right. Now this first big key is to the door of the kitchen, and you know a man always favors his stomach. This second one is the key to the bedroom, and he doesn't like to be shut out from that either. And this last key is the key to the cradle, and he doesn't want to be cut off from his generations at all. So now you take these keys and go lock up everything and wait until he comes to you. Then don't unlock anything until he uses his strength for your benefit and your desires."

The woman thanked him and told him, "If it wasn't for you, Lord knows what us poor women would do." So she started off, but the Devil stopped her. "Just one more thing: Don't go home bragging about your keys. Just lock up everything and say nothing until you get asked. And then don't talk too much."

The woman went on home and did like the Devil told her. When the man came home from work she was sitting on the porch singing some song about "Peck on the wood make the bed go good." And when the man found those doors fastened that used to stand wide open, he swelled up like pine lumber after a rain. First thing he tried to break in because he figured his strength would overcome all obstacles. When he saw he couldn't do it, he asked the woman, "Who locked this door?" She told him, "Me." "Where did you get the key from?" "God gave it to me."

He ran up to God and said, "God, woman has me locked away from my food, my bed, and my generations, and she said you gave her the keys." God said, "I did, man, I gave her the keys, but the Devil showed her how to use them."

"Well, Old Maker, please give me some keys just like them so she can't get full control." "No, man, what I give, I give. Woman has the keys." "How can I know about my generations?" "Ask the woman."

So the man came on back and had to give his respect to the woman. And when he did, she opened the doors. Man is proud, so it took a lot out of him, but he did what he needed to do, and the woman opened the doors.

After a while he said to the woman, "Let's divide up. I'll give you half of my strength if you let me hold the keys in my hands." The woman was thinking that over when the Devil popped up and told her, "Tell him no. Let him keep his strength, and you keep your keys."

So the woman wouldn't trade with him, and the man had to mortgage his strength to her to live. And that's why the man makes and the woman takes. You men is still bragging about your strength and the women is sitting on the keys and letting you blow off till she ready to put the bridle on you.

Stepped on a pin, the pin bent,
And that's the way the story went.

—*Florida*

3
BRINGING MEN
AND WOMEN TOGETHER

Long ago, it used to be that women
lived in one village and men in another. No man had ever gone to the
women's village and survived, but Anansi the Spider was tempted to try.

Anansi started out and soon approached the place where the women
lived. There, between their village and the river where they got water,
a giant tree had fallen across the path. Anansi hollowed out the trunk
of the tree and bored a hole through the bark. Then he climbed inside,
lay on his back, and stuck his penis (which had, meanwhile, grown to
considerable size) up out of the hole. It wasn't long before a woman
came along the path on her way to fetch some water. As she stepped
over the tree, she noticed that her buttocks were moving in a peculiar
way, and that she felt a strong urge to linger. Later on, she told her
sister about the strange sensation she had had and sang a song about the
"sweetness" of the wood. Her sister wanted to see this tree for herself;
once she had tried it, she could barely be pulled away. "What kind of
wood is it that's sweet the way this wood is sweet?" she wondered aloud.

Back at the tree, Anansi worked his way through all the women until
not a single one remained to be experienced. Time passed, and the first
woman to have crossed the hollowed-out tree began to feel peculiar. Her
belly hurt and her body didn't seem well. Then the same thing happened to her sister and, finally, the others felt it too, until every woman
was in the same condition. They were bewildered and were sure they
would die. Finally, the first woman gave birth to a daughter. She called
her sister and said, "Look at this thing I've delivered! It's made just the
way we are!" She was frightened at what had happened to her and
wanted to kill the thing, but her sister dissuaded her. Soon her sister also
gave birth, but to a boy. She noticed that it had something between its
legs, and terrified of its unnatural form, she wanted to kill it. But her
sister persuaded her to wait and see what would happen. Soon all the
women in the village had given birth, some to girls and some to boys; not
a single one had a (recognized) father. The children grew up; and after
a while the ones that were made like the women and the ones that were
made differently began noticing each other. Nothing more really need be

said about what happened after that; their work was all cut out for them. Anansi was pleased at having broken through the isolation of the two villages.

And that's how this way of life began.

—Saramaka (Surinam)

4
THE FIGHT OVER LIFE

One day Cat and Dog found themselves walking along the same way, so while they walked they began to fight as they always do. Of all things, they began to argue about life and death. Cat said, "Man is born to die, and that's it, he dies, that's all and never rises again." Dog argued back, "No, when people die, they can come back." Well, they went on and on like that.

Finally, Cat said, "Let's go and hear what God has to say about all this," and Dog had to agree to go the next day. But as soon as Cat had gone, Dog began to plan a trick on Cat so he could get to God first. Knowing Cat loved butter, he put a little butter all along the road so that Cat would stop for a while at each place, while he could run on ahead. But Cat was thinking too, and he did he same thing, only with bones for Dog.

The next morning, they set out early. They came to one of the places where Dog had put some butter, and Cat put his nose in the air, smelled it, and knew about Dog's trick. So Cat just went on. But when they came to the first bone, Dog stopped; he couldn't resist a bone to gnaw on. This happened each time Cat smelled the butter, and each time Dog found the bone. So Cat arrived at God's house long before Dog did.

Cat bowed to the Lord and asked him humbly if man died and remained dead or if he was raised again? God said, "Well, what do you think?" And Cat said, "I think that when people die that's all there is; they just stay dead." So God said, "Well, that sounds right to me the way you put it."

Now, along came Dog, and he asked God the same question. Well, God said to him that it was the very same question Cat had asked and they had decided that when people died they just died. "Cat said it, and it sounded right to me. But you, Dog, you are too late because you couldn't even keep your mind on what you were coming here for. Every time you passed a bone you just had to stop. It shall be as Cat has said it then: People when they die will not come back to life again."

And that's the way it has been since.

—Guadaloupe

5
THE WIND AND
THE WATER FIGHTING

——

The wind is a woman, and the water is a woman too, and they love to talk together. Mrs. Wind used to go sit down by the ocean and talk and patch and crochet. Mrs. Wind and Mrs. Water were just like all lady people, talking about their children and bragging on them.

Mrs. Water would say, "Look at my children! I got all kinds; the biggest and the littlest in the world. Every color in the world, and every shape!"

The wind lady bragged louder than the water woman: "Oh, but I got more different children than anybody in the world. They fly, walk, swim; they sing, they talk, they cry. They got all the colors from the sun. Lord, my children sure are a pleasure. Nobody has babies like mine, nobody."

Tired of hearing about Mrs. Wind's children, Mrs. Water got so she hated them. One day a whole bunch of Mrs. Wind's children came to her and said: "Mama, we're thirsty. Can we get a cool drink of water?"

She said, "Yeah, children. Run on over to Mrs. Water, but hurry right back."

When those children went to quench their thirst, Mrs. Water grabbed them all and drowned them.

When her children didn't come home, the wind woman got worried. So she went on down to the water and asked for her babies. "Good evening, Mrs. Water. Have you seen my children today?" The water woman told her, "No-oo-oo."

Mrs. Wind knew her children had come down to Mrs. Water's house, so she passed over the ocean calling her children, and every time she called the white feathers would come up on top of the water. And that's how come we got whitecaps on waves. It's the feathers coming up when the wind woman calls her lost babies.

When you see a storm on the water, it's the wind and the water fighting over those children.

About that time a flea wanted to get a haircut, so I left.

—*Florida*

6
THE WORD THE DEVIL MADE UP
——

The Old Devil looked around Hell one day and saw that his place was short of help, so he thought he'd run up to Heaven and kidnap some angels to keep things running till he got reinforcements from Miami.

Well, he slipped up behind a great crowd of angels on the outskirts of Heaven and stuffed a couple of thousand in his mouth, a few hundred under each arm, and wrapped his tail around another thousand. And he darted off toward Hell.

When he was flying low over the earth looking for a place to land, a man looked up and saw the Devil and asked him, "Old Devil, I see you have a load of angels. Are you going back for more?"

Devil opened his mouth and told him, "Yeah," and all the little angels flew out of his mouth and went on back to Heaven. While he was trying to catch them, he lost all the others. So he had to go back after another load.

He was flying low again and the same man saw him and said, "Old Devil, I see you got another load of angels."

Devil nodded his head and mumbled, "unh hunh," and that's why we say it that way today.

—Florida

7
THE KNEE-HIGH MAN TRIES
TO GET SIZABLE

The knee-high man who lived by the swamp wanted to be big instead of little. One day he said to himself: "I am going to call on the biggest thing in the neighborhood and find out how I can get sizable." So he went to see Mr. Horse. He asked: "Mr. Horse, I come to get you to tell me how to grow as big as you are."

Mr. Horse said: "Eat a whole lot of corn and then run round and round and round until you have gone twenty miles. After a while you will be as big as me."

So the knee-high man, he did all Mr. Horse told him to do. And the corn made his stomach hurt, and running made his legs hurt, and the trying made his mind hurt. And he just got littler and littler. Then the knee-high man sat in his house and thought about how it was that Mr. Horse didn't help him at all. And he said to himself: "I'm going to go see Brer Bull."

So he went to see Brer Bull and he said: "Brer Bull, I come to ask you to tell me how to get as big as you are."

And Brer Bull, he told him: "Eat a whole lot of grass and then bellow and bellow, and first thing you know you will get as big as I am."

And the knee-high man did everything that Brer Bull told him to do.

And the grass made his stomach hurt, and the bellowing made his neck hurt, and the thinking made his mind hurt. And he got littler and littler. The knee-high man sat in his house and he thought about how come Brer Bull didn't do him any better than Mr. Horse. After a while, he heard old Mr. Hoot Owl in the middle of the swamp preaching that bad people are going to have bad luck. The knee-high man said to himself: "I'm going to ask Mr. Hoot Owl how I can get to be sizable," and he went to see Mr. Hoot Owl.

And Mr. Hoot Owl said: "Why do you want to be big?" The knee-high man said: "I want to be big so that when I get into a fight I can win it." And Mr. Hoot Owl said: "Anybody ever try to pick a fight with you?" The knee-high man said no. So Mr. Hoot Owl said: "Well, if you don't have any cause to fight, then you don't have any reason to be any bigger than you are." The knee-high man thought about that and finally said: "But I want to be big so I can see a long way." Mr. Hoot Owl, he said: "When you climb a tree, can you see a long way from the top? You know, when it comes down to it you don't have any reason to be bigger in your body; but you sure have got a good reason to be bigger in the BRAIN."

—Alabama

8

PIG'S LONG NOSE
AND GREEDY MOUTH

Take notice that no good ever comes from being greedy, no matter how hungry you feel. And notice too that most troubles began way back there during the week when the Good Lord was so busy in creating the world. The fact is that he didn't have nobody to help him except the Angel Gabriel, and it kept him mighty busy mixing the mortar, and when anything went wrong there wasn't anybody to look after it. Of course Old Nick was there, but he was the kind that always gets himself and other folks into trouble.

Well, when the Good Lord made the pig he made him with a great long nose like an elephant so that he could pick up things and put them in his mouth, and he could scratch his own back with the end of his nose, and things like that.

But the pig, he had such a big appetite that he was just naturally hungry all the time, and that appetite of his got Mr. Pig into trouble right there at the start, and it's been getting him into trouble ever since.

You see, the Good Lord made the pig on a Friday, and that was an unlucky day to begin with. Then the acorns and the pumpkins weren't ripe yet so he didn't have anything to eat till Saturday morning, and he was so hungry by that time that he didn't know what he was going to do next.

Well, when they went out Saturday morning to feed the stock and they threw some corn over the fence, that pig ate the corn with his mouth and fed it in with that long nose so fast that the other animals couldn't so much as get a taste of anything.

When the Good Lord saw the way things were going, he knew that it wouldn't ever do. So he reached over the fence and picked up the pig by the middle of his back and laid him on a block and took a hatchet and chopped his long nose square off, close up to his mouth. Then he turned him loose and told him he had to root for his living the rest of his life. And that's how his nose come to be square across the end, like nobody's else's.

But if you ever had your nose cut off you know it hurts mighty bad, and when Mr. Pig begins to root with that square nose of his, it hurt so much that he can't help but grunt, and he's been grunting ever since. And every time you scratch Mr. Pig on the back it reminds him of the time when he had a long nose to scratch his own back, and he didn't have to work so hard to get a living, and that makes him grunt even harder. But the pig, he hasn't ever quit being greedy.

—*American South*

9
GETTING COMMON SENSE

Once upon a time, Anansi thought to himself that if he could collect all the common sense in the world and keep it for himself, then he was bound to get plenty of money and plenty of power, for everybody would have to come to him with their worries, and he would charge them a whole lot when he advised them.

Anansi started to collect up and collect up all the common sense he could find and put it all into one huge calabash. When he searched and searched and couldn't find any more common sense, Anansi decided to hide his calabash on the top of a very tall tree so that nobody else could reach it.

So Anansi tied a rope around the neck of the calabash and tied the two ends of the rope together and hung the rope around his neck so that the calabash was on his belly. He started up the tall tree, but he couldn't climb very well or very fast because the calabash kept getting in his way. He was trying and trying so hard when all of a sudden he heard a voice burst out laughing in back of him. And when he looked he saw a little boy standing on the tree's root: "What a foolish man! If you want to climb the tree front-ways, why don't you put the calabash behind you?"

Well, Anansi was so angry to hear that big piece of common sense coming out of the mouth of such a little boy after he had thought he had collected all the common sense in the world that Anansi took off the calabash, broke it into pieces, and the common sense scattered out in the breeze all over the world. Everybody got a little bit of it, but no one got it all. It was Anansi who made it happen that way.

Jack Mandora, me no choose none.

—Jamaica

10
HANKERING FOR A LONG TAIL

One time, when the summertime had come and the hot sun liked to burn up everything, mosquito and sandfly and gnat, always buzzing, used their mouths too much and bothered Brer Rabbit too much. He didn't have anything to brush off the pests, so he began jumping around uselessly and soon ran out of breath.

So he went to scheming to see what he could do to get rid of them. He noticed Brother Bull Cow standing under a tree, chewing his cud in a satisfied way, and every time those bugs lit on him, Brother Cow switched his tail and knocked them, and they flew away and left him alone. Just then Brother Horse came along the road, and a fly buzzed around his haunches, and he just switched his tail and killed it dead.

Brother Rabbit was eating himself up with envy, vexed because he didn't have a long tail. He thought that when things like that were handed out he should have gotten a tail like they had. It made him mad to remember how he had been obliged to cry and beg with Sister Nanny Goat just to fool her into giving him even that stumpy little bit of cottontail he had now. There isn't any way in this world to take away the shame of having something that is nothing at all, like his stub of a tail. Fly and flea just buzz around, laughing at that poor excuse for a switch. A long tail would also have made a fine figure of a fellow! But there wasn't any way to go back to those times; the question he faced was how he was to get a sizable tail right now.

He went home and he thought about it and thought about it until suddenly he hatched out a plan. It was a right bodacious plan too, but then Brer Rabbit is a right bodacious creature. There isn't anything so outrageous that he won't try to do it at least one time. And Brer Rabbit put on his store clothes, with his blue breeches and his yellow shoes, all fine. And he cocked his hat and he took the path that went to Heaven to ask God if he wouldn't be so kind as to give him a long tail like those other creatures have.

It wasn't easy for Brer Rabbit to find the way because everybody he asked seemed to have a different notion about how to get there. Brer

Rabbit listened to everyone and paid no attention to most of them, but kept a steady head about him and kept pushing on. And, bye and bye, it seemed as if the narrow path kind of rambled and rambled in front of him. And he went on and on until at last he was right at the front gate of Heaven and at the head of the long avenue of the Beautiful City. And he pushed in and walked along the grand boulevard and at last there he was, right in front of the Big House.

That house sure is big! Brer Rabbit had to walk a mile or more around the veranda to the back porch plaza. When he got there he took off his hat and he put it on the step. He took his bandana and dusted his yellow shoes and wiped his forehead and threw the rag into his hat. Then he reached over and knocked on the floor of the porch at the back door. Tap! Tap! Tap!—sort of easy-like.

His heart almost failed him, but nothing happened. He waited a little while. Then he rapped again. Maybe God isn't in—but no fresh tracks led away from the house. He decided to rap again, a little louder this time. And this time, God hollered out in the house in a great big voice, "Who is there?" Brer Rabbit was really scared. He said in a timid kind of whisper, "It is me, sir."

God eyeballed him and said, "Who is me?" "Well just me, Brer Rabbit, sir." And God asked mighty severely, "What do you want, Brer Rabbit?" "Just a little something, sir. Won't take you barely a minute to do it."

"Humph! What sort of business are you up to now?" God said. "Sit down and I'll be out right away."

Brer Rabbit sat down on the steps. And after a long time while he mostly wished he had never come, God finally came out. The first look Brer Rabbit had of God, he was so scared that he almost took off and ran away. But when he thought about how badly he wanted that long tail he held his ground.

He jumped off the step and displayed his best manners, pulling his forelock and scraping the gravel with his feet. "Now, Brer Rabbit," God said, sort of gruffly, "what is the thing that you want so badly that you have gotten bold enough to come way up here like this?" Brer Rabbit pulled his forelock again and answered, "Master, this weather is so hard on us poor creatures, I don't see how we survive. Looks like Brer Mocking Bird is the only one that can enjoy himself, and he has to go away out to the top of a tree in the woods before he can jump around and sing the way he does. We who have to stay on the ground have Satan's own time. Every sort of devilish biting and stinging and troubling thing just trying to stay alive, we have to contend with. The gnats, and green head flies, and sandflies, and the redbugs, and the ticks, and the chiggers, and all kinds of varmints like that bother us from first day clean to dark. They work from can to can't, and they work faithfully! And when darkness comes and they leave off, the mosquitoes and the gallinippers join hands to take their place and suck out blood and annoy us until the first day brings its light.

Even then, Master, some creatures make out better than the rest because they have a real tail, not just a leftover stump like Sister Nanny Goat gave me. I noticed what nice tails Brother Bull Cow and Brother Horse were given. When a fly bothers them, all they have to do is wave their tails in the air and the flies and the mosquitoes are scared if they don't fly off. *Ping!* That long tail cracks down and they are dead. Now, sir''—Brer Rabbit got mighty bold and brash, but his voice came out as sweet as molasses—''I just came here to ask you to do something for me, Master! Please, sir, if you could be so kind as to give me a long tail so that I can brush away those pesky critters too.''

God cast his eyes down at Brer Rabbit and squinched up his forehead and looked him over. Then he puckered up his mouth like he had been biting a green persimmon. And he said, ''You are made like you are made. You have been contrary about that tail from the first day. Sister Nanny Goat did just as I told her, and she was kind to give you any tail at all. Even with all the blessings you already have you come here to me to get a tail like the very best of creatures have. Hmm! You are mighty little to have a long tail. Brother Horse and Brother Bull Cow are big and stand high off the ground, but your belly mostly drags in the dust. You can jump around in the grass to keep those flies off.''

''That's what I have been doing, sir, but it just wears me out.''

God looked at him closely. ''You just want to be in high fashion, don't you?''

''Who, sir? Why do I have to think about fashion, sir! I am thankful for what I have got. The flies are the only thing that brought me here!'' But Brer Rabbit was so scared he couldn't keep from trembling just a little bit.

God kind of smiled at him and then sort of squinched up his face. ''Well, you are smart enough to get here, and that is more than most, so I reckon I'll set you a task to see just how smart you are. That will keep you from bothering me for a while. And if you do it, I might give you a long tail.''

With that he turned around and went into the house. He came right back out again with something in his hand.

Brer Rabbit jumped up from where he had been sitting and became polite again. God gave him a crocus bag and said, ''Take this bag and bring it back to me full of blackbirds.''

Poor Brer Rabbit cried out at that. But God looked sour at him, cocking his eye, and Brer Rabbit shut up.

Then God gave him a hammer and said, ''Knock out Brother Alligator's eye teeth with this hammer and fetch them to me.''

This time Brer Rabbit was so upset that he could only grunt.

Last, God took a little calabash and said, ''This you must fill with Brother Deer's eye water. You understand? Now, you get away from here. And don't come back bothering me until you have done the whole lot.'' Then he turned on his heel and went back in the house and slammed the door.

Brer Rabbit felt so cut down to size that he could scarcely pick up his hat to put on his head and go home. His heart was heavy and he dragged his feet along the ground. He walked along and he thought. He shook his head and he thought. How could he catch blackbirds by the sackful? He wasn't a hawk! Why would anyone with good sense go anywhere near Brother Alligator's mouth—so how could he knock out his teeth with a hammer?

And getting Brother Deer's tears! Brother Deer is so foolish and skittery, if you just ask him about anything he gets scared and runs off. God fixed it so that it's mighty hard to get a long tail. It didn't look like he was ever going to get his.

Now, you know, Brer Rabbit is little, but he is as quick as a whip. And he worked his mind day and night on how to get a sack full of blackbirds. At last he figured out a scheme. During the fall, the white folks burn off the rice-field bank where the grass grows all summer and stands heavy. The fire just goes along, and the smoke rolls along ahead of it, and then all the birds living in the grass get foolish about the smoke and fly about like crazy.

So when they started that year, Brer Rabbit went down on the bank and got a big clump of grass, just a little way in front of where they were beginning to burn. And when the fire came that way and the heavy smoke reached them, the birds flew around madly, lighting on one bush and then another, just running away. At last they came down right in front of Brer Rabbit's clump of grass. He jumped out and caught a bird and put it in the sack, and he jumped around again and caught some more. The birds were so slippery he got his sack full at last, and he was very proud.

Next, he began to think about the problem of Brer Alligator's teeth. One fine day, he got his fiddle and he went down to the rice field by the river. Now Brer Rabbit worked the fiddle in his own devilish way at all the dances and picnics in the country, and made people lose their religion. And a whole lot of them had been turned out of their churches because they had crossed their feet to his dancing tunes, because when Brer Rabbit played, there aren't any feet around that can take any notice whether they are crossing or not!

Now, this day, Brer Rabbit sat down on a stump and started to play and sing and pat his foot. And when he did that something began to move, because he knew no animal could resist that music, expecially Brer Alligator. Brer Alligator, who was way down at the bottom of the river, yelled at him and came to the top of the water, poked his big eyes out, and looked about to see who it was playing like that. But Brer Rabbit didn't pay any attention to him. He sang and he played and he patted his foot.

Right away that music started to pull Brer Alligator out of the water, and he swam over to the bank. Still Brer Rabbit didn't pay any attention to him. He went on singing and playing and patting his foot just like no one was around.

Brer Alligator crawled out on the edge of the marsh and then climbed right up on the bank and sat down by Brer Rabbit; he popped his eyes up at him and listened.

Brer Rabbit stopped at last. Brer Alligator praised him to the sky for his singing and fiddling. Then he asked Brer Rabbit, "Can you teach me how to play like that? I sure would like to play and sing like that, yes sir!"

Brer Rabbit made like he was thinking a little while and then said to him, "Can't say about the singing because it depends on how a man's mouth is made if he can learn to sing or not."

"Look in my mouth, Brer Rabbit, and tell me if it is right." Brer Rabbit pretended like he didn't care. He told him it was hard to teach anyone to sing anyway. "Do, Brer Rabbit!" he begged him. But Brer Rabbit pretended like he hadn't heard him. He just kind of scratched his head and started to hum a tune.

"Brer Rabbit! Man! You've got to stop that just for a minute. Look and see if I have the kind of mouth that you can teach how to sing," Brer Alligator kept on begging.

Brer Rabbit just yawned and stretched himself and looked down at Brother Alligator, shaking his head and making clucking sounds.

"All right, then, maybe I can, but you have to listen to me close and do just as I say." "Sure! Sure! Brer Rabbit. Anything you say!" "Then shut your eyes tight till I tell you to open them again."

Brer Alligator shut them. "Open your mouth wide—*real* wide—and hold it that way." And Brer Alligator did just as he was told.

Brer Rabbit grabbed a little lightwood knot, and he jammed it into Brer Alligator's jaws to keep them wide open, clear back by the corners of Alligator's mouth, so he couldn't shut it down. And he said, "Bite on that a minute and hold still."

Then he whipped out his little hammer that God had given him and—*Crack! Crack!* He knocked out both of Brer Alligator's eye teeth. And then just as quickly he ran off with them.

Brer Alligator hollered and yelled and thrashed around looking for Brer Rabbit. But Brer Rabbit didn't pay any attention to him. He just scampered on home. And every time he thought how Brother Alligator's jaws might have scrunched down on him, he had to wiggle himself to feel if he was all there. Brer Rabbit was mighty satisfied with himself then, yes sir.

The last thing Brer Rabbit had to do was to get that calabash full of Brother Deer's eye water, and then he would have all the tasks done. But he knew that getting the eye water would be the hardest task of all. He could hardly sleep again because he was so bothered by the problem. He couldn't think of anything except to ask Brer Deer directly to help him. But that wasn't any use because Brer Deer knew Brer Rabbit too well and would figure out that he was going to play some kind of trick on him. Deer would take off so fast when he saw Brer Rabbit that no one would even be able to catch up with him to argue the point.

The problem got so hard Brer Rabbit almost gave up the whole thing, but then he saw Brer Horse and Brother Bull Cow with their nice long tails switching and swinging and it reminded him of how fine he would look, walking on the Big Road, if he just had one of those long tails. He could sure sashay along the road and shake that tail about and just look so handsome. So he began to scratch his head again and think about it some more. Man, he is a schemer, that Brer Rabbit! And finally he got a notion.

Brer Deer lived way down deep in the woods. A long time ago, he used to live in the settlement. He and Brer Dog even planted land together. But Brother Deer, or one of the family, had a fight with Brer Dog; and what with one thing or another it got to be such a goings-on that Brer Dog and his family made Brer Deer and his family run away every time they got a chance. That's what made Brer Deer begin a little place way off by himself. Poor Brer Deer was scared of nearly all the animals because of that experience; in fact, he was the most frightened creature in the woods.

Brer Rabbit counted on that, and he went deep in the woods till he came to the little clearing where Brer Deer had his house. And he found Brer Deer lying down in the hot sun in his yard. Brer Rabbit passed the time of day with him. They talked a little bit about crops and weather and who had been turned out of church, and who had gotten killed at the picnic, and such things.

At last Brer Rabbit said, "Brer Deer, you know I am your friend, right?" "Sure, Brer Rabbit, I know that well." "You know I always do stick up for you, right?" "Yes, man!" "Very well, then, I have to inform you that they have been throwing your name about so much up in the settlement that I had to come and tell you about it."

"What! What did they say?" "They said that you are no good at jumping any longer—that Sister Nanny Goat takes the prize for jumping nowadays."

"Now! Brer Rabbit—who could say that? Why, I can jump three times higher than that no-count little thing!"

"Brer Dog said you couldn't, and I told him that just wasn't so. And I came here to give you the chance to show me how you can still jump higher than anyone. Now I saw Sister Nanny Goat jump a bush almost as high as that one over there, and she could jump it good, too. Can you jump that high?"

Brer Deer sucked his teeth and shook his head and just kind of smiled. He said, "Man! When I was a little fellow, before I could ever walk, I could jump bushes like that one."

"Well then, why don't you go on? That bush goes awful high up in the air for anyone to jump! But if you can make it, I would sure like to see it, so I could pass the word along in the street to Brer Dog."

Brer Deer got up and he ran down his yard and then he came back over the bush just high and fine and graceful. Brer Rabbit looked astonished. He whistled. He slapped his leg praising Brer Deer for how high and far he could jump. "That isn't anything," said Brer Deer, and he jumped over another bush a little higher, just to show what he could do.

Brer Rabbit loudly sang out his praises. "Brer Dog is sure going to have to shut his lying mouth now when I carry the tale to everyone about how fine you jump. Man! you look nice doing that! I reckon you could even jump that big bush yonder?"

And Brer Deer took that one as well. So Brer Rabbit pointed to higher and higher bushes, till at last he fixed on one that wasn't a bush—it was more like a young tree, and it had a heavy fork and was all tangled up with jasmine and cat briar and snailox and supplejack and other kinds of vines.

When he looked at the three with jasmine, Brother Deer sort of hesitated. But Brother Rabbit encouraged him with so much praise that he reared back and jumped it. He leaped very high in the air—but he didn't quite make it. He landed slam bang right in the middle in the big fork!

The jump knocked his breath out of him. When he twisted around to get out, he got so tangled up in that jacktwine and briar that it got harder to move. He hollered for Brer Rabbit to come help him.

Brer Rabbit made sure that he was caught fast and he said, "Man, I can't help you. You're too heavy and you might fall on me and bust my back. But I will go right away to the settlement and find some help to get you out.''

With that, he ran down the path until he was out of sight and then he threw himself on the ground and he rolled and cackled and laughed at the way he had fooled Brer Deer and the way he was going to get his way now. Brer Rabbit laughed till he was crying.

And then he got up off the ground and pulled his handkerchief out of his pocket and ran back to Brer Deer wailing and sobbing: ''Brer Deer, you better get out of that bush now. Don't waste a minute because Brother Dog—'' And he made out like he couldn't speak, he was crying so. ''What's the matter, Brer Rabbit?'' Brer Deer was so scared that his voice trembled.

''You better come out right now because Brother Dog and his whole family are right behind me, and they're going to kill you and eat you if you stay in that bush. When I got close to the settlement, I saw them running down the path coming this way.''

Brer Deer shook and kicked himself. He pulled and he pushed but all he did was tangle himself more tightly in the jacktwine. ''Get out of that bush, Brer Deer! Get out of that bush before they get here and kill you right in front of my eyes.'' And Brer Rabbit bowed his head and mopped his eyes with his handkerchief.

Then Brother Deer burst out crying. He struggled and cried, and then he struggled and then he cried some more. And all that time Brother Rabbit made out as if he was helping him out, but all he was doing was tangling the vines around Brother Deer's foot. Then he held out that little calabash that God had given him and caught every drop of that eye water which ran out of Brer Deer's eyes.

Every time Brer Deer looked like he might let up, Brer Rabbit screeched out, ''Oh, poor Brother Deer! You are going to be caught today!'' And Brer Deer would bawl out some more.

But even so, the calabash wasn't quite full yet, so Rabbit called out, ''I see them getting closer, Brer Deer, howling for your meat! Hurry, Brer Deer, and get loose, or no one can save you!''

Brer Deer struggled the best he could, but he couldn't move himself and he went on crying. And so with all of that Brer Rabbit filled the calabash with eye water. Then he picked up a little calabash and he wiped his own eyes and he didn't say anything else. He just walked away and left Brer Deer high up in the tree fork.

Now that Brer Rabbit was all done with the tasks God had given him, he didn't waste any time. He went home, put on his store clothes, and picked up the three things that God had asked for. He took the path to God's house and all the way he swaggered.

When he got there this time he didn't go to any back door, no sir! He walked right up to the front door, and knocked bold and loud. *BAM! BAM! BAM!*

God was in the house and hollered out, "Who is there?" And Brer Rabbit answered, "It's me, sir, Brer Rabbit!"

"What?" God's voice sounded kind of curious. "You're back already, are you? You haven't done all the tasks I set you to do?" "Yes, sir." "You mean to tell me you got all those things I told you to get?" "Yes, sir. They are all right here, sir." "Take care with your foolishness, Brother Rabbit! You don't lie to me?" "No, sir. I have them all, sir."

God didn't make any sound for a while, but after such a length of time he came out to the door. Brer Rabbit kind of puffed himself up. He felt so pleased with himself that he was just grinning all over his face. Then he noticed that God looked vexed. And Brer Rabbit straightened up his face, put down the sack of blackbirds, then reached down in his side pocket and pulled out a little handkerchief and unwrapped Brer Alligator's two eye teeth, and handed them to God. There they were for sure, and the blood was still on them. And he hunted in his coattail pocket and pulled out the calabash full of Brother Deer's eye water.

God tasted it, and smelled it, and then he said, "You are smart, aren't you, Brother Rabbit! Very well, then!" He pointed to a loblolly pine tree out in the yard. "You go and seat yourself underneath that pine tree till I can fix you up." And he turned around and went into the house and slammed the door after him. *BAM!*

Now Brer Rabbit went and did as he was told and sat down under that tree. But he didn't like the way God had slammed the door at all. And he didn't like the way God had talked to him. And he noticed that God's eyes showed red like fire when he looked at the pine tree. And Brer Rabbit couldn't rest easy because he was getting more and more scared. He scuffled around on his haunches—little bit by little bit—till he got to the other side of the tree trunk from the Big House, and sneaked away real quietly, keeping the tree between him and the house, till he got away over in the corner of the yard where he could hide himself under a heavy sucklebush.

Well, sir! He was hardly in the sucklebush before, *BRAM! BRAM! BRAM!* Out of the clear sky that didn't have so much as a cloud in it came the biggest thunder and lightning bolt that ever was seen. Wow! It just crashed down on the loblolly where Brer Rabbit had been! And the next minute, where that pine tree stood, there wasn't anything at all except a pile of kindling, and that was afire. Brer Rabbit didn't stop for anything! He took his feet in his hands and hit the avenue to the Big Gate and he screamed.

About that time, God in the Big House looked out the window and saw a little something just running lickety-split down the avenue. And he looked close and sure enough it was Brother Rabbit. He leaned out the window and put his two hands to his mouth and he hollered: ''Ah-hah! Ah-hah! Ah-hah! You think you are so smart, eh! You are so drat smart! Well, get a long tail yourself!''

—*North Carolina*

11
THE DEVIL'S DOING

When the Devil gets a good hold of you he's bound to leave his mark on you; and what's more, he'll leave that mark on your children and your grandchildren.

And that's the way it was with the catfish. If he'd kept out of the Devil's hands, he'd been a whole lot better-looking than what he is, and so would his children. You've noticed that the catfish doesn't have any scales like the other fish, but he wasn't always that way. It happened more or less like this.

It was a Friday morning that the Good Lord created the fish, and when he turned them all loose in the river it was a mighty fine sight, I'll tell you. And there wasn't any more handsome fish in the crowd than the catfish. He was all covered with red and yellow and blue scales according to the kind of catfish he was, and he was one of the finest fishes in the river.

Well, the Good Lord created all the different kinds of fish in the forenoon, and he set out to make all the chickens and the turkeys and the geese in the afternoon. When it come dinner time, he put away the tools and locked the door and put the key in his pocket and went along up to the Big House to get something to eat.

After dinner, the Good Lord and the Angel Gabriel were walking along back down the Big Road, picking their teeth, and talking about whether they ought to make the birds with scales, like the fish, or with feathers, when who did they bump into by the side of the road but Old

Nick, and he was scraping the scales off some catfish he had just caught. And the Good Lord said: "Look here, Nick, what in the name of common sense are you doing with those fish?"

Old Nick said, "Well, I noticed it was Friday, and I thought I'd just have a fine fish dinner, and so when I saw how crowded the fish were in the river, I thought it would sort of help matters if I'd just thin them out a bit. So I reached down and grabbed a few of the catfish that were handiest, and I was just getting them ready to fry when you came along."

And the Good Lord came right back: "Well, you look here; you just put those fish back in the water and go on about your business, you trifling good-for-nothing black rascal!"

He made Old Nick put all the fish back in the water. Now, where the scales had been scraped off it hurt so that the catfish went down to the bottom and rolled over in the mud to try and do something about the pain. Bye and bye, the pain went away, but the scales never grew back, and from that time on the catfish haven't had scales.

And that's what makes me tell you that you better always keep out of reach of the Devil, because if you don't, he'll make trouble for you and all your kinfolks.

—*American South*

12
THE JOHN CROWS LOSE THEIR HAIR

In a time before time, there lived a man who hated the John Crows (which is what we call those buzzards) because they were so greedy. Eat, eat, eat, they just always sat around preening themselves, waiting to eat. So he wanted to get rid of them if he could. But, one way or another, he never got the chance, and the John Crows kept on vexing him.

But John Crow thought of himself as a dandy, and it grieved his heart that he had never been christened. So he called a meeting of all his friends and relations, and they resolved to go ask the man to give him a proper name.

When the man heard this he rejoiced greatly, and he said to himself, "Cunning is better than strength. Now I'm going to get back at Old John Crow for all these years."

So he named a day, and told John Crow to make a feast, and to kill a big hog, and to buy a little rum and a little port wine and plenty of salt fish and yams and other vittles, and to invite all the folks to come along to the big party. On the day he had picked, all the John Crows of that country gathered themselves together. And one brought beef, and another brought ham, and another a suckling pig, and another fowls; and there were yams and cocoas and sweet potatoes and everything, and plenty of liquor.

And when the man came to the place where the eating match was to be, he brought with him a big barrel full of white flour, which he said was his contribution to the feast. Then all the John Crows clapped their wings with joy and said: "Hi! the good buckra [white man]!" But the man only smiled to himself and said, "Today is for me, tomorrow for you; you shake my hand, but you don't shake my heart!" Then he turned to the John Crows and told them to light the fire, for he said he would need to boil the flour and water together to make a grand cake for the christening.

When the barrel of flour was empty and the water was boiling, bubbling up upon the fire, he called all the John Crows around him and said, "You see this barrel here?" They all said, "Yes, we see it." "Very well," he said, "come around and put all your heads into it, and you mustn't lift up your head or look around till I tell you, because I have something secret to make ready for the christening." So they all put their heads into the barrel. Then the man took the cauldron of boiling water and stepped up behind them softly, softly, and he lifted the pot and poured all the boiling stuff on their heads. And he laughed and said, "Now listen to this and listen well: I now christen you, John Crow!"

Now, they all got scalded that way, but after all they didn't die. When they got better they found all their heads peeled bald where the boiling water had fallen on them.

And this is why John Crows have bald pates to this day.

—Jamaica

13
TADPOLE LOSES HIS TAIL

When the people don't do what they're told to do, they always get into trouble sooner or later. And that's just what happened with the tadpole.

Now, the Good Book doesn't say anything about the creation of the frogs. But this business of the tadpole explains why it happened. The fact of the matter is that the Good Lord didn't make the frog; he just made the tadpole, and the frog, he came along a few days later.

If you've ever made any tadpoles, you've noticed that it's just as easy to make a hundred of them as it is to make one. And that's the reason why the Good Lord, when he first made the tadpole, he didn't make just one; he made a whole lot of them so they would be company for each other.

Well, he made a whole lot of tadpoles, just like I said, and when they were all finished there were so many that they were all around on the ground, in everybody's way, and you couldn't walk about without stepping on a lot of them. So the Good Lord, just to get them out of the road as much as anything else, told them to go along down to the cornfield next to the creek and do some pulling weeds. And the tadpoles all went down in that field, but it was a mighty hot day and they felt mighty lazy. And Old Nick, he came along there about that time, like he always does, and he said, "Boys, there's a mighty fine swimming hole right down there in the creek."

And the tadpoles, they said, "Yes I guess there is, but the Good Lord sent us down here to pull these weeds."

And Old Nick, he said that of course they should pull the weeds, but they could pull them up a whole lot faster if they just had a little swim first. Then he persuaded them that it wouldn't do any harm just to take a look at the water. Well, no sooner did the tadpoles get a sight of that water then they forgot all about pulling weeds, and every one of them jumped in the creek and went swimming. They never did have such a good time.

The Good Lord was awfully busy in those first days, and he just completely forgot about the tadpoles. But one day Old Nick went up and remarked in a kind of offhand way that some of these new animals that the Lord was creating were pretty trifling when it comes to doing what they've been told. The Good Lord asked him what he's talking about; and Old Nick reminded him that he had sent those fool tadpoles to pull up the weeds in the cornfield but instead of that they'd all gone swimming, and they hadn't pulled a single weed, and the cornfield was getting to be terribly overgrown.

So the Good Lord called up the tadpoles and asked them what they had been up to, and they told him that they had been in swimming. And he told them that he didn't so much mind their going swimming, but he couldn't have folks around that didn't act like he told them. And he told them that he's going to cut their tails off because they didn't mind him. And the tadpoles began to cry and to beg him not to chop their tails off because they couldn't swim without them and if they happened to fall in the water they'd be drowned unless they could swim. But the Good Lord told them he's going to give them legs so that they could swim a little, but he wanted them not to forget that there was something else to do in this world other than swimming. So he chopped off all their tails, but he gave them some legs and made frogs out of every one of them. Then he told them to go on about their business.

And to this day, you notice that the tadpole, when he grows up, he loses his tail, gets legs, and turns into a frog. And to this day, tadpoles are mighty poor hands at pulling weeds.

—American South

14
THE OWL NEVER SLEEPS AT NIGHT

Have you noticed that whenever a creature starts in this world with a habit, it stays with him all his life? Not only that, he passes it along to his children and his grandchildren. Whether the creatures have two legs or four legs or more legs, it works just the same. Another thing is that if you want to see anything, you must open your eyes.

There's the case of the owl. At the very first, he was like the other birds; he had the same kind of eyes as the other birds, and he flew around and sang in the daytime, and when it came dark he went to roost and stuck his head under his wings and slept till daybreak, just like the others. But it wasn't long before he got into the habit of sitting up nights and calling out *"Who-who,"* and he never has stopped that to this very day.

Here's what happened. During the week that the creatures were all created and were just learning how to keep house, the Good Lord noticed that there was something going wrong in the night and he felt mighty nervous about the whole thing. One morning he found the pig's tail curled up; the deer's tail and the goat's tail were cut clean off; the possum and the rat had had their hair all pulled off their tails; the duck had lost his forelegs, the snake had lost all of his; and the guinea hen and the turkey gobbler had lost all the hair off their heads; and nobody knew what was going to happen next. God had a suspicion that it was some of Old Nick's doings, but he never said anything to anybody. He just asked the owl if he wouldn't stay up that night and keep a lookout and see what the matter was and how it all happened. And the owl said he'd be mighty proud to stay up, only he's afraid he couldn't see very well in the dark. Then the Good Lord told him that all he had to do to see in the dark is to open his eyes wider. So they fixed it up that way.

And when it turned dark, the owl never went to bed; he just opened his eyes a little wider, and got out in the open where he could look around over the countryside. And every time it got a little darker the owl would open his eyes a little wider, and he didn't ever have any trouble seeing all the carryings-on.

And sure enough, along about midnight he saw Old Nick tying knots in the horses' manes. And the owl called out, "*Who-who, who-who, who-who-ah?*" With that, Old Nick was so scared that he ran away and left the horses, and struck out across the country in the dark. But the owl opened his eyes wider than ever, and he followed after him, and every once in a while he'd call out, "*Who-who, who-who, who-whoo-ah!*"

Well, he sure scared Old Nick away; but when it became day, Mr. Owl had his eyes so wide open that he couldn't shut them, and the bright sun gave him a terrible headache. Then the Good Lord told the owl that as he'd been up all the night before he could find himself a shady place and sleep all day to make up for the loss of sleep the night before.

But when night came around again the owl was rested, and he didn't have his headache anymore, and he felt so wide awake that he stayed up that night too. After that, he got the habit, and he's had it ever since.

—*American South*

15
WHY HENS ARE AFRAID OF OWLS

Once upon a time, hens had dances every Saturday night. They employed Mr. Owl for a fiddler. He was always careful to go away before daylight so that the hens might not see his big eyes. The last time he fiddled for them, daylight caught him, and when the hens had a look at his eyes they were frightened into fits and all went squalling out of the room.

Ever since then, the hen cannot even bear the shadow of an owl.

—*Kentucky*

16

THE GIFTS OF DIPPER
AND COWHIDE

It was famine time. Terrapin had six children and Eagle had three. Eagle hid behind a cloud and he went across the ocean and got palm oil and seed to feed his children with. When Terrapin saw it, he said, "Hold on. It's hard times. Where did you get all that to feed your children? Can't you show me where you get all that food?" Eagle said, "No, I had to fly across the ocean to get it." Terrapin said, "Well, give me some of your wings and I'll go with you." Eagle said, "All right. When shall we go?" Terrapin said, "Tomorrow morning by the first cock crow we'll leave." So tomorrow came, but Terrapin couldn't wait until dawn. Three o'clock in the morning, Terrapin came in front of Eagle's house and said *"Cuckoo—cuckoo—coo."* Eagle said, "Go on home now and lay down. It ain't day yet." But Terrapin kept on. *"Cuckoo—cuckoo—coo."* And bless the Lord, Eagle came out and said, "What you do now?" Terrapin said, "You put three wings on this side and three on the other side." Eagle pulled out six feathers and put three on one side and three on the other side of Terrapin. Then Eagle said, "Let's see you fly now." So Terrapin began to fly. One of his wings fell out. But Terrapin said, "That's all right, I got the other wing. Let's go." So they flew and flew; by the time they got over the ocean, all the eagle feathers had fallen out and Terrapin was about to fall in the water. Eagle went out and caught him and put him under his wings. Terrapin said, "Gee, it stinks in here." Eagle let him drop in the ocean.

So he went down, down, down to the underworld. The King of the Underworld met him there. He said, "Why are you coming here? What are you doing here?" Terrapin said, "King, we are in terrible condition on the earth. We can't get anything to eat. I have six children and I can't get anything to eat for them. Eagle, he only has three, and he went across the ocean and got all the food he needs. Please let me have something to feed my children." King said, "All right, all right," so he gave Terrapin a dipper, and he said to him, "Take this dipper. When you want food for your children, say:

> *Bakon coleh*
> *Bakon cawbey*
> *Bakon cawhubo lebe lebe.''*

So Terrapin carried it home and went to his children and said to them, "Come here." When they all had come, he said:

> *Bakon coleh*
> *Bakon cawbey*
> *Bakon cawhubo lebe lebe.*

Gravy, meat, biscuits, everything appeared there in the dipper. His children had plenty to eat now.

Now, one time he said to his children, "Come here. This will make my fortune. I'm going to sell this to our king." So he showed the dipper to the king. He said:

> *Bakon coleh*
> *Bakon cawbey*
> *Bakon cawhubo lebe lebe.*

And all kinds of things came out of dipper, and he was able to feed everyone. So the king went and called everybody to see this miracle. Pretty soon everybody was eating and they ate and ate everything, meats, fruits, all kinds of things. So he took his dipper and went back home. He called his children, but now when he tried to get food, nothing came out of the dipper. When it's out, it's out.

So Terrapin said, "All right, I'm going back to the King of the Underworld and get him to fix the whole matter up." So he went down to the Underworld and said to the king, "King, what is the matter? The dipper doesn't give me food to feed my children anymore. So the King of the Underworld said to him, "Take this cowhide and when you want something, say:

> *Sheet n-oun*
> *n-jacko*
> *nou o quaako.''*

So Terrapin went off and he came to a crossroads. Then he said the magic:

> *Sheet n-oun*
> *n-jacko*
> *nou o quaako*

The cowhide began to beat him. It beat, beat. Cowhide said, "Drop, drop." So Terrapin dropped down on the ground, and the cowhide stopped beating. So he went home. He called his children in. He gave them the cowhide and told them what to say, then he went out. The children said:

> *Sheet n-oun*
> *n-jacko*
> *nou o quaako.*

The cowhide beat the children. It said, "Drop, drop." Two children were dead and the others were all sick.

So Terrapin said, "I must go to the King of the Underworld and find out what he has done to us." So he called the local king, he called all the people. All the people came. So before he had the cowhide beat, he had a mortar made and he got in there and got all covered up. Then the king said:

> *Sheet n-oun*
> *n-jacko*
> *nou o quaako.*

So the cowhide beat, beat. It beat everybody, beat the king too. That cowhide beat, beat, beat right through the mortar that was on Terrapin and beat marks on his back.

And that's why you never find Terrapin in a clean place, only under leaves or a log.

—Alabama

17
BUH NANSI SCARES BUH LION

Buh Lion and his wife had eight children, and once upon a time he decided to build a house because he had too many children for the one they were living in. So he started. But Buh Nansi saw what he was doing and he saw a chance for himself— he's such a selfish person, you know. So for every board put on the house, Anansi came at night and put up another. When Lion put on one board, Anansi would go and put on one, too. Lion went to feed his cattle, and when he came back, he thought that something strange was going on. He asked his wife, "What is happening here? I find more boards than I put up myself. Girl, haven't you seen anything?" She said, "What?" He said, "Well I put on one board and go away and come back, and I see that there is another one next to the one I put up."

Anyway, that went on for a considerable time. For every board he put on, he counted the number and went away. And Anansi always sneaked in there and put on one more. Finally, Anansi saw that the house had gotten to the stage where someone could live there, and you know who that was going to be.

So one day he picked up his fiddle and went into the house. As Buh Lion was coming in the house, Buh Nansi started a song out on the road and everybody started to sing and dance with him.

> *I killed ten thousand Lions yesterday,*
> *Lions yesterday, Lions yesterday.*
> *I killed ten thousand Lions yesterday,*
> *What do you think about ten today?*

Now, when Lion heard that, he got a little worried because he knew Buh Nansi was a clever, clever fellow, and he thought maybe he had found a way of capturing lions and eating them. Lion went to the house. He yelled out, "Eh, Buh Nansi, you having a fine time, man." He said, "Yes, Buh Lion." Lion said, "But, Buh Nansi, with all this music you are playing here, you must want something to drink. You do drink rum, no?" Nansi answered, "Yes, man." Lion said, "Well, man, I'll send one of my children for a bottle. Child?" he called. "Yes, Papa." "Go by Mr. Noname's and tell him I said to send liquor here, because we are having a fete." When the child went off a little distance, Lion followed him and said, "Child?" "Yes, Papa." "Wait there at the shop. Don't come back, you hear?" "Yes, Papa." He was worried that Buh Nansi was going to eat all his children.

So they sat there waiting for a considerable time. Finally, Buh Nansi got restless again and started to play his fiddle:

> *I killed ten thousand Lions yesterday,*
> *Lions yesterday, Lions yesterday.*
> *I killed ten thousand Lions yesterday,*
> *What do you think about ten today?*

Even more he worried when he heard everybody dancing and singing that song again. Buh Lion sat down; he said, "Buh Nansi, it's been awhile since the child's been gone." "Why worry about that child? Maybe he lost his way." After a while, Buh Nansi said, "Well, what are you going to do?" Lion said, "Man, I guess I must send another one." He called to the next child and said, "Child, come here. Go by Mr. Noname and tell that child when he comes back I'm going to flog him." He went on, "Go by Mr. Noname's shop, tell him I sent for a bottle of liquor because we have a fete going on here." When that child got a little way down the road, Lion said, "I wonder why that first one didn't understand me. Let me make sure this one does." So he said, "Child, wait for me," and his child stood off waiting. Lion said, "When you go, don't come back." And this was what Buh Lion did with all the children. Each time Buh Nansi started playing his fiddle afresh, harder and harder:

> *I killed ten thousand Lions yesterday,*
> *Lions yesterday, Lions yesterday.*
> *I killed ten thousand Lions yesterday,*
> *What do you think about ten today?*

Buh Lion said, "Buh Nansi, I'm so angry with my children, I'm going to have to send my wife to see about them, because they must be playing some kind of game or going a different way than they are supposed to. She should know where they are." Buh Nansi said, "Well yes, I understand, Buh Lion." Lion told his wife, "Go and find those children and flog them for me, and tell them to make haste home. Make haste to come back, you hear?''

His wife set out. He said, "Buh Nansi, I don't feel good about all this. Let me tell my wife once more." Buh Nansi said, "All right." "Oh, wife," Lion said, calling her. "Wait there for me." When he caught up with her, he said, "When you go, don't any of you come back."

He went back, and Buh Nansi was still playing the fiddle and singing and dancing:

I killed ten thousand Lions yesterday,
Lions yesterday, Lions yesterday.
I killed ten thousand Lions yesterday,
What do you think about ten today?

He played on and on. Finally, Lion decided that he was going himself. He said, "Buh Nansi, this is just taking too much time. I have to go and see where my wife and those children are, you hear? You wait here and I'll come right back." Lion lit out, never to come back. He had to leave the house and give it to Buh Nansi because of that song.

So Lion always has to live in the bush, while Buh Nansi lives in the house.

—*Tobago*

18

TESTING THE GOOD LORD

One day Brer Lizard and Deacon Frog were trying to get through a crack in a split-rail fence. Now, in those days, Brer Lizard sat up straight like Deacon Frog does today. Old Deacon Frog said: "I'll get through this crack here if the Good Lord spares me." He tried it and, bye and bye, he squeezed through just fine. Brer Lizard was more uppity. He said, "I'll get through this crack here whether the Lord spares me or not." He tried it, but, *kerflip*, down came a log and smashed him flat.

That's why the lizard is flat today and crawls in the dust on his belly, while the frog sits straight and hops around.

—Mississippi

19

MR. POSSUM LOVES PEACE

One night, Brer Possum called by for Brer Coon, according to a previous arrangement. After gobbling up a dish of fried greens and smoking a cigar, they rambled forth to see how things were getting along. Brer Coon was one of these natural pacers, and he raced along like a pony. Brer Possum, he went in a hand-gallop; and they could cover a heap of ground, man. Brer Possum, he got his belly full of persimmons, and Brer Coon, he scooped up a good many frogs and tadpoles along the way. They ambled along just as sociable as a basket of kittens until, bye and bye, they heard Mr. Dog talking to himself way off in the woods.

"Supposing he runs up on us, Brer Possum. What are you going to do?" asked Brer Coon. Brer Possum sort of laughed around the corners of his mouth. "Oh, if he comes, Brer Coon, I'm going to stand by you," said Brer Possum. "What are you going to do?" "Who, me?" asked Brer Coon. "If he ran up to me, I'd give him one big scratch!"

Mr. Dog, he came, and he came a-zooming. He didn't wait to say "Howdy" either. He just sailed into the two of them. The very first pass he made, Brer Possum put on a grin from ear to ear, and keeled over like he was dead. Then Mr. Dog, he sailed into Brer Coon, and right there is where he really found himself in trouble because Brer Coon was cut out for that kind of business and he fairly wiped up the face of the earth with him. You better believe that when Mr. Dog got a chance to make himself scarce, he took it—at least what there was left of him. He went yelping through the woods like he was shot out of a musket. And Brer

Coon, he sort of put his clothes back into shape and dusted himself off. Brer Possum, he still lay there like he was dead, until finally he raised himself up carefully, and when he found the coast was clear, he scrambled up and scampered off like something was after him.

Next time Brer Possum met Brer Coon, Brer Coon refused to respond to his greeting and this made Brer Possum feel bad as they used to make so many excursions together. "What makes you hold your head so high, Brer Coon?" asked Brer Possum. "I'm not running around with cowards these days," said Brer Coon. Then Brer Possum got pretty mad. "Who's a coward?" he asked. "You are," said Brer Coon, "that's who. I'm not associating with anyone who lies down on the ground and plays dead when there's a fight going on," he said.

Then Brer Possum grinned and laughed fit to kill himself. "Lord, Brer Coon, you don't expect that I did that because I was afraid, do you?" he said. "Why I wasn't any more afraid than you are this minute. What was there to be scared about? I knew you'd fool Mr. Dog if I didn't, and just lay there watching you shake him up, waiting to get in the fight when the right time came," he said.

Brer Coon turned up his nose. "That's a likely tale," he said, "when Mr. Dog didn't even touch you and you keeled right over and lay there as still as a board." "That's just what I was going to tell you about," said Brer Possum. "I wasn't any more scared than you are right now, and I was fixing to give Mr. Dog a sample of my teeth in his neck, but I'm the most ticklish fool that you ever laid eyes on, and no sooner did Mr. Dog put his nose down along my ribs than I got laughing, and I laughed until I lost the use of my limbs, and it's a mercy unto Mr. Dog, because a little more and I'd eat him," he said. "I don't mind fighting, Brer Coon, any more than you do, but I just can't stand tickling. Get me in a fight where there isn't any tickling allowed and I'm your man," he said.

And down to this day, Brer Possum's bound to surrender when you touch him in the short ribs, and he'll laugh if he knows he's going to be smashed for it.

—*Georgia*

20
GET BACK, GET BACK

God did not make folks all at once but sort of in his spare time. One day, for instance, he had a little time on his hands, so he got some clay, seasoned it the way he liked it, then he put it aside and went on to doing something more important. Another day, he had some spare moments, so he rolled the clay all out, and cut out the human shapes, and stood them all up against his long gold fence to dry while he did some important creating. The human shapes all got dry, and when he found time, he blew the breath of life into them. After that, from time to time, he would call everybody he had made back up to him and he would give them new-made spare parts. For instance, one day he called everybody and gave out feet and eyes. Another time, he gave out toenails that Old Maker figured they could use. So then, one day he said, "Tomorrow morning, at seven o'clock sharp, I'm going to give out different colors. Everybody be there on time. I've got a lot of creating to do tomorrow, and I want to give out colors and get the whole thing over with. So everybody has to come round the throne at seven o'clock tomorrow morning!"

So next morning, at seven o'clock, God was sitting on his throne with his big crown on his head and seven suns circling around it. Great multitudes was standing around the throne waiting to get their color. God sat up there and looked east, and he looked west, and he looked north, and he looked south toward Australia. So he looked over to his left and moved his hands over a crowd and said, "You'll all be yellow people!" They all bowed low and said, "Thank you, God," and they went on off. He looked at another crowd, moved his hands over them, and said, "You're red folks!" They made their manners and said, "Thank you, Old Maker," and they went on off. He looked toward the center and moved his hand over another crowd and said, "You're white folks!" They bowed low and said, "Much obliged, Jesus," and they went on off.

Then God looked way over to the right and said, "Look here, Gabriel, I miss a lot of multitudes from around the throne this morning." Gabriel looked too, and said, "Yes, sir, there's a lot missing." So God sat there an hour and a half and waited. Then he called the angel again and said, "Look here, Gabriel, I'm sick and tired of this waiting. I have too much creating to do this morning. You go find them folks and tell them they better hurry on up here if they expect to get any color. If they fool with me, I won't give out any more."

So Gabriel ran on off and started hunting around. After a long while, he found the missing multitudes lying around on the grass by the Sea of Life, fast asleep. So Gabriel woke them up and told them, "You better get up from there and come on up to the throne and get your color. Old Maker is getting mighty worn out from waiting. If you fool with him, he won't give out any more color."

Soon the multitudes heard that, they all jumped up and went running toward the throne, hollering, "Give us our color! We want our color! We got just as much right to color as anybody else." So when the first ones got to the throne, they tried to stop and be polite. But the ones coming on behind got to pushing and shoving so, till the first ones were thrown against the throne so hard that the throne was careening all over to one side. So God said, "Here! Here! Get back! Get back!" But they were keeping up such a racket that they misunderstood him, and thought he said, "Get black," and that's been their color ever since.

—*Florida*

21
NO JUSTICE ON EARTH

Well, the Devil was talking with someone, complaining that no matter how much he might try to do good that he would never get a good name for his deeds. There just wasn't any justice on this earth. When the other person said he didn't know whether that was really so, the Devil said, "All right, I'll show you what I mean."

So the Devil went to God and asked him if he would be so good as to put out a big stone in the path, so that he could put out a bag of money on it. God put out the stone and the Devil set the money on it. And along came someone walking down the path without looking where he was going, and he stumbled on the rock. "What the Devil," he said, "I stubbed my toe on this stone.'' Then someone else came along and he saw the money. He grabbed hold of the bag and looking upward, he said, ''Praise God; I say to you many thanks for sending this money my way!''

Then the Devil said to the man, ''You see what I mean. Didn't I tell you there is no justice on earth?''

—Surinam

Part II

MINDING SOMEBODY ELSE'S BUSINESS AND SOMETIMES MAKING IT YOUR OWN

INTRODUCTION

O_{ne} of the storytellers' favorite
ways to get the action going is to have a character stir things up by
bringing news to the neighborhood and thus piquing the interest of other
characters, sometimes making one of them angry. The collision of interests or wills then ignites the rest of the plot. The first story in this
section, "Meeting the King of the World," is one of the many Afro-
American tales about how problems first came to beset humans.

The consequences of the coming of trouble are compounded because
some people get full of themselves and feel the need to challenge everyone
around with regard to their successs and their importance. Thus, in both
"Mr. Bamancoo Gets Dropped" and "Tiger Becomes a Riding Horse,"
boasting turns into a competition between two old friends about who is
going to have the most girl friends, the objective being not only to be
the most successful in courtship but also to embarrass and even kill off
rival males.

We can naturally expect the trickster to put his nose into such situations, and included in this section are a number of stories, such as "Making the Stone Smoke," in which Trickster comes from outside the
community, competes with all the most powerful "insiders" for the hand
of the king's beautiful daughter, and manages not only to boast effectively
but to pull off a trick that makes good on his boast.

In some of the stories included in this section, a small animal manages
to become involved in, and control, the behavior of seemingly more
powerful creatures by acting as an intermediary and provoking fights,
as in "The Signifying Monkey" and "The Tug-of-War between Elephant
and Whale." The desire to assert masculine power animates most of
these stories, usually to the detriment of those who choose to carry out a
project in a boastful manner. Indeed, two basic strategies of male attempts at dominance are confronted in most of these tales: operating by
brute strength and using one's wits. For the most part, neither approach
produces winners; we might even say that these are parables of how to
be a vigorous loser.

One rendering of this pattern has a smaller animal, usually a trickster
type, figure out a way of pitting the larger animals against each other,
to hilarious results. In some cases, such as "The Tug-of-War between
Elephant and Whale," we can laugh along with Rabbit at how these big
guys can be manipulated. But in "The Signifying Monkey" we are

amused not only by the details of the fight between Lion and Elephant but also by the antics of Monkey, who is caught at his nonsensical game.

This last story is given in *toast* form—that is, in rhyme. This story, which is told widely in the United States, has been collected in a number of Afro American communities and has been a part of several phonograph recordings of folktales.

In other stories in this section, the confrontation is brought about by a father who pits his children against each other to see which one loves him better—the King Lear story in a very different setting! In ''The Singing Bones'' and ''Making the Stone Smoke,'' both the father and his contest are regarded as foolish by the audience; in other tales, more serious issues regarding the rituals of death arise. The arranged contest between children is, of course, an elaboration of the conflict between parents and children, especially fathers and sons. This theme will emerge in a number of other sections in an even more basic fashion, in stories in which the king attempts to have all his male rivals killed, including his sons (as in ''The Old Bull and the Young One''). This display of masculine insecurity usually emerges in comic form, however, even when the comedy leads (as it does) to acts of mayhem and death. Indeed, the reader may be struck by the emphasis on death that pervades these amusements; the subject becomes a little more understandable when we recall that most of these tales are often told at wakes.

22
MEETING THE KING
OF THE WORLD

$\mathbf{O}$h, this was way before your time.
I don't remember just when myself, but the old folks told me about it.

John was riding along one day, with his long legs thrown around his
horse, when the grizzly bear came running out in the middle of the road
and hollered: "Hold on a minute! They tell me that you are going
around telling everybody that you are the King of the World."

John stopped his horse and said, "Whoa! Yeah, I'm King of the
World, don't you believe it?" "No, you aren't King of anything. Not
until you whip me. Get down here and fight it out with me."

John hit the ground and then the fight started. First, John grabbed
a rough-dried brick and started to rub the fat off of the bear's head. The
bear just fumbled around until he got a good hold on John's middle,
then he began to squeeze and squeeze. John knew he couldn't stand that
much longer. He'd be just one more man whose breath had given out. So
he reached into his pocket and got out his razor and slipped it between
the bear's ribs. The bear turned him loose, keeled over, and just lay there
in the bushes. He had enough of that fight. John got back on his horse
and rode off.

The lion smelled the bear's blood and came running to the grizzly and
started to lap up his blood. Now the bear was really scared that the lion
was going to eat him while he was lying there all cut up and bleeding
nearly to death. So he hollered and said, "Please don't touch me, Brer
Lion. I have met the King of the World, and he cut me all up."

Now that really got the lion's bristles all up. "Don't you just lay
down there and tell me that you met the King of the World if you're not
talking about me! I'll tear you to pieces!" "Oh, don't touch me, Brer
Lion! Please let me alone so I can get well." "Well, don't you call anybody else King of the World, then!"

"Well, Brer Lion, you just sit behind these bushes and see what is
coming by here before long."

Lion squatted down by the bear and waited. The first person he saw
going up the road was an old man. Lion jumped up and asked Bear, "Is
that him?"

Bear said, "No, that's Uncle Yistiddy, he's used-to-be!"

After a while a little boy passed down the road. The lion saw him and jumped up again. "Is that him? he asked the bear. Bear told him, "No, that's little tomorrow, he's going-to-be. You just stay quiet, and I'll let you know when he gets here."

Sure enough, after a while John came down the road on his horse. But now he had his gun with him. He wasn't taking any more chances. The lion jumped up again and asked, "Is that him?"

Bear said, "Yes, that's him! That's the King of the World."

Lion reared up and cracked his tail backward and forward like a bull-whip. He boasted, "You wait till I get through with him and you won't be calling him King anymore!"

He jumped out into the middle of the road right in front of John's horse and laid his ears back. His tail was cracking like torpedoes. "Stop!" Lion hollered at John. "They tell me you call yourself King of the World!"

John looked him dead in his eye and told him, "Yeah, I'm King. If you don't like it, you don't have to take it from me."

Lion and John stared at one another for a minute or two and then the lion sprung on John. Well, you never saw such fighting and wrestling since beginning, when the morning stars sung together in the celestial choir. Lion clawed and bit John, and John bit him right back.

Now, after a while John got to his rifle and he raised the muzzle right in old lion's face and pulled the trigger. Long, slim black feller, he snatched it back and heard it beller! Now that was too much for the lion. He turned around and started to run off into the woods. John leveled on him again and let him have another load, right in his hindquarters.

The old lion gave John the back of his tail. He was into the woods where the bear was hauling some heavy loads.

"More over," he told Bear. "I need to lie down, too."

"How come?" the bear asked him, knowing the answer all too well.

"I have met the King of the World, and he has ruined me."

"Brer Lion, how did you know you met the King of the World?"

"Because he made lightning flash in my face and thunder at my hips. I know when I've met a king; now move over."

—*Florida*

23
MR. BAMANCOO GETS DROPPED

___

I'm going to Heaven today-o
Titty flam, titty flam-o-day.
All of us are flying to Heaven today-o
Titty flam, titty flam o-day.
I'm going to Heaven today-o
Titty flam, titty flam o-day.
To see those Chateaubelaire *girls*
Titty flam, titty flam o-day.
To see some lovely girls up there
Titty flam, titty flam o-day.

This is one about Mr. Bamancoo* and Mr. Chickenhawk. Compé Chickenhawk and Compé Bamancoo were *compé* and *mackmé*—they were best friends and divided everything. But both of them loved those girls, and one time Compé Chickenhawk decided he didn't want to share them anymore. So, one day, Mr. Chickenhawk went up to Heaven and came back talking about how all the girls up there on the other side belonged to him. Mr. Bamancoo wouldn't believe it. He said, ''Well, what we have to do is for me to go up there so you can prove it.'' Mr. Bamancoo wanted to see all those pretty girls anyhow, you know, because he had lots of girl friends too. So Mr. Chickenhawk said, ''Well, so be it, then, but you have to remember that I'm a man who flies very fast. So if you want to come, you'll have to ride on my back!''

Titty flam, titty flam o-day
Titty flam, titty flam o-day.
Going to Heaven
Titty flam, titty flam o-day.
Going to Heaven
Titty flam, titty flam o-day.
To see those pretty girls there

* Refers to someone with huge genitals because of elephantiasis.

> Titty flam, titty flam o-day.
> *I'm going to see those pretty girls there*
> Titty flam, titty flam o-day.

Crick!

Now listen, Compé Bamancoo got on Compé Chickenhawk's back and they really flew fast, so fast and so long in fact that Compé Bamancoo started to get very worried, but he hung on. And Compé Chickenhawk started to sing again:

> Titty flam, titty flam o-day
> Titty flam, titty flam o-day.
> *To see those pretty girls there*
> Titty flam, titty flam o-day.
> *I'm going there to see them*
> Titty flam, titty flam o-day.

Now, listen to what happened. You know Compé Chickenhawk flew lower and lower, but got faster and faster. Compé Bamancoo said he wanted to get off, and Compé Chickenhawk said that would be all right, so when he got close to the ground—about as high as the top of a coconut —he let him go, *Boop!* And Compé Bamancoo busted when he hit the ground, and the people who were down there when he hit were washed downstream when he hit, his grains were so filled with water.

And I was there and danced with all the ladies that came to see what happened.

—St. Vincent

24
THE TUG-OF-WAR BETWEEN ELEPHANT AND WHALE

One day Compere Rabbit and Compere Bouki were making a trip together. When they reached the shore of a sea, they saw something that was so strange that they stopped to watch and listen. An elephant and a whale were talking.

The elephant said to the whale: "Compere Whale, since you are the largest and strongest around in the sea, and I am the largest and strongest on land, we rule over all beasts; and anyone who doesn't like it, we'll just have to kill, all right, compere?" "Yes, compere," agreed the whale. "You keep the land and I'll keep the sea, and between us we'll rule everyone."

"You hear that?" said Bouki. "Let's get going. We better not get caught listening in on their conversation." "Oh, I don't care," said Rabbit. "I know more tricks than they do. Just watch how I am going to fix them." "No," said Bouki, "I'm scared. I'm going." "Well, go if you can't have a little fun because you are scared of everything! Go ahead and leave, and quick because I'm sick and tired of you."

Compere Rabbit went to get a rope that was long and strong. Then he got his drum and hid it in the grass. He took one end of the rope, and went up to Elephant, complimenting him: "Sir, Compere Elephant, you who are so good and so strong, I wonder if you could do me a favor? You could help me a lot and save me from losing my money, too, if you would do me a favor." Elephant always enjoyed hearing such fine compliments, so he said: "Compere, what do you want? I am always ready to help my friends."

"Well," said Rabbit, "This cow of mine is stuck in the mud down on the coast, and I have tried and tried, but I'm just not strong enough to pull her out. I hope you can help me. If you could just take this rope in your trunk, I could tie it to the cow and you could pull her out. When you hear me beat the drum, if you will pull hard on the rope, we'll soon have her out of that mud." "That's all right," said Elephant. "I guarantee I'll pull the cow out, or the rope will break." So he tied the rope around the neck of Elephant.

Then Compere Rabbit took the other end of the rope and ran toward the sea. He went up to Whale and paid her some of the same compliments. He asked her if she wouldn't help him free up his cow that was stuck in the woods in a bayou. He was so convincing that no one could ever refuse him anything. So Whale took hold of the rope and said: "When I hear the drum beat, I'll pull." "Yes," said Rabbit; "begin pulling gently, and then harder and harder." "Don't you worry," said Whale; "I'll pull out the cow, even if the Devil is holding her." "That is good," said Rabbit. And he went off aways from both Whale and Elephant so they couldn't see him and began to beat on his drum.

The elephant began to pull so hard that the rope was stretched to the breaking point. Whale, on her side, was pulling and pulling, but she was losing ground and being pulled to the land because she didn't have any ground to plant herself on. When she saw that she was being pulled onto the land she beat her tail furiously and plunged headlong toward the depths of the sea. Now Elephant found himself being dragged into the sea. "What is happening? That cow must be really scared!" So he twisted the rope around his trunk and planted his feet so well that he was able to pull so hard that he pulled Whale onto the shore.

When he looked back he was astonished to see that his friend Whale was on the other end of the rope. "What is this? I thought I was pulling Compere Rabbit's cow," he said. "Rabbit told me the same thing," said Whale. "I think he must be playing a trick on us." "He'll pay for that," said Elephant, "if I ever catch him on land." "And if he comes near the sea, I'll get him," said Whale.

Hearing all this, Compere Rabbit said to Bouki: "It's getting pretty hot; I guess it's time for us to get out of here." "You see," said Bouki, "you are always getting us into trouble." "Oh, don't worry, I'm not through with them; you'll see how I'll fix them yet."

So they went away and after a while they separated. When Compere Rabbit arrived in the wood, he found a little dead deer. The dogs had worried the hair off its skin in many places, and when Rabbit skinned the deer and put it on his back, he looked just like a wounded deer.

He passed limping by Elephant, who said to him: "Poor little deer, how sick you look." "Oh, yes, I'm really suffering," he said sadly. "You see, Compere Rabbit poisoned me and put his curse on me, because I wanted to stop him from eating grass on land. Take care Mr. Elephant, Compere Rabbit has made a bargain with the Devil; he will be hard on you too, if you don't take care."

Now Elephant got frightened. He said, "Little deer, tell Compere Rabbit that I am still his friend. When you see him, send him my regards."

A little later the deer met Whale in the sea. "Poor little deer, why are you limping so? You seem sick today." "Oh yes, Compere Rabbit did that. Take care, Compere Whale, for Rabbit can poison anyone he wants because the Devil gave him the power to do so." The whale was frightened too, and said: "I don't want anything to do with Devil; send Compere Rabbit my regards when you see him again."

Now Rabbit met Bouki and he took off the deer's skin and they both laughed until their sides ached. "No matter who's the largest," Rabbit said, "I'm still the strongest—at least when I use my head!"

—*Louisiana*

25
TIGER BECOMES A RIDING HORSE

Once upon a time, long before now, Anansi and Tiger used to go out romancing those girls together. But as things will happen, one day they found that they were both courting the same young lady, and they got very jealous of each other. So you know Anansi, he went to this lady's yard and he started in on his boasting, claiming that Tiger was nothing better than his father's old riding horse. Of course, it wasn't any time before Tiger came by to call upon this girl he thought was his sweetheart. But the young lady said to him, "Go along with you now! How can you just come around courting when I heard that you are nothing but an old riding horse?"

"What do you mean?" asked Tiger. "Who is telling you this? It looks like somebody has been telling stories about me, and they have filled your ears with big lies, ma'am. But I tell you what I'll do. I'll go straight to my friend Anansi, and he'll tell you that all of this is just something somebody is stirring up. I never have been his father's old jackass riding horse." So the lady told him to get going.

So Tiger took up his walking stick, and put his pipe in his cheek, and walking out as respectably as he can he went straight to Anansi's yard. He found Anansi lying there on his bed moaning with fever. So he lifted the latch, and called out, "Brer Anansi! Brer Anansi!" Anansi heard him very well, but he just said so soft and sicklike, "Brer Tiger, you call me?" He knew that Brer Tiger was going to be mad at him, you know.

Tiger said, "Yes, I called you! I came right over to your house because someone has been telling lies about me and I wanted to find out if it was you. I want to hear it from your own mouth. If you said those things, I'm going to make you prove it."

"Oooh," Anansi groaned. "Can't you see I have a fever? My stomach is hurting me bad, and I have just been to the doctor and taken some of his medicine!"

"Is that so?" said Tiger. "I don't believe you."

"I just ate two pills, Brer Tiger, so how can you think I could even get up and go to any lady's yard to prove anything tonight?" "I don't want to have any argument with you, brother," replied Tiger, "but I think you better come with me anyhow to tell that lady tonight that I am not your father's old jackass riding horse."

"Oh, Lord!" cried Anansi. "This pain in my breast just won't let me be, it's burning so bad! But if you insist, I could try to go with you to see the lady. But I'm feeling so sick."

Then Tiger said, "Well, since you're so sick maybe I could help you get there. How can I help?" So Brer Anansi said, "Well, just lift me up a little and see how I feel." So Tiger lifted him, and Anansi said, "Oh, Lord, I'm feeling dizzy." So Tiger said, "Just grab on here on my neck, and don't worry; I will carry you on my back." "Wait a minute, then, brother, and I will get out of bed here and help out." But he fell back, and he cried out, "Oh, Lord, I just can't get up at all. I beg you, brother, come lift me up again." So Tiger raised him up again, and again Anansi fell back. Now Tiger didn't know what to do. Brer Anansi looked up and said, "Well, why don't you get that saddle up there in the rafters and put it on and I could maybe grab hold of that and you could carry me."

So he went to the rafter, and took down Brer Anansi's saddle. Brer Anansi said, "Now just put that on your back, brother, and I can sit down soft."

Then Anansi got up on his saddle and got his bridle and reins. "Hey!" said Tiger, "what are you going to do with that?" Brer Anansi said, "If you just put that through your mouth, brother, and then I can tell you if you are starting to go too fast and I am going to fall off. "All right then," said Tiger; "put it on."

So Anansi took out his horsewhip. "Hey!" said Tiger. "What are you going to do with that?" "If a fly comes on your ear or back, brother, I will be able to take this whip and lick it off." Tiger said, "Well, O.K."

So Anansi put on his spurs. "Hey!" said Tiger. "Now what are you going to do with those?" "If flies come on your side, brother, I can brush them away with my spurs and make them fly away." "O.K., never mind then," said Tiger; "put them on."

Then Anansi moaned, "Well, Brer Tiger, if you stoop down, I can get on." And that way Anansi mounted on his back, and Tiger then began to walk off. But as he went along Anansi pulled him up with the bridle. "Stop, brother! Take your time, will you; my head is hurting me so!"

So Tiger went on about a mile or so, and after a little while, Anansi took his whip out and gave Tiger a lick on the ear. "Hey!" said Tiger. "What's that for?" "Well, there was a stupid fly on your ear! Shoo fly!" "All right, brother," said Tiger, "but next time don't hit so hard."

Tiger went on for another mile or so and Anansi stuck his spur into his side. Tiger jumped and cried out, "Now wait a minute! What is that you're doing?" "Those bothersome flies, brother. They are biting your side hard."

Then Tiger went on for another half-mile, till he came to the lady's yard. Now the lady's house had two doors, a front one and a back one. Just as he came to the entrance of the yard, Anansi rose up in his saddle, just like jockeys run races on the Kingston racecourse, and he took out his whip and he lashed Tiger hard! "Hey!" cried Tiger. "You lick too hard!" But Anansi lashed him more and more until Tiger really started to run. Then Anansi took his spurs and stuck them into Tiger's side and he made him run right up to the lady's door-mouth.

Then Anansi took off his hat and waved it above his head and said to the lady, who was standing at the door, "Good morning, mistress, didn't I tell you the truth that Tiger is nothing but my father's old riding horse?" He leaped off Tiger, and went into the lady's house, and Tiger was so embarrassed that he galloped off, and never was heard of no more.

—*Jamaica*

26

THE TELLTALE PEPPER BUSH

Once there was a king and queen who had a daughter and a son. The queen died. There was an old witch who had the power to make herself beautiful when she wanted. And when the king saw her she had changed herself into a beauty, and he wanted to marry her, and he did. Now that woman didn't like the little girl at all because she was so jealous of the king's love for his daughter.

One day, after the king had gone off to work, the woman told the little girl that she was going to the river, and she hung up a bunch of bananas in a tree. Now, birds love to eat ripe bananas when they are just hanging out in the open air like that, but she hung them there just to give that girl a hard task to do. She told the girl that if she saw any birds coming, she must chide them and make them fly away so that they won't peck on the fig-bananas.

So the woman took her washbasin and all the washing and went to the river. The girl stood there in the yard trying to do her sweeping and up came a blackbird. So the beautiful young girl started to sing:

> Do Blackbird, do blackbird
> Don't take that fig;
> Do Blackbird, do blackbird
> Don't take that fig;
> Do Blackbird, do blackbird
> Don't take that fig;
> My mommy will bury me alive.

The blackbird heard what she was singing, took pity on her, and didn't take the fig.

But then a pigeon flew down into the yard toward the bananas, and the girl started to sing again:

> Do Pigeon, do pigeon
> Don't take that fig;
> Do Pigeon, do pigeon
> Don't take that fig;

Do Pigeon, do pigeon
Don't take that fig;
My mommy will bury me alive.

So the pigeon heard her and took pity on her and flew away without touching the bananas.

At last there came an owl. And the girl started to sing again:

Do Mr. Owl, do Mr. Owl
Don't take that fig;
Do Mr. Owl, do Mr. Owl
Don't take that fig;
Do Mr. Owl, do Mr. Owl
Don't take that fig;
For my mommy will bury me alive.

The owl flew down and picked at the fig just as the woman came up the hill to the yard. And that gave her the chance to curse the girl right then. The girl turned to her and said, "But, Mommy, I did everything I could to keep the birds away. But Mr. Owl came last and he picked the fig so fast I couldn't do anything about it."

Now right there in the yard there was a pepper tree. And the father, every time the father ate, he used to like to have a pepper. And she dug a deep hole and she threw the girl into it and buried her right by the pepper tree.

When the father came home, he asked for his beautiful girl, and the stepmother said she didn't know where the girl was, because she had been gone for the whole morning. Well, the father sent his son out to pick a pepper for his dinner. And when the boy went to pick the pepper, the bush started to sing:

Do brother, do brother
Don't mash me hard;
Do brother, do brother
Don't mash me hard;
Do brother, do brother
Don't mash me hard;
For mommy has buried me alive.

Well, the boy was amazed at what he heard. And, of course, he ran and he told his father. The father couldn't believe what he said, and told him he must go and sit down because he wasn't going to listen to all that stupidness he was telling him. So now the mother went out to pick the pepper. But every time she stretched her hand to take the pepper, the pepper tree pulled away from her, and she couldn't get her fingers on a pepper to take back and put in the pot for her husband's dinner.

She went in and he asked where the pepper was for the pot. She told him that she couldn't pick the pepper. So now the king came out and he went to the tree and picked the pepper right away. But the bush started to sing in the little girl's voice:

> *Do father, do father*
> *Don't mash me hard;*
> *Do father, do father*
> *Don't mash me hard;*
> *Do father, do father*
> *Don't mash me hard;*
> *For mommy has buried me alive.*

The father got a shovel and dug up the girl. He was so vexed and ashamed of what the mother had done that he made a big fire and threw it into the bottom of the hole. And he buried the mother there alive, just as she had done to the little girl.

And there is the end of the story.

—*St. Vincent*

27

MAKING THE STONE SMOKE

Well, once upon a time, Massa King had a beautiful daughter. He loved her so much that he didn't want anyone to touch (much less marry) her, so he put her in a showcase behind glass. But the queen and all the others said she must be married to someone. So Massa King pointed to a large stone out in his yard, and he said that anyone who could come and dance this stone into smoke would receive his daughter, and the palace too. So all the men went and danced as hard as they could on this stone, but they couldn't make it smoke.

Well, Little Anansi heard about this beautiful girl, so he decided he wanted to win her. He went to the tailor and had him make a beautiful coat with pockets all the way down to the ground. And he went to the sugar-boiling house and filled every pocket with the ashes he got there.

So he went down to Massa King. He said, "Good morning, Massa King." He told him, "I heard that you had a task to perform here, sir, and I came to see if I could do this wonderful thing and win your beautiful daughter." The king had trouble not laughing at little Anansi, but he said, "Yes, Compé Anansi, that is the girl in the showcase, and there is the stone in the yard. Whoever dances that stone into smoke receives my daughter." He said, "Well, Massa King, let me go and try and see if I can do anything with that stone."

So Compé Anansi went to that stone. And as he was going, his shoes really started into that dance, because Anansi is a wonderful singer and dancer, you know. So he went up to the stone and he started:

> Ying-ee-ding-ee-ding
> *The girl-a for me.*

And he sang that four times.

Massa King stopped him. He said, "Wait, Compé Anansi, what did I hear you saying?" He said, "I was just humming a little tune, sir." Massa King said, "Well, hum that tune again and let me hear it." So he sang it four more times.

Ying-ee-ding-ee-ding
The girl-a for me.

The song made the king want to sing and dance so much that he cursed Anansi and told him to go ahead. And Compé Anansi started dancing and flapping his arms hard against those pockets, up and down his sides.

Ying-ee-ding-ee-ding
The girl-a for me.
Ying-ee-ding-ee-ding
The girl-a for me.
Ying-ee-ding-ee-ding
The girl-a for me.
Ying-ee-ding-ee-ding
The girl-a for me.

And every time he said "the girl-a for me" he slapped his sides. Ashes flew all over the place, so many that Massa King couldn't see where Compé Anansi was dancing anymore. So he made him stop, for he had danced the stone into smoke.

And the wire bended, so my story's ended.

—*St. Vincent*

28
THE LATEST SONG

One day, Anansi and Brer Tiger went to the river to wash themselves, and Anansi looked over at Brer Tiger and saw what a big and handsome man he was. So he said to Brer Tiger, "Brer Tiger, as you are such a big man, if you want to bathe in that nice spot, that big blue hole, with your big balls you're going to drown yourself, you'll be so weighed down. You better take them off and leave them here on the bank." Tiger said to Brer Anansi, "Well, you have the same problem, so you take yours off too." Anansi said, "You take yours off first and then I will."

So Tiger took his off first, and Brer Anansi said, "Go on in the hole, Brer Tiger, let me see how light that makes you." So Brer Tiger got in the water and started to swim, and he didn't pay attention to anything else but how light he was in the water. Brer Anansi never did go in; instead he grabbed the balls that Tiger had left and ate them up.

But Anansi got frightened at what he had gone, so he ran away from the river and went to Big Monkey's town. He found Brer Monkey, and said to him, "Brer Monkey, did you hear the latest song they are singing down at the riverside?" Anansi sang:

> *Yesterday about this time*
> *I ate up Tiger's balls.*
> *Yesterday about this time*
> *I ate up Tiger's balls.*
> *Yesterday about this time*
> *I ate up Tiger's balls.*
> *Yesterday about this time*
> *I ate up Tiger's balls.*

Now Big Monkey was never much of a singer or dancer, so he drove Brer Anansi away, saying that he didn't want to hear songs or any other kind of nonsense.

So Brer Anansi left and went on down to Little Monkey's town, and when he met Little Monkey there, he said, "Brer Monkey, I was down by the riverside and I heard a sweet song there. Everybody there was singing it, it is so sweet." Anansi sang:

> *Yesterday about this time*
> *I ate up Tiger's balls.*

And he sang it all the way through.

Now, Little Monkey, he was one who loved those songs. He said, "Sing that song again, so we can all hear it." So Anansi began to sing again:

> *Yesterday about this time*
> *I ate up Tiger's balls.*

Monkey just fell in love with that song, and had a dance that night just so everybody could hear it. And when Brer Anansi heard that he was glad, because now he could go back to Brer Tiger.

When he got back to the riverside, there was Brer Tiger looking all around for his balls. Tiger said, "Brer Anansi, I can't find my balls any place." Anansi said, "Ha! Ha! Just now I heard them singing a song in Little Monkey's town." And Anansi sang:

> *Yesterday about this time*
> *I ate up Tiger's balls.*

Brer Anansi said, "Brer Tiger, if you think I'm lying, just come with me to Little Monkey's town." So he and Tiger went.

When they got there, Anansi told Tiger they had to hide behind a bush to listen. And when they did, there was Little Monkey dancing and playing that same tune, and Tiger heard. Anansi said, "Brer Tiger, what did I tell you? Didn't you hear me say that they were singing songs about you and calling out your name making fun of you?" And all this time Monkey kept on singing:

> *Yesterday about this time*
> *I ate up Tiger's balls.*
> *Yesterday about this time*
> *I ate up Tiger's balls.*
> *Yesterday about this time*
> *I ate up Tiger's balls.*

Yesterday about this time
I ate up Tiger's balls.

Now Tiger heard that Brer Monkey was going to have a big dance that night. So he marched right up to Brer Monkey and asked him for his balls back. Monkey said that he didn't know anything about his balls, only the song that Brer Anansi had taught to them. So Tiger said that he was going to fight everyone there. But Little Monkey sent a messenger to Big Monkey and asked him to send a lot of soldiers quick to beat Brer Tiger and Brer Anansi too. So when Brer Tiger and Brer Anansi saw how it was going, Brer Tiger took to the bush and Brer Anansi to the housetop. And that's where they have lived ever since.

Jack Mantora, me no choose any.

—Jamaica

29

THE SIGNIFYING MONKEY

Deep down in the jungle where the coconut grows
Lives a pimp little monkey, you could tell by the clothes he wore.
He had a camel-hair benny with belt in the back,
Had a pair of nice shoes and a pair of blue slacks.
Now his clothes were cute little things,
Was wearing a Longine watch and a diamond ring.
He says he thinks he'd take a stroll
Down by the water hole.
And guess who he met? Down there was Mr. Lion.
The monkey started into that signifying.
He said, "Mr. Lion, I got something to tell you today."
He said, "The way this motherfucker been talking 'bout you I know
    you'll sashay."
He said, "Mr. Lion, the way he talking 'bout your mother, down your
    cousins,

I know damn well you don't play the dozens.
Talking about your uncle and your aunt's an awful shame.
Called your father and your mother a whole lot of names.
I would'a fought the motherfucker but looked at him with a tear in
  my eye.
He's a big motherfucker, he's twice your size.''
The lion looked down with a tear in his eye.
Said, ''Where's this big motherfucker that's twice my size?''
That little monkey said, ''I'll show you the way.''
He went down and the elephant was standing by a tree,
And the lion said, ''Hey, motherfucker, I hear you been looking for me.''
Elephant looked at the lion and said,
''Go on, chickenshit, pick on somebody your size.''
The lion made a roar.
The elephant sidestepped and kicked his ass on the floor.
The lion looked up with a tear in his eye.
Says, ''I'm gonna beat you, motherfucker, though you're twice my size.''
He looked back and squared off to fight.
The elephant kicked his ass clean out of sight.
Came back for ride or roar.
Elephant stomped his ass clean on the floor.
The elephant looked about, said, ''What the fuck is this?''
The lion said, ''You know you're a bad motherfucker, put up your fists.''
They fought three days, and they fought three nights.
I don't see how in hell the lion got out of that fight.
Coming back through the jungle more dead than alive,
Here goes the monkey in the tree with that same signifying.
He said, ''Look at you, you goddamn chump.
Went down in the jungle fucking with that man
And got your ass mangled and drug in the sand.
You call yourself a real down king,
But I found you ain't a goddamned thing.
Get from underneath this goddamned tree
'Cause I feel as though I've got to pee.''
The lion looked up, said,
''That's all right, Mr. Monkey, if that's the way you want to play.
The sun's gonna shine in your ugly ass some day.''
Monkey looked down, said, ''Long as the trees grow tall, the grass
  grows green,
You're the dumbest motherfucker the jungle's ever seen.''
Said, ''You motherfucker, I heard you down there pleading for your life.
At the very same time I had my dick in your wife.

You motherfucker, when that man knocked you over the hill,
I was gonna throw a party 'cause I thought your ass got killed.''
The lion strode through the jungle to pick himself up.
The monkey called him back, said,
''Hey, you motherfucker, and oh, by the way,
Don't you come 'round here with that hoorah shit,
Every time me and my wife get ready to get a little bit.''
Monkey started jumping up and down.
The left foot slipped and his ass hit the ground.
Like a bolt of lightning, like a streak of heat,
The lion was on him with all four feet.
Monkey look up with a tear in his eye,
Said, ''Mr. Lion, I'se just kidding, but I apologize.''
Lion said, ''No, you're a signifying motherfucker and you always will.
You gonna fuck around someday and get somebody killed.''
The monkey jumped back, and said, ''Get your feet off my chest and
    my head out the sand
And I'll get up and beat you like a natural-born man.''
Now the lion squared back, he was ready to fight,
But the poor little monkey jumped clean out of sight.
He said, ''I told you, long as the trees growed tall, grass growed green,
You're the dumbest motherfucker the jungle ever seen.
Dumb motherfucker, I done tricked you again.''
So the lion said, ''All right, Mr. Monkey, If that's the way you want
    to play.
The sun's gonna shine in your ass some day.''
Now what do you think? Down on Rampart Street
Who did Mr. Lion chance to meet—
The signifying monkey.
He stomped to the right and he stomped to the left.
Stomped the poor monkey clean to death.
Now I know some people think there is where the story ends.
But I'm gonna show you when it just begins.
You know how news travels in the jungle far and fast,
When it reached the monkey's baboon cousin at last.
He looked in the mirror with a tear in his eyes,
He says, ''I'll get this motherfucker, he's just about my size.''
He told his main whore he had to go
Down to the coconut grove to the water hole.
He packed up his whiskey and his bottle of gin,
He had a long ways to go, but a short time to make it in.
Coming through the jungle, swinging on the limbs,

Come the baddest motherfucker the jungle ever seen.
So by the time he got down to the coconut grove,
All the animals having a party 'round the water hole.
So Brother Lion was there, him and his wife,
When the baboon came up. In his hand he was carrying his knife.
He said, "Hey there, bad motherfucker, you did my cousin in.
Now I come down here to fight, to do you in."
So the lion said, "Look here, Mr. Baboon, I don't want to fight,
I want to get your ass out of my sight."
He said, "Tomorrow I want you to come down here early in the morning.
And be ready to fight."
So the lion went on home, preparing for the next day.
He knowed he had to fight, he had to fight in a hell of a way.
So now coming back to the fight, turn back down to the coconut grove,
Who was standing there looking so outright and fine,
But old Brother Monkey and Billy Lion.
While over there with real bad sight,
They naturally had to pick on Brother Bear to referee the fight.
So he introduced them.
He said, "In this corner we got Brother Lion,
He been bit by a tiger, scratched by a lion,
Tied in a barrel of lye, shot in the ass with a forty-five.
He's a bad motherfucker, but he don't want to die.
And in this corner we got Brother Baboon.
So far he's done licked every ass from earth to the moon.
He's better known as Big Jim,
He's the baddest motherfucker that ever swing from a limb."
So when Brother Bear jumped back off the grass,
Signal for the two motherfuckers to tear their ass.
Now they begin to fight and they begin to scuffle.
Soon the lion's jaw begin to ruffle.
After a while I saw a mighty right to the lion's chin,
And everybody thought the lion had come to an end.
But now when the bell rang for the first round,
The lion went back to his corner.
In his corner they were using Hadacol,
While in the baboon's corner they were saying a prayer to the Lord.
Everybody thought that Big Jim was through.
But when they came back out, that's when it turned to.
Brother Lion hit Brother Baboon to the face, on to the ribs,
Kicked him in the mouth, bust all his jubs.
Hit him in the ribs, hit him in the head.

That time the lion fell out for dead.
Brother Lion's wife jumped up in a mighty roar,
Said, "You just knocked my husband down to the floor."
She said, "I'm gonna have you put in jail.
And there ain't nobody here gonna go you bail."
So the monkey is standing on the corner with the same old signifying,
Said, "Don't worry, I got a friend and his name is Billy Lion.
He's the richest man 'round here in town. He'll get you out."
But where it ends, the baboon's still in jail,
And the monkey's not trying to get a dime to go his cousin's bail.
—Philadelphia

30
THE SINGING BONES

There was a king and queen who
had an only daughter and an only son. The king was getting old and
started to think about who was going to get the kingdom. Now the king
loved flowers and would always send the ladies from all around to go
out and gather roses for him from the forest. So he got this idea that
whichever of his children went into the forest and brought him the more
beautiful bouquet would get the kingdom and all his riches.

So the brother and sister went off into the bush, the boy going one
way and the girl another. And they agreed to meet back in this field. But
where the boy went, he couldn't find any roses at all, while the girl
found six beautiful flowers that she made into a nice bouquet.

When they met in the field, the boy was so vexed to see that bouquet
that he picked up a big stick and hit her over the head. He then dug a
hole underneath a big willow tree that was growing in that field, and he
buried her there. He took the flowers and went back to his father's house,
and gave them to him. They waited and waited for the sister to come but
she never did, which made the king very sad because he loved her so much.

There was a flock of sheep that belonged to the king, feeding in that field one day, and the shepherd boy was walking underneath that willow tree and he heard something singing:

> Shepherd boy, shepherd boy,
> Don't you know this horn you blow?
> My brother he has killed me in the woods.
> And he took my flowers away.
> And he dug a hole and buried me
> Beneath that willow tree.

The shepherd had a dog, and his dog started to scratch the ground when he heard this song, and he dug up a bone. So he brought it to the shepherd boy, and the shepherd boy saw it looked like a fife, so he blew:

> Shepherd boy, shepherd boy,
> Don't you know this horn you blow?
> My brother he has killed me in the woods.
> And he took my flowers away.
> He dug a hole and buried me
> Beneath that willow tree.

So when the shepherd came down to his home that night he wondered what he had found. He blew the bone as he was walking home:

> Shepherd boy, shepherd boy,
> Don't you know this horn you blow?
> My brother he has killed me in the woods.
> And he took my flowers away.
> He dug a hole and buried me
> Beneath that willow tree.

The shepherd was really worried about the bone. "What kind of thing is this?" he asked himself. And he played and listened to it over and over.

So the next day he took the bone with him to the field and played it. And the sheep and the dog descended and led him right to the king.

And when they went, the shepherd came directly in front of him with the bone, and it started to sing:

> *Father dear, Father dear,*
> *Don't you know this horn you blow?*
> *My brother he has killed me in the woods.*
> *And he took my flowers away.*
> *He dug a hole and buried me*
> *Beneath that willow tree.*

And the king was so amazed he took up the bone and tied it in a big white towel and put it on his truck and carried it all around the island. All the people around the island went to hear that bone. And when the truck reached home, he sent a horse and carriage for it, put up a big stand, and put the bone on it so more people could hear that song.

After a while, he sent all about for his people. The more people came, the more the bone would blow. And so the people all came for the brother, but he tried to hide. And they sent out all about until they found him and they brought him to the king. And the king brought him the bone.

> *Brother dear, Brother dear,*
> *Don't you know this horn I blow?*
> *My brother he has killed me in the woods.*
> *And he took my flowers away.*
> *He dug a hole and buried me*
> *Beneath that willow tree.*

The king said, "I don't know what to do to you? What can I do? What do you deserve?" And the king got a cart of pitch and they put him down in the cart of pitch and covered him with the pitch. And he put on top of the pitch some gas. And he sent that cart of pitch with his son covered with pitch all over the island. And the king went up to it and he lit a match and set it on fire. And that was how he killed his only son.

—*St. Vincent*

31
A BOARHOG FOR A HUSBAND

Scalambay, scalambay
Scoops, scops, scalambay
See my lover coming there
Scoops, scops, scalambay.

Once upon a time—it was a very good time—Massa King had an only daughter. And all the young fellows were constantly talking with each other about who was going to be able to marry her. They all came by to call on her, but none of them suited her. Each time one would come, her father would say "Now this is the one!" But she kept saying, "No, Daddy, this fellow here, I just don't like him," or "No, Mommy, this one really doesn't please me." But the last one to come along was a handsome young fellow, and she fell in love with him right away. And of course, when she fell in love, it was deep and wide—she just lost her head altogether. What she didn't know was that she'd actually chosen a boarhog who had changed himself into a human to go courting.

Now the Massa King had another child, a little Old Witch Boy who lived there and did all the nasty stuff around the palace. He was always dirty and smelly, you know, and no one liked to be around him, especially the King's beautiful daughter. One day after work the young fellow came in to visit his bride, and the Old Witch Boy whispered, "Daddy, Daddy, did you know that the fellow my sister is going to marry is a boarhog?" "What? You better shut your mouth and get back under the bed where you belong." (That's where they made the Old Witch Boy stay, you see, because he was so dirty.)

Now when they got married, they moved way up on the mountain up where they plant all those good things to put in the pot, roots like dasheen, tania, and all those provisions that hogs like to eat, too. One day, Massa King came up there and showed him a big piece of land he wanted his daughter and her husband to have for farming. The husband really liked that because he could raise lots of tanias—which is what boarhogs like to eat most.

So one day he went up to work, early early in the morning. Now there was this little house up by the land where he could go and change his clothes before he went to work. He went into one side of the little house, and he started singing:

> *Scalambay, scalambay*
> *Scoops, scops, scalambay*
> *See my lover coming there*
> *Scoops, scops, scalambay.*

And with each refrain he would take off one piece of clothing. And with every piece he took off he became more of a boarhog—first the head, then the feet, then the rest of the body.

> *Scalambay, scalambay*
> *Scoops, scops, scalambay*
> *See my lover coming there*
> *Scoops, scops, scalambay.*

Well, about noon, when he thought the time was coming for lunch to arrive in the field, he went back into the house and put back on his clothes, took off the boarhog suit and put back on the ordinary suit he came in. And as he got dressed he sang the same little song to change himself back into a handsome man.

> *Scalambay, scalambay*
> *Scoops, scops, scalambay*
> *See my lover coming there*
> *Scoops, scops, scalambay.*

After a while, the Old Witch Boy as usual came with the food, but this day he came early and saw what was going on, heard the singing, and saw the man changing. So he rushed home and told his father again, "Daddy, this fellow who married my sister up there really is a boarhog. It's true!" Massa King said "Boy, shut your mouth," and his sister said, "Get back underneath the bed, you scamp you."

The next day, the Old Witch Boy got up very early and went up the mountain and heard the song again:

Scalambay, scalambay
Scoops, scops, scalambay
See my lover coming there
Scoops, scops, scalambay.

All right, he thought, and he went down again and he told his father what he had seen and heard. He even sang the song. Now Massa King didn't know what to think. But he knew he was missing a lot of tanias from his other fields, so he loaded up his gun and went to see what was going on up there in his fields. Mr. Boarhog was up there changing and didn't know he was being watched, but he thought he heard something so he kind of stopped. The Old Witch Boy started to sing, and Mr. Boarhog couldn't do anything but join in with him. And so there they both were, singing:

Scalambay, scalambay
Scoops, scops, scalambay
See my lover coming there
Scoops, scops, scalambay.

And the man slowly changed into a boarhog. When the King saw this he couldn't believe his eyes. He took his gun and he let go, *pow*! And he killed Mr. Boarhog, and carried him down the mountain. The King's beautiful daughter couldn't believe what she saw and began to scream and cry, but Massa King told her what he had seen and what he had done, and then she had to believe it.

They cleaned Mr. Boarhog's body and had him quartered. And I was right there on the spot, and took one of the testicles and it gave me food for nearly a week!

—*St. Vincent*

32
THE WOMAN WHO WAS A BIRD

There was this man who had a son and married a second time, but what he didn't know was that his new wife was really a garlin, or egret. Now every time she cooked him his peas and rice and meat, she would tell him she didn't want any because she wasn't feeling well. Then when her husband went out to work she turned back into a garlin and went out to the pond and caught crabs and ate her belly full, and made haste to come back home and return into a person before her husband came back. Each time, just as her husband left, she would go inside the bedroom and shed her clothes and begin to sing:

> *Kitty Katty kee wang wah,*
> *Kitty Katty wang wah wah,*
> *Kitty Katty kee wang wah,*
> *Kitty Katty wang wah.*
> *Kee bottom, kee bottom, kee pyang,*
> *Kitty Katty kee wang wah, kee pyang.*

Then two wings would come out. She would sing again:

> *Kitty Katty kee wang wah,*
> *Kitty Katty wang wah wah,*
> *Kitty Katty kee wang wah,*
> *Kitty Katty wang wah.*
> *Kee bottom, kee bottom, kee pyang,*
> *Kitty Katty kee wang wah, kee pyang.*

Her feathers would come out on her. She would sing again:

> *Kitty Katty kee wang wah,*
> *Kitty Katty wang wah wah,*
> *Kitty Katty kee wang wah,*

> *Kitty Katty wang wah.*
> *Kee* bottom, *kee* bottom, *kee pyang,*
> *Kitty Katty kee wang wah, kee pyang.*

A bill would come out. And then she would fly out the window and go to the pond and catch crabs.

Now the man's son suspected his stepmother wasn't a person, so he kept watch on her. One day he stayed home after his father had gone, and as he was watching, he heard her sing her song and saw her turn into a garlin again.

And when his father came back that night, the little boy said, "Poppa, this wife that you have isn't really a person; she's a garlin." "What is that you say, boy? This couldn't be." "Yes, Poppa, she is a garlin. If you don't believe me, keep watch on her like I did this morning when you leave for work." And he described what had happened, and sang the song for his father.

The next day the garlin-wife cooked her husband's breakfast. He ate some, and so did the little boy, but she wouldn't eat anything. Her husband asked her why, and she said, "I'm feeling sick. No, no, husband, I just can't eat anything this morning." Her husband went and got his gun, loaded it up and he began to sing:

> *Kitty Katty kee wang wah,*
> *Kitty Katty wang wah wah,*
> *Kitty Katty kee wang wah,*
> *Kitty Katty wang wah.*
> *Kee* bottom, *kee* bottom, *kee pyang,*
> *Kitty Katty kee wang wah, kee pyang.*

Now as he sang that song she burst out crying, "Don't, husband, don't sing that. Every time you sing that song, it makes me remember my dead mother." She knew if he kept going, she would turn into a bird right in front of him, but he sang it anyhow. First time, though, her legs came out, and the second time it was her wings:

> *Kitty Katty kee wang wah,*
> *Kitty Katty wang wah wah,*
> *Kitty Katty kee wang wah,*
> *Kitty Katty wang wah.*
> *Kee* bottom, *kee* bottom, *kee pyang,*
> *Kitty Katty kee wang wah, kee pyang.*

He sang it until her feet came out, her feathers, and then her bill. He took his gun then, and killed her.

—Bahamas

33
MY MOTHER KILLED ME, MY FATHER ATE ME

O nce, a woman killed her little boy, cooked him, and served him to her husband. When he asked where she had gotten the meat, she said that she had bought the meat from one of the neighbors. So the man ate, and the boy's little sister took the bones and carried them off and laid them under an almond tree. Then the little boy's spirit turned into a bird. He flew around and started singing. And he went into a goldsmith shop and sang:

> *My mother killed me, my father ate me,*
> *My sister Marjileta took my bones and laid them under*
> *the almond tree.*

The goldsmith looked at the bird and said, "Sing that song again for me, birdie, and I will give you some golden slippers."

> *My mother killed me, my father ate me,*
> *My sister Marjileta took my bones and laid them under*
> *the almond tree.*

The man gave the little birdie the golden slippers. The bird flew away from there and went to the next goldsmith's shop, and he flew around and flew around and started to sing:

> *My mother killed me, my father ate me,*
> *My sister Marjileta took my bones and laid them under*
> *the almond tree.*

Everybody in the shop was amazed to hear the little bird. They asked the birdie to sing. "May we hear that song?" And he sang the song again.

> *My mother killed me, my father ate me,*
> *My sister Marjileta took my bones and laid them under*
> *the almond tree.*

The people in the shop gave the little bird a tiny golden stone and away he went. He went home and flew onto the housetop. And after he got to the top of the house he started to sing. He sang the same song:

> *My mother killed me, my father ate me,*
> *My sister Marjileta took my bones and laid them under*
> *the almond tree.*

The boy's little sister ran out of the house. As she looked at the little bird he threw the little golden slippers on her feet. She ran inside and cried, "Mama, Mama, run out and see what the birdie will give you. Look! The shoes I have on my feet are the ones that the little bird gave me." Well, the mother ran out. The bird sang again:

> *My mother killed me, my father ate me,*
> *My sister Marjileta took my bones and laid them under*
> *the almond tree.*

The father heard all of this. He went outside and threw the golden grindstone around the mother's neck and killed her. The boy flew down to his mother and said, "Mama, you killed me and I killed you."

—Providencia

Part III

GETTING A COMEUPPANCE: HOW (AND HOW NOT) TO ACT STORIES

INTRODUCTION

No subject is talked about more in Afro-American communities than each other's *business*—which, as we saw in the last section, means the way people behave toward one another. Such notions as respectability and reputation are therefore very important—especially respectability. Moreover, respect given and received is particularly associated with family. Discussions of behaving good and bad are often directed at heads of households, who are expected not only to display how respectable they act but to point to others' behavior as bad or rude.

As I noted in the Introduction, this does not mean that acting bad is forbidden or even unusual. There is a common understanding that one should always expect the worst of others, especially if they are of a different age or sex. A great deal of talk is reported throughout Afro-America about how badly behaved and untrustworthy others are, even those one calls friends. And the most common feature of such maladroit actions are that others engage in talk about you: *he-say, she-say* talk, as many black Americans put it in the 1960s and 1970s. One may make claims to a certain degree of respectability by making negative comments about such gossip.

The other side of the coin is to testify to one's respectability by talking sweetly to others, especially older women, and to encourage good talk in children and grandchildren. In the speech system in which these tales took root, there were a number of traditional *sweet talk* events, that is, ones in which eloquence was called for: courtship speeches and letters, recitations, and speechmaking. The West Indian *tea meeting*, in which children were called upon by the best speechmakers of the community to perform an oration before a contentious crowd, was paralleled by *recitations* in schools in the United States and *testimonies* in churches. Heads of households, in a bid for respect, strongly encouraged their brightest youngsters to take lessons in this art.

Surely, many of the stories in this section found their place in the repertoire by being told by respect-oriented people inculcating good manners on the part of the listening children, both black and white, for the respectable ones were, of course, the ones given charge of raising the planters' children as well as their own. The introduction to "The Doings and Undoings of the Dogoshes," written in Uncle Remus style as a story told by an older black storyteller to her or his white charges, is typical of how the subject was approached directly.

I'll tell you what, honey, good manners'll get you lots further in this world than good looks. And if you want to have good manners, you have to listen to them that knows what good manners is. But then some folks don't want to hear no advice from nobody. And you can most generally be might sure, that kind of folks is going to land right spank in the middle of trouble sooner or later.[1]

Such strong displays of upright character were to form an important part of neighborhood and family life throughout Afro-America. Not only was the ideal of acting sensibly and commanding respect the bedrock of the Afro-American behavior system, but this way of acting was strongly bound up with notions of teaching children to *talk right*, especially on those ceremonial occasions when family continuity was celebrated. At weddings and wakes, on Christmas and Emancipation Day, the speeches taught to the young not only constituted their offerings for the occasion but signaled to the community that these children came from mannerly homes. As the stories here attest, these overtly moral tales have persisted in the repertoire from the Old World, where such stories, usually performed by adults for children, were found in abundance.

In communities that have preserved such occasions of eloquence, the women-of-words or men-of-words, like teachers, see themselves as preservers of order, decorum, tradition, and continuity. In the West Indies one still finds oratorical contests in the form of a tea meeting (an elaboration of a testimonial session, with prizes for the ''ABCDs'': ''A is for Attention, B is for Behavior, C is for Conduct, and D, my friends, is for what we *shall* have tonight, *Decorum*''). In the cities, where the eloquence traditions have devolved almost totally to the churches, men-of-words are still regarded as ''heavy upstairs'' and are sometimes called ''street-corner philosophers.''

As often as not, the stories are cautionary; they illustrate how disorderly and unmannerly people act, and what happens to them when they do. They are moral stories, often in the form of how certain animals got to be the way they are because of their misbehavior. For example, in ''What Makes Brer Wasp Have a Short Patience,'' the strange shape of the wasp is accounted for by his continued unmannerly laughing.

Unlike most of the stories in this book, these tales have strong endings, for that is where the moral truth lies. This point is generally hammered home by the narrator through a generalization about behavior—such as the discussion of promises at the conclusion of ''The Poor Man and the Snake'' or the proverb in ''Being Greedy Chokes Anansi.''

---

1. John C. Branner, *How and Why Stories* (New York: Henry Holt, 1921), 80.

34
WHAT MAKES BRER WASP
HAVE A SHORT PATIENCE

Creatures don't all stay just the way God made them. No sir. With the mistakes made, and accidents, and natural debilitation, and one thing or another, they became different as time goes on, until sometime later they are hardly the same thing at all.

At one time, Brer Wasp looked very different from the way he does today. He was big on company, and he loved to talk, and joke, and cut the fool. He was one person that had to have his laugh.

One day, he was walking on a path, and he met up with Brer Mosquito. Now, Brer Mosquito and his whole family weren't very big at all, but they took themselves mighty seriously. Brer Mosquito and his pa planted a little patch of ground together, but they always called it the plantation. They talked so big about their crops and land and everything that you would have thought that they had a twenty-mile place. Now, Brer Wasp loved to draw Brer Mosquito out on the subject.

That same week, there had been a heavy frost, and all the sweet-potato vines died and turned black and everybody was forced to dig for the early potatoes. And Brer Wasp, after he had passed the time of day with Brer Mosquito, and inquired about his family, asked him about his pa's health and how he had made out with his crop. "We made out fine, Brer Wasp," Brer Mosquito said; "just too fine. We had the biggest crop you ever have seen!" "The potatoes were big, then?" "I tell you, sir! They were huge! You have never seen such potatoes!" "How big are they, Brer Mosquito?" Brer Wasp questioned him. "My friend," Brer Mosquito said, puffing out his chest and reaching down and pulling his little britches tight around his little leg, "Most of our crop came up bigger than the calf of my leg!"

Well, sir! Brer Wasp looked at Brer Mosquito's poor little leg, and as he thought about those "huge potatoes," he had to laugh to himself. Now, he tried to mind his manners, but his chest and face swelled up, and his eye water ran out of his eyes, and he burst out laughing right in Brer Mosquito's face. He laughed and he laughed till his sides hurt him. Whenever he thought he would stop, he looked at that ridiculous leg that stood there like a toothpick, and he laughed more than ever. His sides hurt him so much he had to hold them in with both his hands and rock himself back and forth.

"What makes you have to do that?" Brer Mosquito asked him. "You had better explain yourself. That is, if you can act sensible!" Brer Wasp gasped out, "Good lord, Brer Mosquito, looking for the biggest part of your leg is like hunting for the heaviest part of a hair! How big those huge potatoes must be, if you say they are as big as that!" And he laughed again till his sides hurt so bad that it wasn't enough just to press them—he had to grab them in both his hands and squeeze.

Brer Mosquito was so annoyed that he felt like fighting Brer Wasp right on the spot. But then he remembered that Brer Wasp was kind of nasty when he got in a row. So he just drew himself up, and stuck out his mouth, and said, "Laugh, you no-mannered devil! Laugh! But take care that the day doesn't come when somebody laughs at you the same no-mannered way!" And he went away so blistering mad that his two little coattails stuck straight out behind him.

But that didn't stop Brer Wasp. All the way to his house he had been laughing so hard that he had to stop now and catch his breath. At last he got home and started to laugh some more and tell his family about Brer Mosquito.

Just then his wife got a good look at him, and she hollered out, "For crying-out-loud, Brer Wasp! What's happened to your stomach?" Brer Wasp looked down where his waist had been and he could hardly see it.

He lost all notion of laughing right then. He looked again and he saw what all that shaking, and pushing, and squeezing had done to him. He was almost in two! Even his little hand could reach around his waist. He remembered how big it had been, and he saw how much he had shrunk up, and he was afraid to so much as sneeze.

Then he remembered what Brer Mosquito had said to him. He remembered all those people he had been joking about and laughing at so hard and for such a long time and he thought about how now the others were going to have their turn to laugh at that little waist he had now. He got so that he couldn't get that shameful thing out of his mind. And that is why he has such a short patience! Everywhere he goes he thinks somebody is ready to laugh at him. If anyone so much as looks at him, he gets so mad that he is ready to fight.

And that isn't the worst, because from that day to this day, he can't laugh anymore, because if he does, he will burst in two!

—*North Carolina*

35
BETWEEN THE FIDDLER
AND THE DANCER

———

There was once an old man who had a son, and he taught him to play the fiddle. This was an amazing, magic fiddle, though, and in the hands of a small boy it could really lead him into some bad, bad trouble. So the father told the boy, ''Whatever you do, don't touch my fiddle!'' The boy said, ''No, sir, I won't do that.''

But you know how these boys are, and as soon as his father was gone he went and took down the fiddle and he went down to the crossroad and just started playing away. When he commenced to play, an old witch jumped out of the bush and said to him, ''Son, if you can play longer and stronger than I can dance, you can kill me. But if I can dance longer and stronger than you can fiddle, I will kill you.'' And she went on. ''When you see my two feet peeling and bleeding, and I drop to one knee, you'll see I'll still be dancing. If you see my skin peel off all the way to my elbow, I'll still be dancing. When you see me bleeding, and falling on my head, my feet will still be in the air dancing.''

Just as the boy drew back the bow and was starting to fiddle, his friend the drummer-boy appeared. The boy threw him his tobacco and the drummer-boy tore it in half and threw it back, and away they went, fiddling and knocking the old tambourine.

Now his father could hear the music, it was carrying that far, and he knew his son was in trouble then, one way or the other, because this was a magic fiddle. So he grabbed his cutlass and ran back to the crossroad where he could hear the music. He snuck up on the boy and took the fiddle away while the witch was turned away dancing, and couldn't see him, and he commenced to play. Now the witch danced and danced until she couldn't dance any longer, and the old man took his cutlass and just cut off the witch's head.

From that day to this, they say that ''a hard-headed bird never makes good soup,'' so those boys better listen and mind the older people.

Nine pence to make the heart content;

If you want any more, you got to find it out yourself.

—Bahamas

36
BEING GREEDY CHOKES ANANSI

One time, Anansi lived in a country that had a queen who was also a witch. And she decreed that whoever used the word *five* would fall down dead, because that was her secret name, and she didn't want anyone using it.

Now, Buh Anansi was a clever fellow, and a hungry one too. Things were especially bad because there was a famine, so Anansi made a little house for himself by the side of the river near where everyone came to get water. And when anybody came to get water, he would call out to them, "I beg you to tell me how many yam hills I have here. I can't count very well." So, one by one he thought they would come up and say, "One, two, three, four, *five*," and they would fall down dead. Then Anansi would take them and corn them in his barrel and eat them, and that way he would have lots of food in hungry times and in times of plenty.

So, time went on and he got his house built and his yams planted, and along came Guinea Fowl. Anansi said, "I beg you, missus, tell me how many yam hills I have here." So Guinea Fowl went and sat on one of those hills and said, "One, two, three, four, and the one I'm sitting on!" Anansi said, "*Cho!*" [sucking his teeth], "you can't count right." And Guinea Fowl moved to another hill and said, "One, two, three, four, and the one I'm sitting on!" "*Cho!* you don't count right at all!" "How do you count, then?" Guinea Fowl said, a little vexed at Anansi. "Why this way: one, two, three, four, FIVE!" He fell dead. And Guinea Fowl ate him up.

This story shows that what they say is right: "Being greedy chokes the puppy."

—*Jamaica*

37
THE DOINGS AND UNDOINGS
OF THE DOGOSHES

—————

I tell you, good manners will get you lots farther in this world than good looks. And if you want to have good manners, you got to listen to those that know what good manners are. But then, some folks don't want to hear any advice from anybody. And you can generally be mighty sure that that kind of folks are going to land right in the middle of trouble sooner or later.

Take the dogoshes. As nice critters as there ever was to look at, but they just naturally had bad manners and they wouldn't take the advice of those who knew what was right. That's how it comes about that there aren't any dogoshes in the world anymore. They weren't fit to live because they wouldn't listen to anybody.

The dogoshes were created by the Good Lord, just like the rest of the critters, and on Sunday morning they all went to church meetings along with the other folks. And the preacher told them how they had to behave themselves at church, how they had to stand up when they sang, and how they had to get down on their knees when they prayed, and how they mustn't talk or fool around during the sermon, and how they had to put something besides tin buttons in the contribution box when it was passed around, and how they must be sure not to look around themselves every time somebody came into the church—because all of that was nothing but bad manners.

Well, sir, the dogoshes didn't feel very well acquainted with the other critters because they had just been created yesterday, as you might say, and they didn't have much time to visit around with their neighbors. So they were curious about who had feathers or scales or hair or who had just nothing at all on their bodies. When they got into the church they just had to look whenever they heard somebody walking up the aisle with squeaky shoes on, because they wanted to know who it was or what they looked like and how they were dressed.

But there was only one door in the back of the church, and the folks had to sit with their backs to the door. And when anybody came in, the dogoshes turned their heads around and looked at them until they had come way up in front, and went over to the left-hand amen corner and sat down. By that time somebody else had come in the door again, and before they had time to untwist their necks, they started staring at the new people. And they would watch them until they had passed down to the front and sat down in the left-hand amen corner too.

Well, then, it kept on happening the same way till the necks of the dogoshes were twisted around and around until they just naturally choked to death with their curiosity. And when the Good Lord saw the dogoshes choked to death because they didn't have any manners in church, he said he guessed he better not make any more folks of that kind. And he never did. And that's the reason there aren't any more dogoshes in the world.

And the next time you go to meeting, child, keep your eyes on the preacher, no matter what is happening behind you.

—American South

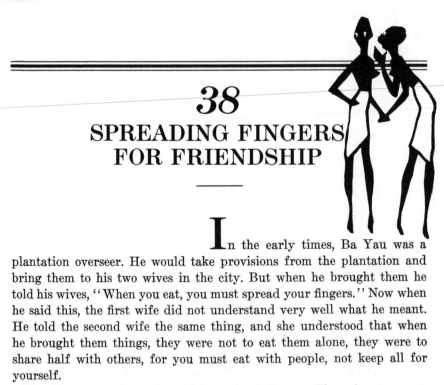

38
SPREADING FINGERS
FOR FRIENDSHIP

In the early times, Ba Yau was a plantation overseer. He would take provisions from the plantation and bring them to his two wives in the city. But when he brought them he told his wives, "When you eat, you must spread your fingers." Now when he said this, the first wife did not understand very well what he meant. He told the second wife the same thing, and she understood that when he brought them things, they were not to eat them alone, they were to share half with others, for you must eat with people, not keep all for yourself.

Now the first wife, whenever she cooked, she ate. Then she went outside, and spread her fingers, and said, "Ba Yau said when I eat I must spread my fingers." Ba Yau brought her much bacon and salt fish, but she always ate it alone. When Ba Yau brought the things for the second wife, she shared with other people.

Not long afterward Ba Yau died, and nobody brought anything to the wife who had spread her fingers to the air. She sat alone. But to the one who had shared things with others, many people brought things. One brought her a cow, one brought her sugar, one brought her coffee.

Now, one day, the first wife went to the second, and she said, "Sister, ever since Ba Yau died, I have been hungry; no one brought me any-thing. But look how many people have brought provisions for you!" The second wife asked her, "Well, when Ba Yau brought you things, what did you do with them?" She said, "I ate them." Then the second wife said again, "When Ba Yau said to you, 'You must spread your fingers,' what did you do?" She said, "When I ate, I spread my fingers in the air." The second wife laughed. "Well, then, the air must bring you things, because you spread your fingers for the air. For myself, the same people to whom I gave food now bring me things in return."

—*Surinam*

39
DON'T SHOOT ME, DYER,
DON'T SHOOT ME

Don't shoot me, Dyer, don't shoot me
Don't shoot me, Dyer, don't shoot me.
With all the pigeons around now dead
And I'm alone, just me here
Don't shoot me, Dyer, don't shoot me.

Well, this is a fellow they call Dyer, who loved to go out hunting. He went up to the mountain shooting pigeons, and he shot so well, and so many, that there was only one pigeon left in the whole world. And this pigeon flew through the pines singing:

> *Don't shoot me, Dyer, don't shoot me*
> *Don't shoot me, Dyer, don't shoot me.*
> *With all the pigeons around now dead*
> *And I'm alone, just me here*
> *Don't shoot me, Dyer, don't shoot me.*

The pigeon, when he saw the hunter, said, "Don't shoot me," but Dyer wasn't going to listen at all, and he let go, *Pow!* and the pigeon dropped to the ground. As he dropped he began singing:

> *Don't pick me up, Dyer, don't pick me up*
> *Don't pick me up, Dyer, don't pick me up.*
> *With all the pigeons around now dead*
> *And I'm alone, just me here*
> *Don't pick me up, Dyer, don't pick me up.*

So Dyer thought to himself, "What is happening here? Why shouldn't I pick you up?" But he is amazed that this dead bird is singing to him, and afraid too. "Well," he said, "I won't pick you up this time, but I'm going to throw you in my bag and carry you home!"

When he went home that night, he took the only pigeon left in the world and put on the kettle with hot water and he threw it in, took it out, and started plucking.

> *Don't clean me, Dyer, don't clean me*
> *Don't clean me, Dyer, don't clean me.*
> *With all the pigeons around now dead*
> *And I'm alone, just me here*
> *Don't clean me, Dyer, don't clean me.*

He said, "What are you saying? I'm going to clean you up and cut you up and cook you and eat you." Well, the bird sang now:

> *Don't cut me up, Dyer, don't cut me up.*
> *Don't cut me up, Dyer, don't cut me up.*
> *With all the pigeons around now dead*
> *And I'm alone, just me here*
> *Don't cut me up, Dyer, don't cut me up.*

He cut him up and threw him in the pot. The bird sang now:

> *Don't stew me, Dyer, don't stew me*
> *Don't stew me, Dyer, don't stew me.*
> *With all the pigeons around now dead*
> *And I'm alone, just me here*
> *Don't stew me, Dyer, don't stew me.*

Even when he was cut up into fine pieces, the bird kept singing. Now, in the pot, he's still singing, "Don't stew me up."

So finally he was cooked and Dyer went to eat him. The bird now started to sing:

> *Don't eat me, Dyer, don't eat me*
> *Don't eat me, Dyer, don't eat me.*
> *With all the pigeons around now dead*
> *And I'm alone, just me here*
> *Don't eat me, Dyer, don't eat me.*

After he ate him, he felt terrible, his belly was all swollen up and getting larger and larger. And he felt like he needed to ease his belly. He went to the toilet, and nothing happened. It kept on like this until the middle of the night, until he couldn't stand it anymore. So he went out in the dark; still nothing happened. Well, you know when you gotta go, you gotta go, and he really had to, but nothing came out. So he went to the side of the river and took down his pants, and the bird started singing again:

> *Don't shit there, Dyer, don't shit there*
> *Don't shit there, Dyer, don't shit there.*
> *With all the pigeons around now dead*
> *And I'm alone, just me here*
> *Don't shit there, Dyer, don't shit there.*

He couldn't understand what was happening to him. He said to himself, "What is this? I eat the bird and still it is singing and my belly is going to burst." So he went to the ocean, and again he took his pants down:

Don't shit there, Dyer, don't shit there
Don't shit there, Dyer, don't shit there.
With all the pigeons around now dead
And I'm alone, just me here
Don't shit there, Dyer, don't shit there.

So he went onto the sand, and still the bird was singing; so he went into the water, until his feet couldn't even touch the sand, and still the song:

Don't shit there, Dyer, don't shit there
Don't shit there, Dyer, don't shit there.
With all the pigeons around now dead
And I'm alone, just me here
Don't shit there, Dyer, don't shit there.

And along came this big swell, and picked him up and dashed him against rocks and tore him to pieces.

And that's why you don't see people going into the sea, even up until today.

—*St. Vincent*

40
LITTLE EIGHT JOHN

Once and long ago, there was a little black boy named Eight John. He was nice-looking, but he didn't act exactly like he looked. He was a mean little boy, and he wouldn't listen to a word the grown folks told him, not a living word. So if his loving mammy told him not to do a thing, he would go straight out and do it. Yes, he was the spite of all the world.

"Don't step on toad frogs," his loving mammy would tell him, "or you will bring bad luck on your family, yes you will." Then Little Eight John would go out and find a toad and squash it.

Sometimes he squashed a lot of toads. And then the cow wouldn't give anything but bloody milk and the baby would have bad colic. But Little Eight John, he just ducked his head and laughed.

"Don't sit backward in your chair," his loving mammy told Eight John. "It will bring the troubles to your family." And so Little Eight John sat backward in every chair. Then his loving mammy's cornbread burned and the milk wouldn't churn. And Little Eight John just laughed and laughed and laughed, because he knew why all this was happening.

"Don't climb trees on Sunday," his loving mammy told him, "or it will be bad luck." So that Little Eight John, that bad boy, he snuck up trees on Sunday. Then his pappy's potatoes wouldn't grow and the mule wouldn't go. Little Eight John knew how come.

"Don't count your teeth," his loving mammy told Little Eight John, "or a sad sickness will come on your family." But that Little Eight John, he went right ahead and counted his uppers and he counted his lowers. He counted them on weekdays and on Sundays. Then his mammy, she coughed and the baby got the croup. All because of that Little Eight John, the badness of a little old boy.

"Don't sleep with your head at the foot of the bed or your family will get weary money blues," his loving mammy told him. So he did it and did it, that Little Eight John boy. And the family, it went broke with no money in the pot. Little Eight John, he just giggled.

"Don't have no Sunday moans, because Old Raw Head and Bloody Bones will come," his loving mammy told him. So he went into the Sunday moans and he had the Sunday groans, and he moaned and he groaned and he moaned. And Old Raw Head and Bloody Bones came after that little bad boy and changed him into a little old grease spot on the kitchen table, and his loving mammy washed it off the next morning.

And that was the end of Little Eight John.

And that's what always happens to never-minding little boys.

—American South

41
THE POOR MAN AND THE SNAKE

One poor man was making a living
by splitting long shingles and cutting timber in the swamp. He had a
wife but no children. Every day, from sunrise till sundown, he went to
the swamp to cut. Though he tried his best, he scarcely could make
enough for his everyday bread to eat.

Once, a very big snake—the father of all those other snakes that lived
in the swamp—noticed the man. He saw how hard he worked and how
little he made and he took pity on him. One evening, just before the
poor man left working, this snake crawled up to the log where the man
had been chopping and said, "Brother, how you making out?" The man
answered, "I don't make out. I work in this swamp from day till dark,
day in and day out, and I try my best, but I can scarcely make vittles
enough for me and my wife to eat." Then the snake said, "I am sorry
for you and willing to help." The man thanked him and asked him how,
and the snake said, "Do you have any children?" The man said, "No!"
The snake asked "Do you have a wife?" The man said, "Yes." The
snake said, "Can you keep a secret from your wife?" The man answered
that he could. Brer Snake told him he was afraid to trust him; but when
the man begged the snake very hard to try him, the snake agreed to do
so. The snake told him he was going to give him some money the next
day, but he mustn't tell his wife where he got the money. The man made
a strong promise, and they parted.

The next day, just before the poor man finished working, the snake
crawled up to him. His belly and his mouth were puffed out. He spit out
two quarts of silver money on the ground right there in front of the poor
man, and he said, "Do you remember what I told you last night? Well,
sir, here is some money I brought to help you. Take it. But remember,
if you tell your wife where you got it, or who gave it to you, it won't do
you any good, and you will die a poor man." The man was so glad to
get the money, he kept saying, "Thank you, thank you, thank you, my
brother; I won't ever tell anyone where I got this money." After he left
the swamp to go home, the snake suspected that he was going to go back
on his promise and tell his wife, so he made up his mind to follow him
and see what happened.

It was dark when he reached the man's house. He crawled up and lay down under the window where he could hear everything that was said inside the house. The wife was turned around and cooking supper. After she and her husband ate, her husband said, "I had a lot of work today, look at this money." Then he pulled out the silver and spread it on the table. Well now, his wife was amazed. She jumped with happiness and said, "Tell me where you got this money." The man said, "A friend gave it to me." His wife said, "what friend?" The man said he had promised not to tell. The wife begged so hard that the man forgot his promise and went and told everything that had happened. Then the wife said, "That snake must have a belly full of silver money, and I will tell you what to do tomorrow. When the snake comes to talk to you, you pick a moment and chop off his head with your ax, and take all the money out of him." And the husband agreed!

Brer Snake heard every word they spoke, and he went to his house in the swamp very vexed because the man that he had befriended had gone back on his promise and made an evil plan to kill him.

The next day, the man watched for the snake. When the sun lay far down, and the man was very tired from splitting one big log, Brer Snake crawled up alongside of the log and showed himself to the man. They talked together, and the snake asked the man, "Have you shown your wife the money I gave you?" The man answered, "Yes, I did." And then he asked him, "Did you tell your wife where you got it?" The man said, "No." The snake asked him again, "Are you sure you didn't tell her you got it from me?" The man said, "I told you once already. What makes you ask again? You think I am lying to you?" With that, he tried to chop off the snake's head. But the snake had had his eyes on him and he drew back against the log. The ax missed the snake and glanced back off the log and cut the man's own leg off. The poor man hollered for someone to come help him. But he was way in the middle of the swamp and out of everybody's hearing. Well, he was bleeding to death, and just before he died, Brer Snake said to him, "Didn't I tell you when you got that silver from me, that if you told your wife you would die a poor man? You promised me you would keep the secret. You went home to your wife and you showed her the money and you told her where you got it. More than that: you and she fixed a plan to kill me, me who had been your friend, and to rob me of the money I had left. Now you see the judgment that comes to you. When you tried to chop off my head, you cut your own foot off. You are going to die in these here woods. No man nor woman is ever going to find you. The buzzards are going to eat you."

And it happened just as the snake said. The man broke his word, and he died a poor man.

Anybody who goes back on his promise and tries to harm the person who has done him a favor is sure to meet up with big trouble.
—*Georgia*

42
THE LITTLE BIRD GROWS

This once happened. There was a good child whose mother had died and whose father had married another woman. This woman didn't like the child and gave him all kinds of trouble, but whenever this would happen the boy would cry for a moment, then he would laugh and be happy and sing all day long. He was that good.

Now, the stepmother had a lot of bags of maize and rice that she sold in town, while the child went around in torn clothes and was always dead hungry. One day, as he was coming from school, he saw in the middle of the road a little bird hopping around. He crept up behind him and grabbed him and put him in his pocket. When he reached home, he sat the bird quietly in front of the kitchen door and he sang to it, but the bird wouldn't sing a note. The child fed him, petted him a little, and whistled for him. Now the bird began to whistle too, making such beautiful music that the stepmother came into the kitchen to see for herself what was whistling this way.

But she couldn't hear the beauty of the song because she just wasn't made that way. She said, "Lazy boy! What kind of noise is this?" He was surprised at her shouting. "Mother, don't be angry! Look at what I found on the road, and listen to the beautiful song this bird is singing!" "You know there are too many lazy people in the house who I have to look after all the time. You alone are too much for me. If it was bigger, I would twist its neck and eat it."

The bird stopped singing. He looked right at the woman, then looked directly in her eye. Well, I'll tell you that woman got frightened. Then the bird sang:

Food, give me food,
Give me food,
Doomeng, Doomeng, Doomeng.

Now she got really mad. "That's what I've been telling everyone. This child is always getting people into trouble. And now this damned bird is asking for food!" The boy answered:

I have no food
To give to my bird.
I have no food
To give to my bird.
The bird said to me:
"Doomeng, Doomeng, Doomeng!"

The little bird flew around in circles over her head and threatened the stepmother, singing: *"Doomeng, Doomeng, Doomeng!"* She was afraid and told the boy: "This bird is a Devil trying to pluck out my eyes and bring me bad luck. Run to my pantry and bring a bag of rice to him to see if you can make him stop singing."

The child climbed the ladder and came back with a bag. The bird gave it but one stroke with its beak, and the bag burst open. He pecked and pecked and pecked. In fifteen minutes nothing was left. He had finished the whole twenty pounds. He grew as big as a hen, his coat shone, he turned all beautiful colors; his wings were blue powdered with yellow. He turned his face, and fixing them in the eye, said, "I forbid you to leave this place." He opened his beak very wide and sang: *"Doomeng, Doomeng, Doomeng!"*

Now the stepmother really started in scolding the boy because she was having to give up all this food. "See what kind of trouble you have gotten us into. You're just a troublemaker. Why did you have to go out and catch this damned bird?"

The bird opened his wings way out wide, flapped them a couple of times, and began to fly around and around in circles again. The stepmother yelled to the boy: "Run to the granary and get all the sorghum you can find. If that doesn't help us, we are all going to be eaten up, I'm afraid." "How can I do that, Mother, when the bird doesn't want me to leave the room." All the time the bird was singing: *"Doomeng, Doomeng, Doomeng!"*

But he followed his stepmother's orders and brought back seven bags of sorghum, hoping it would be enough, but the bird said, "You are my servants. You must stay and watch me while I am eating!" The woman screamed to God, but the bird shrieked and told her to shut up.

She stopped short and watched as the bird crushed the grain like a mill! The more he ate, the larger he grew. By the time he had swallowed the seven bags of sorghum, he was taller than the child. He flapped his wings and the wind blew so hard they had a hard time even catching their breath. Now the bird saw through the door in the distance that a man was coming. The woman could see that it was her husband, and she called, "Ti-Nom! Bring your machete to the kitchen." "Shut your mouth!" the bird cried.

The man didn't hear and kept on coming. The bird let him come very near and told him, "Come on in! You too are not allowed to go out of the room from now on. *Doomeng, Doomeng, Doomeng!*" The crying boy sang:

> *I have no food*
> *To give to my bird.*
> *I have no food*
> *To give to my bird.*
> *The bird said to me:*
> "Doomeng, Doomeng, Doomeng!"

The woman whispered to her husband to choke the bird. The bird looked at her angrily. "I beg your pardon, Mr. Doomeng, I didn't really say anything. Run to the granary and bring whatever maize we have left, down to the last grain, for Mr. Doomeng. Do you see that, Mr. Doomeng, everything I have is yours. May I go now?" "*Doomeng, Doomeng, Doomeng!*" sang the bird. The stepmother snapped, "Go, boy, go quickly!"

Now the little boy came back with seven bags of maize. By now, each wing of the bird was as big as a five-pound can, and still he was growing all the time. When he had finished eating, his head reached the top of the house, he shook his wings, and the whole house shook with it and he boomed out his song: "*Doomeng, Doomeng, Doomeng!*" His voice was thunder. The boy cried out, then sang again:

> *I have no food*
> *To give to my bird.*
> *I have no food*
> *To give to my bird.*

The bird said to me:
"Doomeng, Doomeng, Doomeng!"

So the stepmother shrieked at the bird: "Eat him! He's the one who brought you here!" pointing to the boy. Doomeng looked at the woman and opened his mouth. The woman went to him like a butterfly that goes to a lamp, and Doomeng swallowed her up. Then he looked at the father. The man ran at him with his machete in his hand, and the bird swallowed him whole!

The child was really scared now, and he threw himself flat on the ground; he caught Doomeng's wing and kissed it begging: "Doomeng, he is my father! Dooomeng, give me back my father!" "You are a good child, so I will give you back your father, but promise me you will take me back to where you found me." Doomeng sang:

The wedding knife you see on the highway
Must remain on the highway
What you don't know is stronger than you.

"You have disturbed me while on duty. If I were not so weak toward you, it would not be your family only that would suffer; the whole country would have paid for this disturbance. But I am too good to you —I am forgiving you!"

He spat out the father and then he made his body smaller and smaller, until he was once more a little bird. "Take me to the middle of the highway!" he instructed the boy. And so he did.

—*Haiti*

43
TRICKING ALL THE KINGS

There was once a king who had a deep well that gave him lots of fresh water. One day, he began to notice that some of his water was gone, and the rest all muddied up, and he couldn't tell who had done this to him. He knew he had to catch the thief because the weather was so dry that no one could get any water except from the king's well.

So the king made a man out of tar and set it right by the mouth of the well. He put bread in one of the hands of the tar-man, and in the other, a fish. When the thief comes, the king figured, he will have to have a chat with him, and when he finds the tar-man won't talk, he'll hit him. And so he said, and so it happened. Up came the thief about eleven o'clock that night, and when he came near the well, he was startled. He said, "Good evening to you, sir." But the tar-man didn't respond. He said, "I'm just taking a walk around tonight and I got thirsty, so I wanted to ask you for some water." The tar-man wouldn't speak. The thief said, "I will have to find out who you are." He went right up to the face of the image and he peered at it for a long time because it was so dark. "Oh, I see now, you are a watchman Massa King put here to frighten me away. But you are no good here." And he slapped him in the jaw and his hand stuck.

He said, "Oh hell! You look gummy. Let me go, will you?" The tar-man said nothing. He said, "I'll give you another slap if you won't let me go." And he slapped him, and now his two hands were stuck. He said, "What do you mean by this? You won't let me go? I'll throw you into the well if you won't let me go." He said, "Massa King sent you here to hold me, and you are holding me, but I'm going to toss you into the well and then both of us will be down there, I'll tell you." And he tried to toss him, in his struggle to get away, and he just stuck more and more until he was fastened on from head to toe. And who was the thief? Buh Nansi.

Now, the next morning, the king came and said, "Ah, I've caught the thief and his meat and bones will make my bread today!" And he took him by the shoulder and he pulled him off the tar-man, and he dragged him by the hair to the palace. He called his servant and said, "I caught the thief who has been stealing my water for many weeks, but he won't steal from me anymore." Then he said, "Take him and hold him, and we'll chain him until we can think of the way we can kill him best." The servant asked what his sentence would be, so Massa King said, "Maybe we'll have to burn him." Buh Nansi never said a word. The servant said, "I think the best death for him is to shoot him." Still Buh Nansi kept quiet. Then the king said, "The best way to take his life is to drown him." Then Buh Nansi said, "Oh, Massa King, you mean to pitch me in that blue, blue sea? Massa King, better to shoot me than pitch me in that blue sea water." But the king said, "No, I wouldn't. I'll have you drowned." And he took a bit of rope and put it around Buh Nansi's neck and tied a piece of iron to it and took him to the beach. Massa King and his servant took him out in a boat about three miles out to sea, and flung him overboard. And he went right to the bottom, sat down, loosened the iron from around his neck, and floated to the top, just like he knew he would. He was bobbing along even before the boat moved half a mile, and called out, "Ah, Massa King, you couldn't have done me a better favor than to fling me into this sea water. It's my home."

He dove down again, feeling kind of happy, and he met up with a shark. "Oh, Buh Shark, you're the very man I've been looking for, for three nights and three days now." Buh Shark asked why. And he said, "I want to get together to catch some small fish and go ashore and cook them up for a big feast this afternoon." Buh Shark said, "You would invite me to a big feast?" "Yes, I would. Come on, let's go on and catch some and I'll show you."

Well, they caught plenty, and they went ashore, and Buh Shark said to Buh Nansi, "You must go ashore alone, and leave me in the water, because I can't live out of the water for more than two minutes. You cook them up and just bring me my share." Buh Nansi said, "Well, I'll have them all cooked up then, and I'll bring you your share. You stay in the water and sing some sweet songs thinking about this feast, while I get some kindling and get this fire going."

After the fire was going, he put a big copper pot on it, one that holds two hundred gallons of water. And he filled it with the small fish, and when they were all boiled up and the water was steaming hot, he said, "Buh Shark, come here in the sun for a while, and show me how you can stand on the tip of your tail, and tell some jokes." Buh Shark said, "I'll come, but only for half a minute, you know, because otherwise I'll die." And as Buh Shark came up and stood on the tip of his tail, Buh Nansi took out a bucket of the steaming water and he killed him.

Buh Shark had nothing more to say ever again. Buh Nansi cut him in three pieces and put them in the copper pot with the little fishes and boiled it properly with peppers. And after it was cooked, he took it off the fire. He knew he couldn't eat it all alone, but being so selfish, he was going to throw away what was left over.

But just as he was beginning, up came Buh Lion. Buh Nansi said, "Ah, you are the man I wanted to see. I want you to help me eat some of my fish here. I have caught plenty and can't eat them all." He was afraid of Lion, but just smiled and said, "You just came in time."

And they both sat down to eat. When Buh Nansi ate about six pieces of fish, Lion had eaten just about all the rest. Buh Nansi, who didn't *really* want to share, grumbled to himself. "I have been here all the time, lighting the fire and straining to put that big copper pot on the fire and here you come just in time to eat." Lion said, "What are you saying? If you grumble any more, I'm going to kill you and eat you too. You just look at what I'm doing and keep quiet." Buh Nansi got really scared now, and didn't say anything until they had finished eating.

Then Buh Nansi said to Lion, "Let's play the little game we used to play when we were at school." And Lion said he didn't remember any games. Buh Nansi said, "Sure you do. We take a little piece of string, and you put your two hands behind your back, and we tie you to a tree, and take a little switch and touch your back with it, and when you make a rush you break the string and get away, and the other person has to do the same thing." Lion said to Buh Nansi, "If you let me tie you first, I'll play." Buh Nansi said that was all right, and they got a string and a switch, and Buh Lion tied him. And then when Buh Lion hit him with the switch he made a plunge and got away. Buh Nansi said, "Now let me tie you," and he pulled a cord-rope out of his pocket and tied Buh Lion's hands behind his back. And he took out a whip from his pocket and really started to lick him hard. Lion made a plunge at Buh Nansi with his paw to kill him, but he couldn't touch him, Buh Nansi was that quick. And he shouted out, "My wife, my wife, you and all the children come out and get your licks on Buh Lion. A little while ago he ate all my fish, which I was going to bring home." So all his children started to beat Buh Lion too, until he was half dead. And they just left him there tied to the tree, Buh Lion lying on the ground half beat to death, and they went on home.

Buh Lion saw a woman coming his way on her way home. So he said, "My good lady, please let me loose or else I shall surely die." The lady said, "Who put you there, my good lion?" "Buh Nansi, ma'am." "Why did he tie you?" "He tied me here because we had a little game we played in school and he got me to remember it and play it with him. I tied him first, and he broke the string like we always used to, and he got away. Then he tied me, but not with the same string, but a much stronger cord-rope, and then he licked me, and his wife and children came and licked me and had me completely beaten." "But if I let you loose, my good lion, you will spring on me and eat me." He cried, "Oh now, my good lady, if I tried to do that all the trees and stones around here would cry 'shame.'" She said, "All right, then, I will." And she let him loose, and he immediately tried to spring on her and eat her. And all the trees and all the stones sang out: "Shame, Lion, shame." So he stopped.

So he went home and told his wife what Buh Nansi had done to him. And she said, "I always told you to stay away from Buh Nansi's reach. You are much stronger than he is, but you haven't got the tricks that he has. But we'll think of a way to get back at him."

So she thought and thought, and finally she said to Lion, "We'll have a dance tonight. You know how much Buh Nansi likes to dance. We'll figure out a way to fix him because he will come to the dance—he couldn't stand to stay away. I know, we'll get a revolver and shoot him."

Well, Buh Nansi heard about how everybody else had been invited to the dance, and he wanted to go. So he told his wife to wrap him up in a white sheet and he would go as a little baby, and she could carry him into the dance. And if anyone notices that it is him, she should just throw him out of the window in the sheet. So said, so done. And the music struck up and they got right into the dancing. And Lion noticed a mother with this baby. And he said, "I don't think a baby has bones that big. It must be Buh Nansi pulling a trick." So he found out by pulling on the sheet, and Buh Nansi told his wife to throw him out of the window. But his wife was so taken up in the dancing that she didn't hear him.

So Nansi gave a little jig and started to run, Lion behind him. He ran until he saw a crab hole just beside a pepper tree. So he grabbed some peppers and jumped down in the hole. He put the peppers in his mouth and crushed them up. Lion came to the hole and started to dig. He dug until he could just about see Buh Nansi, and then Buh Nansi spat out the mouthful of peppers into Buh Lion's eyes and made him blind. He rubbed both eyes out of his head with his paws, it hurt so much. And he died from the pain, and out came Buh Nansi and chopped him up and flung him on his shoulder and carried him home, piece by piece, to his wife. He said, "My wife, we can walk out proudly forever, day or night, because I have killed this great king of the woods, and we have Lion to eat tonight for dinner." So he got the pot on the fire and got some limes and made a lion soup.

I went to this feast and enjoyed some of it, and I came directly here to tell you this big lie. That's why you see that today you must never do evil. You must always do good to your friends, and never do evil. You must always do good to your friends even if they do you bad.

—*St. Vincent*

44
THE FEAST ON THE MOUNTAIN AND THE FEAST UNDER THE WATER

It was Anansi's birthday, and he invited all the animals to come to his feast and eat with him, and Tortoise came along too. But Anansi didn't want him, and before they went to eat, Anansi suddenly said that all the animals who were going to eat must wash their hands before they came to the table. Now Tortoise went to wash his hands, but as he walked back, his hands got dirty again. He tried over and over, but he could not walk any other way. So he never got to eat at Anansi's table.

Tortoise went away. He said, "Anansi tricked me, but I am going to get even with him."

Tortoise decided he would also have a big feast, and he sent a call to all the animals to come and eat with him. He knew that Anansi would come, of course. When they arrived he said his feast would be under the water; he knew Anansi was too light to swim down to where they were eating. But Anansi borrowed a pair of breeches and a coat, and he dressed himself in that. He picked up stones and put them in his pockets so that he might swim below. Now, when he was heavy enough, he went down into the water. The table was set and all were beginning to eat. Tortoise looked and saw that Anansi had put stones in his pockets. Immediately Tortoise said to them all, "Before you come to the table, you must all take off your coats."

Anansi was troubled when he heard this. He thought about it and said to himself, "If I take off my coat, then I am going to float up to the top again, because the stones that are in my pockets hold me." So he kept his coat on. But when Anansi came to the table, Tortoise at once said, "When you gave a feast, you did what you liked. When I give mine, I can do what I like too. You have to take off your coat."

So Anansi took his coat off. No sooner did he do so than he rose to the surface of the water. So he did not get any food that day.

Greed caused this to happen to him. So when you eat, you must eat with others.

—Surinam

45
HIDE ANGER UNTIL TOMORROW

There was a man who had to go off to town to work. In town he met this old man who was wise in all things, and who said to him, "I am going to tell you the two things you need to know: When you get angry, hide it until tomorrow; and all that your eyes see, you must not believe."

Now, this man had a wife at home, but they had no child. He had to remain away from home for a long time, but finally he was able to return. But when he came home, he found a man in bed with his wife and they were both asleep. He drew his revolver to shoot the man, but suddenly he remembered what the old man had said to him: "Hide your anger until tomorrow." So he didn't shoot him.

When the morning came and they were all awake, his wife told him of their good luck; for when he left she was pregnant, and this was their boy who was sleeping with his mother. The child had grown so big! If he had shot him, he would have killed his own child.

That is why it is well to listen to a person who says, "Hide your anger till tomorrow, and all that you see you must not believe."

—Surinam

46
BUYING TWO EMPTY HANDS

—

Well, once upon a time, Massa King built a great, large building and sent all over the West Indies for great men to come to look at it to see if there was anything wrong with it. He was proud of that building, so proud that he wanted it to be perfect. And all those men went into it, and no one could find any fault with it at all. But still the king worried.

Now, Anansi heard about this and he thought he would just look into it and see what he could see in the building. So he went down there and paid his manners to Massa King. He said, "Good morning, Massa King." He said, "Good morning, Anansi." Anansi said, "Well, sir, I heard you had a great building built down here." King said, "Oh yes." Anansi said, "I heard that you had a lot of important people come and look at it, and they all said it is beautiful, and no one could find any fault with it." He said, "Well, I came to look at it, too, if I could?" King said, "Go in the building and look around, for I am very proud of it."

Well, Anansi went in and sat down and he looked around and he thought about Massa King and how proud he was and he began working out a plan. He went up to Massa King and said, "Well, Massa King, the building is very beautiful and well built, but I did find one fault that worries me." Now, Massa King was surprised and asked him what the matter was. He said, "Massa King, the only thing missing in this building is two empty hands." King said, "Well, how can I get them?" Anansi said, "Well, Massa King, I know a gentleman at Sion Hill who always has empty hands to sell so I could probably get some for you." And Massa King said, "Well, what do you think he would charge me?" Anansi said, "They are going to cost you sixteen cents. If you give me that, I am already on my way to get them and bring them to you."

So Massa King gave Anansi sixteen cents. And Anansi took the money and went to the shop at Sion Hill, where he bought a quarter-pint of strong rum for eight cents and a loaf of bread and some fried fish for the other eight cents.

Then he took a little of the rum and he rubbed down his skin all over and he went where he knew Compé Lion always passed. And he lay down on the road and played drunk. Compé Lion came down the road toward him carrying a great load of wood on his head. When he saw Anansi lying there he threw down the wood and stooped down and said to Anansi, "Compé, what are you doing here?" Anansi said, "Compé, I was drinking all night, and I tried to get home, and Compé, I just couldn't make it. If you think I am telling you a lie, look in my pocket there, you will see the bottle." Compé Lion took out the pint and he held it up to his mouth and he tried and tried but he couldn't get even one drop out of it. This made Compé Lion angry, because he loves rum, you know. So when he passed he kicked Anansi again and again, and Anansi just lay there on the ground, rolling in the dust and mud until his whole skin got mudded up.

Now he went to Massa King. And with big tears in his eyes. And Massa King said, when he got there, he said, "Well, Compé Anansi, what's wrong now?" Anansi said, "Compé Massa King, I went to the shop and when I got there the shopkeeper wasn't there. And they told me he was leaving on the boat, so I ran down and caught him just as he was getting on the boat to go away. And he sold me the last empty hands that he had, sir. I was bringing them to you, and on my journey coming back, Compé Lion beat me up and took away the two empty hands, sir." So Massa King said, "Well let's get Compé Lion here." And off Anansi went.

When Compé Lion came, he said, "Good morning, Massa King," because he didn't know what was happening. Massa King greeted him back, "Good morning, Compé Lion," he said, "and how are you?" And so they talked for a while like that. Finally, Massa King said, "Well, come in and get a little supper with us." He said, "Well, Massa King, I just had some supper, but I wouldn't want you to be ashamed by me not eating anything. So I will take a little bit." When he finished, Massa King called in Compé Anansi and said, "Well, Compé Lion, do you know this man?" He said, "Sure I know him well." He said, "Did you see him this morning?" He said, "Yes, sir, when I was going home from the forest with a load of wood, I met him on the road." He said, "Well, did he have anything with him?" Compé Lion said, "No." Compé Anansi got up and said, "Compé Lion, I had nothing with me?" Compé Massa King said, "Compé Lion, I sent this man to buy something for me and he told me that you took it from him." Lion said, "Oh, Compé, I did not take anything from this man. When I was coming, I met this man with nothing but two empty hands." Massa King said, "Well, that's just what I sent the man to buy." He said, "Hand my gun to me." Compé Lion ran away when he heard that, and went to the forest.

And he lives in the forest from that day on until today.

—*St. Vincent*

47
CUTTA CORD-LA

————

One time, food got very scarce. The rice crop made nothing and the fish were swimming too low to catch and the birds too high to shoot. Really hard times had come on every day— all the animals got really hungry way down in their bellies, and that's the truth. Brer Rabbit and Brer Wolf decided to put their heads together to see if they couldn't figure out what to do.

After a while, Brer Rabbit, weeping bitter tears, said that they would just have to kill and eat their grandmothers. Brer Wolf, he just kept on crying. Brer Rabbit said, "If you're going to take it so hard like that, Brer Wolf, it would be better for you to kill your grandmother first and get it over with so that way you'll be done with your grieving fastest."

Brer Wolf dried his eyes and killed his grandmother. And together they went off and they ate and ate day and night until it was all gone. Soon after, Brer Wolf went visiting Brer Rabbit and said, "Brer Rabbit, I am hungry through and through. Let's kill your grandmother so we can have something to eat."

Brer Rabbit lifted up his head and he burst out laughing. He said, "Brer Wolf, you think I'm going to kill my own grandmother? Oh no, Brer Wolf, I couldn't do that!"

Now, this made Brer Wolf so mad, he tore at his hair with his claws and he howled like an Indian. He said that he was going to make Brer Rabbit kill his grandmother somehow. Brer Rabbit said they would see about all this nonsense later.

Now, Brer Rabbit took his grandmother by the hand and led her *way* off into the woods and hid her at the top of a huge coconut tree and told her to stay there quietly. (In those days there were lots of coconuts, you know.) He gave her a little basket with a cord tied to it, so that he could send food up to her.

The next morning, Brer Rabbit went to the foot of the tree, cleared his throat and hollered in a fine voice:

Granny, granny, o granny! Cutta cord-la.

When the grandmother heard this, she let down this basket with the cord, and Brer Rabbit filled it with things to eat. Every day he came back and did the same thing; every day Brer Rabbit came to feed his granny, saying:

Granny, granny, o granny! Cutta cord-la.

And she let down the basket.

Brer Wolf, he watched and he listened. He crept up close and listened some more. Bye and bye, he heard what Brer Rabbit was saying and he saw the basket swing down on the cord and go back up again. When Brer Rabbit went away from there, Brer Wolf came up by the root of the tree. He hollered, saying:

Granny, granny, o granny! Shoota cord-la.

Now, Old Granny Rabbit listened closely, she listened well. She said, "Now what's happening here? My grandson doesn't talk like that. He never said 'shoota cord-la' like that."

So when Brer Rabbit came back to his grandmother, she told him about how someone was hollering "shoota cord-la," and Brer Rabbit, he started laughing and he laughed so hard he couldn't laugh anymore. Brer Wolf was hiding close by and heard Brer Rabbit cracking his jokes and laughing, and so he got very mad!

When Brer Rabbit went away, Brer Wolf came back under the tree by the roots and hollered:

Granny, granny, o granny! Cutta cord-la.

Granny Rabbit held her head to one side and listened hard. "I'm very sorry, my son, that you have such a bad cold; you know your voice is sounding very hoarse, my son." Then she kind of peeked out of the branches and saw Brer Wolf. "You can't fool me like that," she said. "Go on away, now, you hear?" Now Brer Wolf was really mad. He grimaced and snorted until his tusks were all shiny. He went to the swamp, scratched his head, and started to think about his problem. Bye and bye, he went to the blacksmith and asked him how he could make his voice less hoarse-sounding, so that it could sound fine like Brer Rabbit's voice does. The blacksmith said, "Come on, Brer Wolf, and

I'll run this hot poker down your throat and it will make you talk nice and easy like Brer Rabbit.''

Then the blacksmith ran his red-hot poker down Brer Wolf's throat, and it hurt so bad that it was a long time before Brer Wolf could even say anything. Finally, he took his long walk back to that coconut tree. And when he got there, he hollered:

Granny, granny, o granny! Cutta cord-la.

The voice sounded so nice and fine to Granny Rabbit that she thought it must be Brer Rabbit's voice, and she let the basket down. Brer Wolf shook the cord like he was putting food in the basket, and he just got in it himself. Brer Wolf just sat there as still as can be. Then Granny Rabbit pulled on the cord. She said, ''Lord, this load seems heavy. My grandson must really love me to bring me so much food.''

Brer Wolf, he was just grinning away when he heard this, but he kept still. Granny Rabbit pulled, she pulled hard. She pulled until she was tired and had to rest, and there was Brer Wolf almost to the top of the tree. Brer Wolf looked down and his head started to swim. He looked up and his mouth started to water. He looked down again and he saw Brer Rabbit. He got scared then, and he jerked on the rope a little. Brer Rabbit hollered then:

Granny, granny, o granny! Cutta cord-la.

Well, Granny Rabbit cut the cord and Brer Wolf fell down and broke his neck.

—*Sea Islands*

48
BRER BEAR'S GRAPEVINE

Brer Bear used to be very, very fond of grapes. He was a good farmer, so he went out in the woods and dug himself up a grapevine and set it out on his farm.

Brer Bear tended his grapevine like it was a baby, hoeing and watering it in the summertime, and wrapping it up in the wintertime. This went on for two years, and Brer Bear was really proud of himself when he saw the flowers on it the third spring that rolled around. He went into the house that morning and he said to old Missus Bear, "I am going to have the best grapes you ever saw this fall, you just wait and see."

Missus Bear started to grumble because she was ill-natured anyhow, and she said, "You ought to make some grapes, you nurse that old vine all the time. I suppose that the birds will eat them up before they get ripe, though." Brer Bear said, "You are the crossest woman I've ever seen. You wouldn't see a bit of sunshine in a pot of gold, that's what you wouldn't, and I know it." With that he went back out to the grapevine.

Brer Possum came along and stopped to watch Brer Bear working. When he saw that Brer Bear really had himself a grapevine, he laughed to himself. Then he just went on about his business because the grapes weren't ripe yet.

The summer wore on, with Brer Bear always nursing that grapevine and watching the little grapes grow. When they began to grow and when they started turning purple, Brer Bear was so proud that all day long he watched them to see that the birds didn't peck at them. Meanwhile, Missus Bear just fussed and fussed at all the work he was putting in.

Brer Bear's grapes were ripening. One day, he said to himself that he wanted to eat some of them, but he just ate a few, because he wanted them to get nice and ripe before he ate them all up.

That same evening, Brer Possum woke up from a long nap and remembered the grapes and decided to go see for himself how they were coming along. He sneaked up to the garden where the vines were and he looked around for Brer Bear. When he saw that Brer Bear wasn't anywhere to be seen, he sneaked up and tasted one of the grapes. He just meant to taste the grapes to see if they were sweeter than the woods' grapes as Brer Bear said they were, but they were so good that Brer Possum kept on tasting them for a long time.

After a while, Brer Possum heard somebody coming and he climbed up on top of the vine just as Brer Fox crept up and started eating Brer Bear's grapes quietly. Brer Possum lay there quietly until Brer Fox got a taste and left, then he started eating again.

Soon he heard somebody else coming and he had to hide again. This time it was Brer Bear's cousin, and I tell you, this Brer Bear could sure say grace over a powerful heap of grapes. Before Brer Bear left, Brer Raccoon came, and poor old Brer Possum had to lay there almost all night. At last it was getting to be daylight, and Brer Possum knew that Brer Bear would be there soon to shoo the birds away. He got up and he couldn't see any grapes to save his life, but when he heard Brer Bear opening the door he jumped off the vine, and I tell you, he flew away from there.

Brer Bear, when he found he didn't have any grapes left, he went wild, at first with grief, then with anger, and he began to look for tracks of the thief. The other animals had stepped lightly, but Brer Possum when he had jumped off of the vine had planted his tracks in the soft dirt and there was no mistake about that being old Brer Possum himself that had left the tracks.

Brer Bear was so mad that he looked for Brer Possum for a week to kill him, but Brer Squirrel warned Brer Possum and Brer Possum stayed hidden for a long spell. He had another advantage too, for Brer Possum slept during the daytime and Brer Bear slept at night.

After that, Brer Bear never planted another grapevine, and he never had any use for Brer Possum anymore either. Until this day they don't have a thing to do with each other, and Brer Possum is scared of Brer Bear. Of course, Missus Bear said to old Brer Bear, like a woman will, "Old man, I told you so, didn't I?"

—*North Carolina*

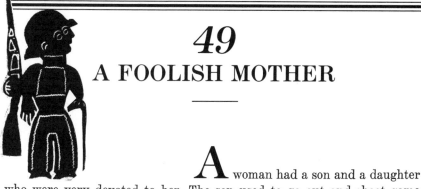

49
A FOOLISH MOTHER

A woman had a son and a daughter who were very devoted to her. The son used to go out and shoot game every day so that they could have something to eat. And every day that son would come back with his bag full of pigeons. One day, while traveling through the bush, he came upon a house. There was only one person— a girl—living in that house. He went in and fell in love with the girl. And after that, when he went out to shoot game, he left a portion of his catch for the girl before he went home.

Seeing the bag wasn't full, his sister said to the mother, "Mama, why do you think that Brother is not bringing as many pigeons as he used to? He must be giving them away to somebody." The mother said, "I was thinking that, my child. I will find out if he is giving them away."

She thought about it and took his shot bag and put some ashes in it. In the morning, when the sun woke up, he took up the bag and he went out and paid no attention to what was in the bag. On the road he took, those little ashes made a track as he was riding along, and his mother followed the track. When she got way up in the bush she heard her son singing, and she got up close to hear what he was saying:

> *My sweet Arlegen, my sweet Arlegen,*
> *Ye virgin, open the door,*
> *My sweet Arlegen.*

The girl opened the door and he went in now and stayed there with her for a little while. When he left he went into the bush, and when he came back out he left a portion of pigeons and went home. The next morning, his mother followed him again. She went, and she heard the song:

> *My sweet Arlegen, my sweet Arlegen,*
> *Ye virgin, open the door,*
> *My sweet Arlegen.*

Well, she opened the door and he passed a little time there and went out again. Now, the mother wanted to kill the girl. After the fellow went into the bush, the mother went by the door and began to sing, softly and lightly:

> *My sweet Arlegen, my sweet Arlegen,*
> *Ye virgin, open the door,*
> *My sweet Arlegen.*

But the girl knew that it wasn't the boy's voice, and she wouldn't open the door. Well, after she saw that the girl wouldn't open the door, the mother went back and she went to a blacksmith, and asked him to put hot lead down her throat to give her the voice like her son, and he did.

Next day, the fellow went again and sang, and the door opened. After the fellow left and went into the bush, the mother went up to the door of the house and sang:

> *My sweet Arlegen, my sweet Arlegen,*
> *Ye virgin, open the door,*
> *My sweet Arlegen.*

Now that she had the same voice as the man, the girl got up and opened the door. And the mother went inside and she chopped off the girl's head, and she wrapped her up and put her back on the bed, and she went out and closed the door. When the man came back, the man sang:

> *My sweet Arlegen, my sweet Arlegen,*
> *Ye virgin, open the door,*
> *My sweet Arlegen.*

Now, the door didn't open, and he said to himself, "How deep you must be sleeping that you can't hear me." And he jerked open the door. He went in and pulled the sheet off of the girl, and her head dropped on the floor.

Well, he took the head and put it back carefully and covered her up, and went on home. He carried his bag full of pigeons this day now, and thrust it at his mother. And he turned back and he went and he dug a grave deep and wide, and he threw himself down into the grave and broke his neck.

Now, the mother and the daughter were still waiting for his food, but he never came. The next day and the day after, he still didn't come back, and now they were hungry. With nothing to eat and no one to go to, they started to eat each other's shoulder, and they ate each other's hands until they got as far as their mouths could reach, mother and daughter, and the two of them died like that.

—Providencia

50
OLD GRANNY GRINNY GRANNY

One time, Brer Rabbit was traveling around to all the neighbors. He had been mad at Brer Wolf for some time, but he decided to be a friendly neighbor that day. He came past Brer Wolf's house, but he didn't see anything, and he didn't hear anything. So he hollered: "Hi, Brer Wolf! Why aren't you answering when I'm coming by to say 'hello'? Why are you making such a worried face for me?" He waited and he listened and still there was no answer. Brer Rabbit hollered again: "Come on out and show yourself, Brer Wolf, come on out and show yourself! It would be a shame not to come out when your old acquaintance came visiting you where you lived."

Nothing answered at all, and Brer Rabbit really began to get mad. He got so mad, in fact, that he stamped his feet and bumped his head on the side of the fence. Bye and bye, he got a little courage and he opened the door and looked inside the house. The fire was going in the chimney, a pot was set on the fire, and an old woman sat by the pot. The old woman was Old Granny Wolf. She was crippled in her legs, and blind in her eyes, and almost deaf in her ears. In spite of her deafness, she had heard Brer Rabbit making a fuss at the door, and she cried out: "Come in and see Old Granny, my grandson, come in and see Granny. The fire is burning, the pot's boiling. Come on in and get something to eat, my grandson." She just couldn't tell it was Brer Rabbit and not Brer Wolf.

So Brer Rabbit went on in and made himself comfortable by the fire. Bye and bye, he hollered: "Hi, Granny, I've been crippled myself. My eyes have come to blindness. You must boil me in the water so my leg can get better and my eyes can see again." Now, Brer Rabbit really liked tomfoolery, so he took a chunk of wood and dropped it in the pot, *kerchunk*. He then said, "Now I'm feeling better, my granny. My leg is getting stronger and my eyes can almost see."

Granny Wolf shook her head and cried: "My one leg is crippled and my other leg is crippled; my one eye is blind and my other eye is blind. Why don't you put me in the pot and make me feel better?" Brer Rabbit laughed and said, "Hold yourself still, Granny, and I'll fix one place in the pot where you'll be able to get back the strength in your legs and the sight in your eyes. Hold still, now, Granny." And Brer Rabbit took the chunk of wood out of the pot and put Granny in its place. She touched the fire and hollered, "*Ow*! Take me away from this." Brer Rabbit said she wasn't in there long enough yet. Granny Wolf hollered, "*Ow*! Take me away from this, it's too hot." Brer Rabbit didn't take Granny Wolf from the pot, and finally she died and was cooked. Brer Rabbit took the bones out and threw them away, but he left the meat. He took Granny Wolf's cap and turned it around and put it on. Then he sat by the fire and waited, holding himself in the chair the same as Granny Wolf.

Bye and bye, Brer Wolf came back. He walked into the house and said, "I'm hungry, Grinny Granny, I'm really hungry." "Your dinner is ready, Grindson Grandson!" Brer Wolf looked in the pot and smelled it and stirred it, and served himself up a big plateful. He ate his dinner and he smacked his mouth.

Brer Wolf ate the dinner and then called in his children and asked them if they didn't want something to eat. But they said, "We can't eat Grinny Granny," So Brer Rabbit knew he was going to get caught and he scampered away from there. But he hollered back, "Brer Wolf, you just ate Grinny Granny."

Brer Wolf got so mad. He heard Brer Rabbit holler and he tired to cach him. His feet just tore up the grass the way he was running along. Finally, he ran down Brer Rabbit, he was pushing himself so hard. Brer Rabbit had run and run till he couldn't run any more, so he hid underneath a leaning tree. Brer Wolf found him there, but couldn't get to him. Brer Rabbit hollered, "Hi, Brer Wolf, come quickly and hold up this tree before it falls down, for the world is coming down. Come on and hold it up and I'll run and get a prop for it." Brer Wolf was scared now, so he held up that tree for Brer Rabbit; he held it until he got tired, and Brer Rabbit was gone.

—*Georgia*

51

YOU NEVER KNOW
WHAT TROUBLE IS
UNTIL IT FINDS YOU

 One time, Brer Alligator's back used to be smooth and white as a catfish skin. When he came out of the water and lay down to sleep in the hot sun on the mudbank, he shined like a piece of silver. He was mighty proud of that hide, and mighty pleased with himself in every way.

He and his wife and his family lived down in the river at the edge of the rice field. They had plenty of fish to eat and never had to bother any of the animals on the land, unless they strayed into those bogs of mud by the riverside, or fell in the water. They just threw themselves in the bottom of the ditches and canals, and they had a gang of children so their house was always full up without them asking in no company. And they were so satisfied with themselves that they thought that there wasn't anybody quite like them. And they had no notion how true that was!

Well, one hot day in the fall, Brer Gator was resting himself upon a rice-field bank, letting the sun soak into that bright back of his, when along came Brer Rabbit.

Now Brer Rabbit had no love for Brer Gator, but he stopped all the same to pass the time of day with him, to have a little conversation with him, because Brer Rabbit loved to talk with anyone. Rather than keep his mouth shut he goes out of his way to talk, if it's only with one of those ridiculous animals that don't know any better than to live in the water.

"Howdy, Brer Alligator. How is Sister Alligator, and all the young alligators making out?" Brer Gator didn't bother to reply at first. It just seemed like he didn't care what any other animal thought about him, or how they were getting along themselves. But after a while he fixed his cat-eye on Brer Rabbit and told him, "Please God, they're getting on just fine. But it's no wonder that those children are smart and pretty and raised right, because they live right here in the river. I swear to God, I can't see how you others get by living up on top of that dry, drafty land. And you and all the other animals that aren't fit to live in the water. You seem to spend all of your time fighting with each other until you must be worn out before the day is half finished!"

Brer Rabbit got really angry with Brer Gator for being so set in his notions and so superior in his manners; so he got it in his mind to just tell him what he thought of that kind of talk. But you know how, even when he's angry, he can hide it, so Brer Rabbit just stayed calm and pretended that Brer Gator is a wise man. He sighed and he shook his head and said, very mournful like, "Maybe so. We sure have been seeing a lot of trouble up here lately."

"Who is that you're talking about, Brer Rabbit—Trouble?"

Brer Rabbit thought that Brer Gator must be joking with him.

"What's that, Brer Alligator! You never heard of—Trouble?"

Brer Gator shook his head. "No. I never heard about him, nor have I seen him. What does he look like?" Brer Rabbit couldn't believe his ears. "Oh, for crying out loud, Brer Alligator! Old as you is, and you haven't seen Trouble yet?" "I tell you, Brer Rabbit, I ain't never know nothing about this here Trouble. What does Trouble look like?"

Brer Rabbit scratched his head. He figured that if Brer Gator is so stupid, and so satisfied with himself, and so ridiculous and unmannerly about everything that lives on land, that now he has a chance to teach Brer Gator his right place. And Brer Rabbit is so mischievious that he schemed about how he was going to have the most fun at Brer Gator's expense. "I don't know that I can tell you exactly what Trouble looks like. But maybe you'd like to see him?" he asked. "Of course, I can show him to you, Brer Alligator, but I don't know that I really want to. Maybe you won't like him so well when you actually meet." "What are you talking about? I'm not worried about that. I just want to see him. If I don't like him, that won't matter to me at all." "Well, I'm pretty busy right now," Brer Rabbit pretended. "Come now, Brer Rabbit! You have time for a lot of inconsequential things, after all, and it is me, Brer Alligator, that is requesting this from you, don't forget that!"

"Of course. How can I forget that!" Brer Rabbit mocked him, only Brer Gator did never recognize that Brer Rabbit meant to trick him. "But I have to fix my house up, and Sister Rabbit is not feeling well, and the children have to be watched, and—"

"*Tchk*! All that'll take care of itself!" And Brer Alligator coaxed and begged and begged and coaxed until at last Brer Rabbit agreed to show him Trouble.

"Meet me here as soon as the dew is dry on the grass next Saturday. That's a good day. Trouble may have some time off on Sunday." And Brer Rabbit bid him good morning, and went along down the road.

On came Saturday, and Brer Gator got up before dawn and started to make himself presentable. Sister Alligator woke up and asked, "Where are you going?" Brer Gator never opened his mouth but continued to fix himself up. That just got Sister Alligator into the mood to bother him. "Where are you going?" she asked again. And she questioned and she questioned until after a length of time Brer Gator saw that the woman was not going to shut up until she found out. He gave up at last. "I am going out with Brer Rabbit." "Where are you going?"

Brer Alligator made a long mouth and tried to pay no more attention. But Sister Alligator knew the ways to get around that fellow. And after another length of time, Brer Alligator told her: "I am going to see Trouble." "What is Trouble?" "How do I know? That's what I am going to see." "Can I go along?" asked Sister Alligator.

He said no, but after her talking and persuading, talking and persuading, finally Brer Alligator said, "All right, you can come along," but his patience was worn thin.

So she started to fix herself up. What with all the talking and persuading, all the little alligators woke up by this time. They looked at their pappy and their mammy, both fixing themselves up, getting ready to go out, and they ran to Brer Gator and asked him, "Where are you going, Pappy?" "None of your business!" They ran to Sister Alligator, and they cried out, one after another, "Where are you going, Mammy?" But all Sister Alligator said is, "Get away and let me alone now."

Then they ran to their father, and they teased him: "Pappy, Mammy said for you to tell us where you are going." Brer Alligator was mad, but he saw that it wouldn't do him any good to hold back. "I'm going to see Trouble," he grunted. "Pappy! Can we go with you? Can we go with you?"

Now the children jumped up and down, hollering and begging him to go along. Brer Alligator told them, "No!" So they ran to their mother and asked, "Mammy, can we go?" And she told them, "If pa says you can go, you can go; but if he said no, then it's no."

So they went back to their father: "Ma says that we can go if you let us." Now, Brer Alligator was just worn out with all the fuss, so he said, "Well, all right, but fix yourselves up nice and pretty. And you have to act well-mannered now! You have to show Brer Rabbit how much better water children are than woods children."

They ran to fix themselves up nice, and soon they were all dressed up for going out. They had on their best, with mud on their heads, and marsh on their backs, and moonshine on their tails, and didn't they think they looked fine! About this time, Brer Alligator looked out the door and saw that the dew was almost gone, so he called them all to come on. And they all came out, crowding each other, going down the rice-field bank to wait for Brer Rabbit.

They hadn't been there long before Brer Rabbit came along, smoking his pipe. When he got to where they were, he was surprised to see the whole family there. He laughed to himself, but he didn't say anything but "Howdy" to Brer Gator and his wife. And he told them, "How nice your children look today!" But all the time he was saying to himself, "Oh, Lord! This is an ugly gang of people, aren't they? And just look at those clothes!"

Brer Gator didn't even apologize for bringing such a big crowd with him. All he said was, "They all begged me so that I had to give in and let them come along."

Brer Rabbit said, "There's plenty of room for everybody. I hope you will all enjoy yourselves."

"Thank you!" they all told him. And the children were so glad that Brer Rabbit didn't send them home that they all danced around with joy.

They looked so funny that Brer Rabbit almost laughed in their faces. But instead of that he knit his eyebrows and looked at his watch, and said, "Time to get going, I guess."

So they all started down the rice-field bank, Brer Rabbit and Brer Gator leading off, with Sister Alligator walking behind to make the little alligators behave themselves. But they wouldn't hardly mind her, they played along, or dawdled, or fought until they almost drove her crazy.

Brer Rabbit led them up through a patch of woods until he got to a field grown over with broomgrass and briar! The grass stood like pure gold. The path they took went straight through the field, and it was a big field too. Brer Rabbit led, and after a while they got to the middle of the field and then he stopped. He took his pipe from his mouth and cupped his ear, and pretended that he was listening for something. *"Sh! Sh!"* he told the children. Sister Alligator said, *"Sh! Sh!* Or I'll lick the tar out of you!"

After Brer Rabbit listened some more, he shouted out, "Who is that calling Brer Rabbit?" Then he pretended that he heard something more, and he yelled back, "Yes. It's me. What do you want with me?"

He cupped his hand to his ear again, and then he said, "I am coming right now." And he turned to Brer Gator and told him, "I beg your pardon, but somebody is calling me away for a minute on business. Please excuse me. Wait right here, and I'll be right back." "We aren't going anyplace," Brer Gator promised.

Brer Rabbit made a low bow and ran along the path out of sight. That deceitful devil ran until he got to the edge of the woods, and he sat down and chuckled to himself like he was tasting the fun before he started it. Then he got down to business.

He smelled the wind and looked which way it was blowing. Then he pulled a handful of that long, dry broomgrass, and he knocked out the hot coal from his pipe into it, and he blew on it till the grass caught fire good. Then he ran along the edge of the field with the fire, and set the field blazing all around. When he was finished, he got up on a safe high stump where he could see good, and he sat down and waited.

All this time, the alligators were down in the middle of the field. They were tired because they had walked so far, and were satisfied to rest themselves awhile.

Sister Alligator was just that kind who liked to know just what she was going to see. She pestered and bothered Brer Gator with which-and-why talk: "Which way are we going to find Trouble? Why didn't you make Brer Rabbit tell you more about this thing you're looking for? How long do we have to wait?" He didn't answer her, but just sat still and grunted every now and then. Once in a while, Sister Alligator called to the children who were running around, "Stop that noise!" And they sat, and they sat. The fire burned and burned. At last the wind caught it and it flared up high, and the sparks and flames flew away up in the sky. One of the little alligators saw that and he hollered out, "Look there! Look there!" But, just then, Sister Alligator asked Brer Alligator another question, and she shut up the children to answer him.

But all the rest of the little alligators looked toward where their brother had pointed and they sang out too, "Look-a dere!" And one got a notion and he yelled out, "That must be Trouble." And Sister Alligator turned and looked, "Look, Pa! Is that Trouble for true?"

Brer Gator was so ignorant he didn't know. He lived in the water and mud, and he hadn't ever seen fire until now, but he didn't feel easy in his mind. "I guess maybe Brer Rabbit got lost or something?" he asked Sister Alligator, without answering her question. Then one of the children sang out, "Trouble is pretty!"

With that, all of the brats raised up their voices and hollered: "Trouble is pretty! Trouble is pretty! Trouble is pretty!"

Brer Gator said, "If that is Trouble, he sure is pretty! The child speaks the truth." And he and his wife sat staring with their big eye up in the air watching the fire coming on, and they forgot all about Brer Rabbit. And all the children stared too, same as their mother and father, and kept quiet as if they were afraid that they might scare Trouble away.

At last a hot spark landed right on one of the little alligators' back. And he screamed and cried, "Trouble hurts!" His mother smacked him in the jaw and told him to mind his manners and shut up, and to look at how pretty Trouble is. But just as she did that, a big spark lit on her and burned her bad. And she started to jump around and holler. "It's true; Trouble hurts!" And they remembered then who they had forgotten. "Brer Rabbit! Brer Rabbit! We don't want to see no more

Trouble, Brer Rabbit!'' Well, about that time the sparks began to burn the whole bunch. They were so mixed up they didn't know what to do. And they ran around and ran about, this way and that way, to get away, but everywhere they turned was the fire. And they hollered out, and hollered out, ''Brer Rabbit, where are you? Call to Trouble, Brer Rabbit! Come for us!''

But Brer Rabbit didn't come, and he didn't say anything. And very soon the fire got so close to those gators that they couldn't hold their ground any longer. They stopped calling Brer Rabbit, and got ready to get through the fire the best they could. They didn't have any notion left in their head but Get Home!

Sister Alligator hollered, ''Children, follow your pa.''

And right through the scorching fire they burst, Sister Alligator pushing them along. They don't walk so fast every day, but this was a very special day, with that hot fire blistering and frying them. After they got through, they didn't slow down. They went past Brer Rabbit on the stump, but they didn't see him, they were running so fast. And they looked so funny that Brer Rabbit almost fell off the stump, laughing so hard.

''Wait, Brer Alligator!'' he shouted, ''I guess you have seen Trouble now! Get back in the water where you belong. And don't ever hunt Trouble anymore!'' Those gators were just too busy running to stop and argue with him. They didn't stop until they got to the rice-field bank and jumped in the river. And they were still so hot from the fire when they went over the bank that as the water hit them, it went ''*Swiish-sssssssss-sh!*'' And the steam rose up like a cloud.

They didn't come out again the whole day or that night either; but when they got a chance to look at each other they found that the fire had burned them so bad that their white skin was just as black and crinkly as a burned log of wood, and as rough as a live oak bark.

And from that day to this, alligators have a horny hide.

—*South Carolina*

52
HE PAYS FOR THE PROVISIONS

Blacksnake and Buh Nansi were very good friends. They went to church one day and they heard a preacher preaching and telling about a famine that was coming. After he went home, Blacksnake told Nansi that they must work a garden. Anansi said he was not going to work at any garden; he'd rather live as a thief.

The next day, Blacksnake started to work on his garden, planting yams, potatoes, okras, tanias; and as everything came into bloom, the famine started. All this time, Blacksnake was expecting to see Anansi come to help, but he never saw him. Anansi came home and saw the garden and asked Blacksnake for something to eat. Blacksnake decided to give something to Anansi, but he told him that each time he must give him a lash with his long tail, and you know how strong that Blacksnake is. But Anansi saw that might give him some chance for even more food.

Anansi went one day and Blacksnake gave him a bunch of plantains, a few yams, some potatoes, okras, and callaboo bush (the leaves of the dasheen taro), and Anansi went home and made a big pot of food for himself. Then, the next day, Anansi got a little kettle drum and he started to beat it, singing:

> *Ah me Buh Nansi—O*
> *Ah me Buh Nansi—O*
> *Good feast here tonight*
> *Good feast here tonight—O*

Buh Goat heard that, heard the singing, and he went up. "Buh Nansi." "Yes, Buh Goat?" "What's happening?" Say, "Oh God, man, I have bush peas, man, bush peas and lots of other food left over from a feast last night." Well, Buh Goat being the kind of person who will eat anything, he really went at some of the leavings. And he got so full he lay down to sleep and decided to spend the night.

Around twelve o'clock, Blacksnake came. "Buh Nansi." "Yes, sir." He whispered to his guest, "Buh Goat, open the door, man come." And as soon as Buh Goat got up and opened the door, Blacksnake gave a lash

in the dark and cut Buh Goat in half. Nansi got up and he saw Buh Goat lying there. He said, "Son of a bitch, I'm going to have some food tomorrow." Early in the morning Buh Nansi cleaned Buh Goat, cut him up, put him in the pot, seasoned him, cooked up a big pot full of goat-water stew. But he needed some provisions—yams, peas, taro, and other roots. So he went back to Blacksnake's garden now. Blacksnake said, "Buh Nansi, you aren't dead?" He said, "No Blacksnake, look at me, Buh Nansi, here!"

And he begged another bag of provisions. So Blacksnake gave Buh Nansi some plantains again, some yams, some greens, potatoes; and Buh Nansi went home and he made a big feast for the second night. After Nansi had eaten, he started to dance and sing again:

> *Ah me Buh Nansi—O*
> *Ah me Buh Nansi—O*
> *Good feast here tonight*
> *Good feast here tonight—O*

Brer Hog came up. Soon, Buh Hog got there, *"Hunh, huhn, hunh, hunh."* Buh Nansi said, "Oh God, man, I have nice things to eat tonight, nice things, a big feed going on here, big feed." Buh Nansi said, "People came here last night and for the whole night we had a big spread." So Buh Hog ate a belly full, and he fell asleep too.

Just at twelve o'clock, Blacksnake came again, just as he had the night before. As soon as Blacksnake called at the door, Buh Nansi said, "Buh Hog, would you get up and open the door? Somebody's knocking." As soon as Buh Hog opened the door, Blacksnake lashed out and cut Hog right in half, and he dropped dead.

Buh Nansi got up, cleaned Hog, seasoned up Hog the next day and made another big cook-up. But again he needed provisions for the pot to go with the meat. So he went back to the field. Blacksnake was really surprised now, "Buh Nansi, you mean you are still alive?" He said, "Yes, Blacksnake. You both beat me and you feed me."

Blacksnake gave him the same thing as usual. Well, by this time Buh Nansi was finding it hard to find anyone who would be friends. Nansi walked all around the house and started in with his drumming and singing again:

> *Ah big music here tonight*
> *Big spree—O, big spree*
> *Neighbors all come,*
> *Come a here.*

[spoken] *Big spree tonight, big spree*
[sung] *Ah neighbors—O*
[spoken] *Come join me we get by spree.*

Well, Mr. Tattoo the Armadillo was there, and Buh Tattoo decided to go. Now Tattoo does not eat cooked food like that, he lives on rotten wood and worms. But he was interested in all this singing and dancing and whatever was going on. So Tattoo did not partake of anything that Buh Nansi was cooking. When night came, Anansi went and lay down on the bed, but Tattoo went and dug a hole right in front of the door in the dirt and he lay down there.

At twelve o'clock, when Blacksnake came and called Anansi, Anansi called out: "Buh Tattoo, Buh Tattoo, will you open that door?" Tattoo said, "It's your house, it's for you to open the door. Don't you know good manners?" Blacksnake called, "Buh Nansi." Buh Nansi said, "I'm coming, sir. Buh Tattoo, the man is knocking loud. Get up and open the door. Man, I'm not feeling good. I've got a fever." But Tattoo said, "It's your house, it's for you to open the door and invite your friends inside. I'm not going to open anyone else's door." Well, Anansi cannot get Tattoo to get up and Blacksnake was getting angry outside. So Anansi put a sofa, a chair, and a table on top and he got under all that. And as Buh Nansi got under all of that there, Blacksnake gave a lash with his long tail and it cut the table, chair, and everything else around in half and nearly cut Buh Nansi in half too.

And from that day, Nansi doesn't beg but works for himself. There is the story.

—Tobago

53

THE CUNNING COCKROACH

T he cockroach can be a big creature, almost as big as your hand. You find cockroaches on the roof, where they make a noise like this: *"Crum, crum, crum, crum, crum, crum!"*

Cockroach and Fowl were once friends. They bought land to cultivate together. Each day, the fowl would go to the field to work the land. Cockroach would find an excuse not to go. So the fowl would just leave and go to the field. Now, Fowl is not a very smart fellow, you know? When he was gone, Cockroach would get out of bed and start to play. This cockroach fooled Fowl day after day.

Fowl said, one day, "You must come to work the field." "I can't go out there. I'm too sick." This is what Cockroach told Fowl every day. And he would not get out of bed. As soon as Fowl was gone, he jumped out and started to play and sing also:

> *Cockroach a* cunnyman, *a* cunnyman, *a* cunnyman,
> *Cockroach a* cunnyman, *a* cunnyman, *a* cunnyman.

He kept fooling this fowl about work. And he would not go out.

> *Cockroach a* cunnyman, *a* cunnyman, *a* cunnyman,
> *Cockroach a* cunnyman, *a* cunnyman, *a* cunnyman.

Fowl got suspicious. He got one of the neighbors to watch what Cockroach did when he wasn't there.

One morning, he set out to go. As usual, Cockroach said he couldn't go. "I'm too sick, I can't go out." And he didn't go. Fowl tried to persuade him, but he wouldn't go. Fowl went to the field, and as usual Cockroach jumped from his bed, happy, playing and singing:

> *Cockroach a* cunnyman, *a* cunnyman, *a* cunnyman,
> *Cockroach a* cunnyman, *a* cunnyman, *a* cunnyman.

And the neighbor saw him doing this and he went out to the field and told Fowl what Cockroach was doing. Now Fowl got really mad. He came back and grabbed the cockroach, and he killed him. He swallowed him up that quick!

That is why fowl will catch cockroaches today.

—*Antigua*

54
LITTLE BOY-BEAR NURSES THE ALLIGATOR CHILDREN

One time, there was a big, strong old Mother Bear who lived way back in the swamps where she kept her den in a hollow tree. She had one, two little bears there in this den, and she loved them as she loved her life. One day, she got hungry, so she told her children that she was going off a little ways to get something for them all to eat, so they must be good children and stay near home, and she would bring back some nice fish for their breakfast. And she left them there.

The little bears slept until they couldn't sleep any more because the sun was shining and things started to get very warm inside their den. The little boy-bear rubbed his eyes and said that he was going to go outside just a little ways and play for a little while. The girl-bear said, "What will our mammy say?" But he just laughed and said, "I'm just going down by the side of the creek and catch a few fish before Mammy comes back." She looked scared then, and said, "Our mammy said that something's going to get you, you remember that?" But the little boy-bear, he just kept laughing, and said, "Sure, sure, she'll never know unless you tell on me. If you don't tell her anything I'll bring you back a *big* fish."

Then the little boy-bear, he just took off. He went down there by the side of the creek and took his hook and line to catch some fish. And when he got there, he saw something just lying there in the mud. It looked like a big log to him. He laughed to himself and said, "That is one big log, for sure. I think I'll just stand on top of it so I can catch a big fish for my little sister."

The little boy-bear jumped down and got on that log and fixed his line for fishing. After a while, the log started to move, and the little boy-bear started to holler, "Oh my Lordy!" He looked down almost scared to death. That log was really one *big* she-alligator, and she swam away with the little boy-bear caught in her two hands. She was grinning *wide*. She felt the little boy-bear with her nose and said, "I'm going to take away your life; my children are going to have you for their breakfast."

The gator swam toward the hole in the bank where she lived and carried the little boy-bear in there. She called for her children and said, "Come see what a fine breakfast I brought you." Old Gator had seven children in her hole there.

Now, the little boy-bear was scared. He hollered and cried and begged. He said, "Please, Missy Gator, give me a chance to see what a fine nurse I am. Whenever you need to swim away, I'll just mind your children for you so you won't have to worry about them."

Old Gator flipped her tail and said, "Well, I'll try you just for one day. That might not be such a bad idea. If you take good care of them, I let you be."

So the old gator went away and left the little boy-bear to mind the children. She swam away to get them all some breakfast. The little boy-bear sat down there and waited and waited. Bye and bye, he got hungry himself, but he waited and waited, minding the children. He got so hungry that he could hardly hold up his head. He sucked on his paw, and that didn't help, but still he waited. The gator didn't come back.

He said to himself, "What now? I'm not going to starve myself when there is plenty to eat right here." So the little boy-bear grabbed one of the little gators by the neck and took him to the side of the creek where the bushes grow and he just ate him up. He didn't leave anything behind, not even the head or the tail.

He went back to where the other little gators were still huddled up in bed. He rubbed his stomach when he saw them and said, "What now? I feel too good to worry about anything. I'll think of something when the old gator comes back. I'll have plenty of time then." So the little boy-bear lay down, coiled up in the gator's bed, and shut his eyes, and slept like any bear does when he's full.

Bye and bye, when it was almost nightfall, Old Gator came back. She hollered, "Hey, Little Boy-Bear, how can you mind my children when you have gone to sleep right beside them?" The little boy-bear sat up on his haunches and said, "My eyes have gone to sleep, but my ears are wide awake!" The gator flipped her tail and said, "Where are the children I left with you?" Now, the little boy-bear was scared and he said, "They're right here, Missy Gator. Here, let me count them." And he started humming:

Here's one, here's another
Here's two on top of each other
Here's three, piled all together.

The gator opened her mouth and said, "You nurse them pretty well, Little Boy-Bear. Bring me one of them here to wash and get his supper." So the little boy-bear carried one over to his mother, and then carried another and then another until he had carried six. Then he got scared again, because now the gator is going to find out what happened for sure. He stopped and he didn't know what to do. The gator hollered, "Bring me another!" The little boy-bear grabbed the first one, threw him down in the mud and got him all dirty again, and carried him back. So the gator washed him up again good and didn't even know the difference.

Bye and bye, the next day, the gator went away, and left the little boy-bear there to nurse the children. He got hungry again, and he waited again, but this time he knew what to do when the gator didn't come. He just grabbed another little gator and ate him for his dinner. Then, when the old gator came home toward night he did the same thing. When Old Gator asked, "Where are my children that I left you to mind?" he sang:

Here's one, here's another
Here's two on top of each other
Here's three, piled all together.

She called them, one by one, to wash and get their supper, and little boy-bear carried them to her, one by one, carrying two of them back twice this time. Every day he did it this way until it came to the point that he ate the last gator. Then he left the place where the old gator lived. He went down by the side of the creek until he got to the place where the foot-log was lying, and he ran across it *quick*. He got into the bushes and he fairly flew home. And he never left there again.

—*Georgia*

55
THE GIRL MADE OF BUTTER

Once was a time, a very good time,
Monkey chew tobacco and spit white lime.

There was a woman. She had a daughter who was made entirely of butter. Tom and William used to come courting her, and they didn't know this about her. So the woman never let those boys near her daughter, lest she melt with the heat. But, one day, she got so busy cooking for these two boys, the woman forgot to keep watch, and the boys saw their chance. They came and sat down next to the girl. The girl started singing while the woman was in the kitchen cooking, trying to remind her.

> *Momma, come wash my skin,*
> *Momma, come wash my skin!*
> *Move off, Tom! move off, William!*
> *Till my momma has washed my skin.*

The girl started melting because her mother wasn't there to wash her skin with cool water. She melted from her head down to her shoulders.

> *Momma, come wash my skin,*
> *Momma, come wash my skin!*
> *Move off, Tom! move off, William!*
> *Till my momma has washed my skin.*

She started melting more. She melted from her shoulder down to her waist. She started singing again:

> *Momma, come wash my skin,*
> *Momma, come wash my skin!*
> *Move off, Tom! move off, William!*
> *Till my momma has washed my skin.*

She melted from her waist down to her knees. All that time the woman was in the kitchen cooking, while her daughter was melting. The girl started singing again:

> *Momma, come wash my skin,*
> *Momma, come wash my skin!*
> *Move off, Tom! move off, William!*
> *Till my momma has washed my skin.*

She melted from her knees down to her feet. When the woman did remember, she cried out, "Oh, my butter daughter! Oh, my butter baby!" She had forgotten all about her daughter. When she did go back in the house, she only found a pile of melted butter but no one else. Tom and William were gone.

The bow bended, my story ended.

—*Bahamas*

56
POPPA STOLE THE DEACON'S BULL

The reverend had a whole lot of kids, but the reverend didn't have any money, and so he could buy nothing to eat. Deacon had a bull, so the reverend went and stole the deacon's bull. He went and had people over to dinner; he even invited Deacon over. "Come over to my house Sunday, 'cause right after church we're gonna have all kinds of beef." So Deacon said he'd come.

So he came over and he sat down. You know how they do in the country, kids eat first and then the grown-ups. So the deacon sat down, and he said, "This is sure good food. *Um, um, um.* You know one thing, Rev?" He said, "What's that, Brother Deacon?" He said, "You know, somebody stole my bull." He said, "*Um*, ain't that something, people just going around taking other people's stuff." And at the same time he's the one that stole the bull.

So the kids were outside playing. The deacon went outside for a while to get some air after eating so much. And he stopped for a while to watch the kids playing. It sounded to him like the kids had made up a new game. They had each other by the hand, going around in a circle singing:

> *Oh, Poppa stole the deacon's bull,*
> *And all us children got a belly full.*

So the deacon walked over to them and said, "You know, if you sing that song again I'll give each of you a nickel." Being kids, a nickel was a whole lot of money to them. So they started singing louder and louder:

> *Oh, Poppa stole the deacon's bull,*
> *And all us children got a belly full.*

So he said, "How would you all like to make some more money, lots more?" They all said, "Yeah!" He said, "If all of you come to church next Sunday, I'll give you fifty cents apiece to sing that same song right there, just like the choir, because that song carries an important message."

So they were really excited now. They ran and told their mother that they were going to sing in church, and she was so glad to hear that the children were going to get a chance to sing that Sunday. Of course, she didn't know what they were going to sing about!

So the deacon went around to everybody's house, and told them that Reverend Jones's kids were going to be in church that Sunday, singing. He told them of their beautiful voices and the great message of their songs. So everybody wanted to come down to hear it. They said, "The Lord sent these children to bring us this message." Pretty soon Deacon

had gone all around the community spreading the word, and everyone got very excited.

So, finally, Sunday came. The children got all dressed up and cleaned up and went down to church. And were they clean and sparkly looking! Well, by the time they got there, the church was so packed that many people had to sit in the back of the church. So the reverend, their father, was so proud he told them, "Now, when you go up there, I want you to sing loud enough that everyone can hear what you're singing, because there are a lot of people in the back." So they said, "Yes sir, Daddy, we'll sing very loud."

So you know how the preacher does before he brings on the gospel singers. He went to preaching, telling the congregation this and that, building up the people to a great excitement. But they mostly came to hear the song. Finally, the deacon stood up and said, "Ladies and gentlemen, you never know where the word is going to come from. Kids can carry a divine message if you learn how to listen to them." He said, "I

want you to listen closely to this message that Reverend Jones's children are going to bring to you. Now, sing that song, children.'' They got up there and started singing away:

> *Oh, Poppa stole the deacon's bull,*
> *And all us children got a belly full.*

Now, there was so much noise set up when they started in, and the kids had such small voices, that their father couldn't hear them. So he said, ''Sing up louder, now. Come on, you must sing louder so that I can really hear you.'' By that time the people down front are looking at him like he's crazy. So he wondered why they were looking at him. So they started singing again:

> *Oh, Poppa stole the deacon's bull,*
> *And all us children got a belly full.*

Now the reverend heard what they were singing. He just looked at them in the eyes, and started in, ''Well, children—'' he began,

> *When you told them that, you told your last,*
> *Now when I get home I'm gonna kick your ass.*

> —*Philadelphia*

57

THE TROUBLE WITH HELPING OUT

One time, one time there was a big fire in the wood. All the trees were in flames, and nearly all the animals were burned to death. To get away from the heat, Snake slithered into a deep hole. The fire went on for a long time, but was at last put out by a heavy rain. When the danger was over, Snake tried to climb out of the hole, but try as he would, he could not get up the sides. He cried out to everyone who passed by to help him; but nobody dared to help because they were scared of getting bitten by him. To each he promised not to bite, of course, but no one would take the chance.

At last, a hunter came along and took pity on Snake and pulled him out. But as soon as Snake was free, he turned on Hunter and was about to bite him. "You can't bite me after I pulled you out of the hole," said Hunter. "And why shouldn't I?" asked Snake. "Because," explained Hunter, "you shouldn't harm the one who has been kind to you." "But how I am sure that everybody acts this way?" said Snake. "All right," said Hunter, "let's put the case before a competent judge!" Snake agreed. So together they set out for the city.

On the way they met Horse. Hunter and Snake told their story again, and asked if anyone should return evil for good? Horse neighed, saying that he was usually whipped for his good services to man. Then they saw Ass and asked him the same question. Ass hee-hawed, saying that he was beaten with a stick for his good services to man. Then they met Cow and told her the story and asked her if it was right for Snake to act this way. Cow bellowed that she expected to be slaughtered for her good

services to man. Snake then claimed that he had won the case and lifted his head to strike Hunter. But Hunter said, "I don't agree yet; let's put the case before Anansi, who is very wise!" Snake agreed, and so they continued on their way.

Well, they came to the city where Anansi dwelled and it so happened that they found him at home. They told him all that had happened, and what Horse, Ass, and Cow had said, and then asked Anansi to settle the dispute fairly. Anansi looked thoughtful, and shaking his head, said, "My friends, I cannot say who is right until I have seen with my own eyes how everything happened. Let us go back to the exact spot."

Well, then, all three walked back to the hole in the wood out of which Hunter had helped Snake, and Anansi asked them to act out everything just exactly as it had happened. So Snake slid down into the hole and began calling for assistance. Hunter pretended to be passing and, turning to the hole, was about to help Snake out again when Anansi stopped him, saying, "Wait, I will settle the dispute now. Hunter must not help Snake this time. Snake should try to get out without any assistance, so that he will appreciate a kind act." Snake had to stay in the hole, and he was hungry the whole time. At last, after many tries he just managed to get out. But experience had been a good master, and Snake had learned his lesson well.

Well, some time later, Hunter was caught poaching in the king's woods and was thrown into prison. Snake heard of it and made up his mind to help Hunter, so he hastened to the king's palace. Unobserved, he approached the king. When he got a good chance, he suddenly bit the king, and succeeded in making his escape before any one could catch him.

Then he made his way to the prison in which Hunter was confined, and found a way to enter it. He calmed Hunter's fears and said, "A while ago, you did me a favor, and now by experience I have learned to appreciate it. I come to aid you. Listen! I have just bitten the king and he is very sick and will die from the poison. I bring you the only cure for my bite. It is known to me alone. Send word to the king that you can cure him. But that you won't do it unless he promises to give you his only daughter in marriage." So saying, Snake gave Hunter the cure, using three different kinds of leaves, and then he left.

Hunter did as Snake told. He sent word saying that he could cure the king, and asked as reward his release from prison and the king's daughter in marriage. The king was afraid that he was dying and so he consented.

The king was quickly cured to health, and Hunter married the princess, and I know because I got drunk at the wedding.

—*Surinam*

58
THE ROOSTER GOES AWAY
IN A HUFF

Everybody in the farmyard was invited to a big supper and dance in another farmyard—ducks, geese, turkeys, guinea fowls, hens, roosters, and all. Who could pass up a big supper? So everyone went, of course, headed up by the big farmyard rooster, who strutted and crowed as he marched. Never have you heard such merry-making noise with all that quacking, cackling, and gabbling. After a few rounds of dancing to raise their appetites, they were allowed into the supper room. There was a big table sitting there just filled with plates of food as high as the old gobbler's head when he stood all the way up. But when they looked, all the plates seemed to be heaped to the top with nothing but cornbread, pones upon pones, nothing else at all.

Well now, the rooster got upset by all this. He said that he could get all the cornbread he wanted at home. So he went off in a huff. The others, however, were too hungry to care, so they fell to it. No sooner had they eaten the outside of the cornbread than they found inside a huge pile of bacon and greens. And at the bottom of that were pies and cakes and other good things.

Poor Rooster, now, when he looked back and saw what he had walked away from. But it was too late now, for word of what he had said was out and no one ever knew Rooster to take back, even if he had to die for it. But now, you notice, whenever Rooster sees some food in front of him, he always scratches with his feet the place he finds the food, and he never leaves off scratching until he gets to the bottom of it.

—*American South*

Part IV

HOW CLEVER
CAN YOU GET?
TALES OF
TRICKERY
AND ITS
CONSEQUENCES

INTRODUCTION

In contrast to the moral tales of the last section are these stories of Trickster's gross immoralities. Of course, from Trickster's perspective, actions are not to be judged in terms of their consequences so much as whether he succeeds in his ventures or not. It is this very characteristic of outrageousness that places these stories at the imaginative center of the Afro-American repertoire. Trickster's ability to dream up new and ever more clever and boundary-breaking schemes is matched by his extraordinarily nasty habits. Thus we often see him attacking the most basic distinctions between the clean and the dirty. He does not hesitate to steal, assault sexually, kill, and eat other animals. His appetites are immeasurable.

He is a creature who lives on the margins of human society, but who often invades the human encampment as a spider, rabbit, pigeon—even a mangy, homeless dog.

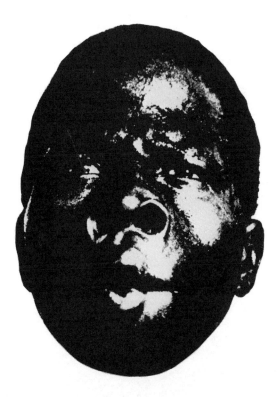

The antics of Anansi, Rabbit, and Pigeon have been exhibited in earlier sections. In these further adventures in outrageous fiction, we can see the trickster's tremendous ingenuity in stirring things up and keeping them boiling; how he gets into a stew of his own making on many occasions, and how, as often as not, he uses his wits to get out of this trouble— often by getting someone else to take his place!

A number of stories illustrate nicely the way in which Trickster establishes patterns of action (or at least seems to), and how others get caught when they try to imitate him. The classic story here, gory as it may seem to some, is "Crawling into the Elephant's Belly." But we also see what happens when Rabbit or Anansi tries his tricks once too often, as in "Anansi Plays Dead."

Trickster's unbridled egotism runs as high as his clever wit. Both characteristics emerge again and again, but nowhere so clearly as in the first story in this section, in which Anansi tricks Master King into agreeing to name all stories for him. In fact, in the West Indies, not only are tales told in his name but so are jokes, riddles, and all other forms of nonsense that come up in wakes and are called *Anansi Story*.

Anansi and Rabbit and the others are great talkers—even when they talk too fast or lisp or stutter—and great performers in general. They are found singing in a number of tales ("The Race between Toad and Donkey"), riddling ("Brer Rabbit's Riddle"), even cutting a caper ("Dancing to the River"). Usually, these antics are carried out in the face of an authority figure, such as Massa King or his watchman, or form part of a contest with other, stronger animals.

59

WHY THEY NAME THE STORIES
FOR ANANSI

Once upon a time, Anansi decided that children should call all their stories after him. So he went to Master King and told him this, and Master King said, "Well, as you know, Blacksnake is a very wise and clever creature. If you can trick him and bring him back to me full-length on a pole, then I will have all those stories named for you."

Well, Nansi really wanted his name to be known this way, but it is very hard even to catch a snake. Nansi knew that Blacksnake really loved to eat pigs, so he went and set a trap for Blacksnake with a pig as bait. Mr. Blacksnake, though, was very clever and saw immediately that it was a trap, so when he got to it he just raised up his tail and slithered right over it, catching the pig in his mouth as he went by. He took it home and had a good dinner for himself.

Well, Nansi then *really* had to think hard about how he was going to catch Blacksnake. So he tried again. He set another trap with a pig, this time in a place that he knew Mr. Snake passed each day of the week to go for water. Again, Mr. Blacksnake saw the trap, so he walked around it, took the pig, and went on his own way. He met Nansi then, and he said to him, "Nansi, you have been setting these traps for me all around. Why are you doing this when you know I am as wise and clever as you and any other creature?"

So Nansi said, "Well, Mr. Blacksnake, I must tell you the truth. They were talking up there in Master King's yard, and everyone was saying that of all the snakes, the longest is Mr. Yellowtail Snake. I tried to tell them you were *much* longer, but they just shouted, and so I bet money that you were the longest. So will you come with me and prove to Master King that you are longer than Mr. Yellowtail Snake?"

Now, Blacksnake was very proud of his length. So he said, "As a matter of fact, Mr. Nansi, I *am* much longer than Yellowtail Snake, and I'm glad you told the king because he should know such things." So Nansi said, "Well, how can we prove it to Master King? Why don't you lay down as long as you can make yourself, and I'll take you to Master King that way and we'll just prove it together." So Blacksnake thought for a while and he couldn't see anything wrong with doing it that way, so he just lay down full-length, and stretched and stretched himself until he was stretched as full as he could get. And Nansi quickly tied him to a pole as tightly as he could.

Nansi just threw that pole across his shoulder and carried him right up to the king: "Well, Master King, you see I brought Mr. Blacksnake to you tied up on a pole." So the king said, "Well, after today, I'm going to call all those stories 'Nansi Stories,' and I'll order everybody else to do the same, because you were able to trick the wisest and cleverest of the creatures."

So that's how we get it that we call all these stories after Mr. Nansi.

—*Tobago*

60
BROTHER RABBIT TAKES A WALK

One time, the other creatures all got the laugh on Brer Rabbit, and this is how it happened. It seemed there was some kind of argument going on among them, and word went out that they all had to meet together somewhere to untangle the tanglements.

When the time came, they were all there, and each one had something to say. They all had their plans, and they jabbered like folks do when they call themselves together just like they were being paid for talking. Mr. Dog got a seat close to Brer Rabbit, and when he opened his mouth to say something, his teeth looked awfully long and so strong, and they shined very white.

Each time Mr. Dog would say something, Brer Rabbit would jump and dodge those teeth snapping away. Mr. Dog, he'd laugh; Brer Rabbit, he'd dodge and jump. It kept on this way until every time Brer Rabbit dodged and jumped, the other creatures would slap their hands together and break out laughing. Mr. Dog, he got a notion that they were laughing at *him*, and this made him so mad that he began to growl and snap.

And it came to that pass that when Rabbit saw Mr. Dog make a motion to say a speech, he'd just drop down and get under the chair.

Of course, this made them all laugh even worse and worse, and the more they laughed, the madder it made Mr. Dog, until he got so mad that he howled, and Brer Rabbit, he sat there and shook like he got a chill and fever.

After a while, Brer Rabbit got sort of on the other side, and he made a speech, and he said there ought to be a law that made creatures who had sharp teeth catch and eat their food with their claws. All of them agreed to this except Mr. Dog, Brer Wolf, and Brer Fox.

In those days, if all the creatures didn't agree, they put it off until the next meeting and talked it over some more, and that's what they did with the Brer Rabbit project: they put it off until the next time.

Brer Rabbit got a sneaking notion that the creatures weren't going to do as he wanted them to do, and he told Brer Wolf that he expected that the best way to handle the problem was to get all the creatures to agree to have Mr. Dog's mouth sewn up because his teeth looked too venomous. Brer Wolf said they would vote for that.

Sure enough, when the day came, Brer Rabbit got up and said that the best thing to do to have peace was to have Mr. Dog's mouth sewn up so his teeth wouldn't look so venomous. They all agreed, and then Mr. Lion, sitting up in the armchair, asked who was going to do the sewing?

Then they all agreed that the man that wanted the sewing done, he was the man to do it, because then he'll know it's been done right. Brer Rabbit, he sort of thought about it, and said: "I don't have a needle." Brer Bear, he felt around in the flap of his coat collar, and he said: "Brer Rabbit, here is a great big one!" Brer Rabbit, he thought again, and then he said: "I don't have any thread." Brer Bear, he unraveled some thread from the bottom of his waistcoat and he said: "Here, Brer Rabbit; here's a long one!"

If it had been anybody else in the round world he'd have begun to feel sort of ticklish, but old Brer Rabbit, he just took it and put his finger across his nose and said: "Just hold him there for me, Brer Bear, and I'll be much obliged to you. It's just about my time of day to take a walk."

—Tobago

61

THE LION IN THE WELL

Now, this tale is about how come Brer Rabbit doesn't have to work no more. That came about this way:

In those days, folks all lived in settlements and such, like they do today, and they were pretty good neighbors to one another and believed in having a good time.

Things were going along mighty well until a big lion—the Boss of the Woods, he called himself—moved into the settlement where Brer Rabbit and Brer Fox and Brer Coon and all the folks lived. And he didn't do nothing, he didn't, but just lay around and destroyed pigs and goats and things, until after a while it looked like he was going to ruin the whole neighborhood and everyone in it.

The folks all got together and held a meeting. And after lots of arguments, first this way and then that, they decided they'd have to tell Brer Lion that they just couldn't stand it any longer, because if he kept up doing as he had been doing, that first and last there wouldn't be anybody left but just Lion. They said they would agreed to feed him, because it wasn't right to starve anybody to death, but if they did feed him, he should have to stay in his house and behave himself. And if he didn't want to do that, they were going to be forced to call in the law on him and maybe put him in jail.

Then Brer Fox, he jumped up and said, "Well, gentlemen, we have gotten this part of the matter settled now. The next thing is, who's going to carry the news to Brer Lion?"

That started another argument, because they knew Brer Lion was a bad man to fool with, and they all were scared. Brer Bear said he wouldn't mind going down to Brer Lion's house and telling him what the folks had to say, but he said he was already behind in his corn planting in his new ground and he just didn't have the time.

Brer Fox said he had to go and dig a well before his stock all perished for water, so he couldn't go.

They all gave first one kind of excuse and then another. Brer Goose said he just had to get in his field and cut grass; Brer Gobbler said Sis Turkey was sick with a terrible backache and he had to get home right away and tend to his children. Brer Pig said he had to go and root up his garden before it rained. It looked like all of them had some important business to tend to, and none of them could carry the news to Brer Lion.

Then Brer Rabbit jumped up, and popped his heels together, and he said, "By golly, folks, if you're all scared of him, I'm not!"

Now, Brer Rabbit was a mighty good man, and a mighty smart one too; but he sure could curse when the occasion came up. He sure could do that.

When I said Brer Rabbit was a good man, I meant he was a good neighbor and kindhearted. You never could rightly call Brer Rabbit a good Christian man, you couldn't, and besides that, in those days things were different from what they are now.

Brer Rabbit, he said, "Folks"—just shaking his head from side to side as if he was mad—"a man's just a man and he isn't any more one than anybody else. I'm like Brer Lion is. And I don't care if you all are scared of him. I am not. Ah'll take the news to him myself."

Then the folks all said, "Shucks, Brer Rabbit, you know you have more sense than that. Brer Lion is two, three times bigger than you are, and he'll eat you up and won't know he's had a mou'ful. Aren't you scared?" "Scared? Who? Me? Why, bless your souls, folks, I thought you already knew I'm not scared of anything or anybody. And just to prove it to you, I'm going down there and tell that old mangy-hided Brer Lion just exactly what we are going to do for him and just exactly what we aren't. And if he doesn't like it, he can just lump it. You wait here for me, folks, and I'll show you."

With that, Brer Rabbit tucked his britches legs down in those red-top boots of his, pulled his white duck-cloth cap to one side of his head, and then, with a big cigar sticking out of his mouth, he sauntered off down the road toward Brer Lion's house, as if he was going to a picnic.

Brer Rabbit walked mighty biggity, he did, as long as the folks could see him; but when he got around a bend in the road, he rubbed that cigar out against a stump and put it in his pocket and he straightened his cap on his head and from then on, he walked differently. He was scared and his knees were shaking.

When he got to the lion's house, he crept up to the door and he knocked on it lightly, *tap-tap-tap*, and he said, "Mister Lion, Mister Lion." And his voice was so weak and trembly he could hardly hear it himself. But the lion heard, and he threw open the door and hollered out loud, "WHO ARE YOU AND WHAT DO YOU WANT?"

Brer Rabbit was just shaking, "This is just me, Brer Rabbit, Mister Lion. The folks had a meeting," he stuttered, "they had a meeting and they sent me down here to tell you that—to explain to you that they have decided—decided that as you are the big boss of the whole world it isn't right for you to have to go out and get your own vittles. And—and they told me to tell you that—that if you'll stay in your house all the time and don't go out foraging, they will send you something to eat every day, right here. And that's just exactly what they told me to tell you, Mister Lion." And he got ready to run off. "WELL, I HAVE TO HAVE FRESH MEAT THREE TIMES A DAY," the lion hollered at him. "IF THEY WILL DO THAT, I'LL STAY IN THE HOUSE. BUT IF THEY DON'T, I'M GOING TO DESTROY EVERYBODY." Brer Rabbit, he said, "Yes sir, yes sir, Mister Lion, yes sir. They will do that for sure! They are going to feed you good, too, because I'm going to see to that myself."

With that, Brer Rabbit took off down the road, lickety-split. As soon as he was out of sight of Brer Lion, he stopped and knocked the dust off his boots, pulled the cap down on the side of his head again, and with that old cigar sticking out of one corner of his mouth, he strutted back to where the folks were waiting for him.

When they saw Brer Rabbit coming, they all ran out to meet him. "Did you see him?" they asked him. "Did you see Mister Lion? What did he say?" Then Brer Rabbit said, all puffy, "Have I seen him? Well, I went down there to see him, didn't I? Of course I've seen him!" Then the folks all said, "Oh Lord, Brer Rabbit! You did? What did you tell him? Weren't you scared?"

When they asked him that, Brer Rabbit snatched his cap off of the side of his head and threw it down on the ground and stomped it. "Scared!" he said. "What in the name of God kind of foolishness are you talking about now? Why, folks," he said, doubling up his fist and shaking it in all their faces, "I'm a man. A *m-a-n*, a *m-a-n* I tell you. And being as I'm a man, I'm not scared of nothing nor nobody, and that means Brer Lion and all the rest."

Then the folks just begged Brer Rabbit to tell them all about it. "Well," said Brer Rabbit, "when I went down to old Brer Lion's house, I knocked on the door, and when he opened it, I went in and sat down by the fire. And I told him that we had had a meeting and decided that he was raising too much disturbance in the neighborhood. And I told him we had decided he'd have to stay in his house and behave himself or else we would beat his liver out, and the Lord himself only knows what else. Then I told him we didn't want to see anybody suffer and starve, so we would feed him, but he'd have to take just what we want to give him and be satisfied with it, or else he could just lump it."

Then the folks all said, "Lord, Brer Rabbit, you sure are brave!" "I'm just a man, folks," said Brer Rabbit, and he picked up his cap and knocked the dirt off of it and set it back on the side of his head. "Just a man, folks, that's all. Ol' Brer Lion, he pitched and he cursed and he roared, but that didn't scare me; and when he saw I meant business, he said he'd do just what the folks want him to do.''

Then the folks tried to decide who would be the first one to go and feed Mister Lion. Everybody said to everybody else, ''You go first, you go first.'' And there they stuck, arguing and quarreling until Brer Rabbit told them, ''Let's draw straws, and the one who gets the short one feeds the lion.''

They agreed to that, they did. Brer Rabbit held the straws, and Brer Goose, he drew the short one. When Brer Goose saw he had the short straw, he began to shiver and shake his wings and he said, *''N-a-a nah! N-a-a nah!''* *''Y-e-h yeh!''* said Brer Rabbit, *''Y-e-h yeh!* Go on down there and feed Brer Lion like you agreed to do.''

So Brer Goose went on down there and Brer Lion ate him up.

The next feeding time, Brer Pig drew the short straw. When he saw he was the next, he started crying and hollering, *''W-a-i-t! W-a-i-t! W-a-i-t! W-a-i-t!''* *''W-a-i-t!* the devil!'' said Brer Rabbit. ''You get on down yonder and feed Brer Lion like you done agreed to or else we'll beat you half to death and drag you there.'' So Brer Pig went on down there and Brer Lion ate him up.

Now Brer Fox and Brer Alligator soon saw that as long as Brer Rabbit held the straws he was going to send everybody else except himself down the road to feed the lion. So next feeding time, they fixed it so that Brer Fox held the straws. And sure enough, this time Brer Rabbit, he drew the short one!

When he saw that he had gotten the short straw, he said to himself, ''Dear God! I sure got my business in a twist now.'' Then he said out loud, ''Folks,'' he said, ''it sure looks like my time has come. We have had a heap of fun and frolics together,'' he said, ''but that's behind us now. And now I must go and feed that old lion's belly. I have been a good friend to you all, folks,'' he said, ''and a good neighbor, too. I visited the sick and fed the hungry and helped to bury the dead. But now it looks like my time is done and I want you all to pray for me and promise me that when your time comes you'll all meet me in the Promised Land where there isn't anybody who goes but the pure in heart. Good-bye, folks, good-bye, everybody,'' said Brer Rabbit, and then he started walking off down the road, slow and mournful.

Brer Rabbit sounded so pitiful that all the folks started crying, and just before he got out of sight, 'round a bend in the road, Brer Hound Dog, who was the gospel carrier, started singing:

> *Am I born to die,*
> *To lay this body down?*

And everybody joined in.

Brer Rabbit, he walked along mighty slow, he did, and then he decided that, even if ole Mister Lion did have to wait for his dinner, he was going to look over his big plantation one more time anyhow.

As soon as he decided that, he took off through the woods to his house. When he got there, he went all around and around. He went to where he was born and he went to the barn and the hog lot and the garden, and he said good-bye to everything. And then he went to the well for a last drink of water. He looked over in that old deep well of his, and when he saw his own face shining up at him from the bottom, it gave him an idea. So he slapped his leg with his hand and slammed the cover shut, and he put out through the woods for the old lion's house. When he got there it was way after one o'clock.

He knocked on the door and he said in a trembly voice, "*U-r-r-r*, Mister Lion, here is your dinner."

The old lion threw open the door and he roared out, "WELL, IT'S MIGHTY LITTLE DINNER YOU BROUGHT ME, AND HERE IT IS WAY AFTER ONE O'CLOCK." And then Brer Lion pulled out his big gold watch and looked at it, and he showed Brer Rabbit his big teeth.

Brer Rabbit looked at them big ol' teeth sticking out of old Brer Lion's mouth and his knees shook worse than ever. Then he said, "Yes sir, Mister Lion, yes sir. I just couldn't get here any sooner. I'm very sorry, Mister Lion, if I am not big enough for your dinner; but if you are real hungry I know where there is a heap of good fresh meat saved for you. And I'll show it to you, too, if you'll come with me, and that's the God's truth."

"WHERE IS THAT MEAT?" the old lion asked him. "It's not far, Mister Lion," said Brer Rabbit; "it's just a little way over toward my house where I got it stored for you." "WELL, IT BETTER BE ENOUGH!" roared the old lion, and with that he and Brer Rabbit ran through the woods to Brer Rabbit's house. Brer Rabbit opened up the well and looked in it and fell back! "Lord God," he said, "if he isn't in there eating your food right now!" When Brer Rabbit said that, the old lion knocked him away from the well and looked down it himself. He thought he saw another lion looking up at him, and he hollered, "WHO ARE YOU?" The voice came echoing back up out of the well, "WHO ARE YOU?"

Old Brer Lion began to get mad and he hollered down the well again, "WHO ARE YOU, I SAY?" And the voice came back up out of the well, "WHO ARE YOU, I SAY?"

Then Brer Rabbit nudged the old lion in his side and said, "You heard him, didn't you, Brer Lion? Didn't you hear him mocking you like that? Are you going to take that from him? All that loose talk, Brer Lion? Confound his fresh-meat-stealing soul," he said. "If he'll come up here, I'll whip him myself!" The old lion looked over into the well again and he hollered, "WHO-0-0-0-0-0-0-0-0-0!" The voice came back up from the well, "WHO-0-0-0-0-0-0-0-0-0!"

Then the lion said, "STAND BACK, BRER RABBIT, HE'S MY MEAT!" And in he jumped!

As soon as Brer Rabbit heard him hit the water—*kerchug!*—he slammed the cover shut and locked it. Then he pulled his cap to one side of his head, took that cigar out of his pocket and lit it, and he sauntered on down the road.

The folks were all debating about who was to feed the lion next, and when they saw Brer Rabbit coming, they thought he was a ghost and they started to run. But he stopped them and then they all asked, hadn't the lion eaten him up? Brer Rabbit said, "Ate who up? Me? No, God. I wasn't aiming to be eaten up by that old lion nor nobody else for that matter." "But what did he say, Brer Rabbit? And what did he do? Lord, Mister Lion is going to come up here right away and destroy us all."

Then Brer Rabbit laughed hard. He said, "There isn't any use in you folks being scared of nothing as long as you got a man with you, and that's me! I'm a man, folks, just like I said. And when I said I'm a man, I mean I'm a man and I can prove it. That big old fool lion didn't say anything and he isn't going to destroy anyone, because when he tried to get rough with me, I beat the scoundrel half to death and threw him in my well and drowned him."

The folks wouldn't believe him, until Brer Rabbit took them all over to his house and opened that well and showed them the old lion drowned down in the bottom. Then they all said, "Brer Rabbit, you are too smart a man to be anything except a king. And from this time on, you are never going to have to work any crops because we are going to do it for you."

And that's just exactly how come it is, that from that day until this, Brer Rabbit has been living on other folks' peanuts and potatoes and things.

—Mississippi

62

A LICENSE TO STEAL

_____

Once upon a time was a very good time
When Monkey chewed tobacco and spit white lime.

Now, Massa Tom was boss of the office and Massa Sam was boss of the
fields. Poor Rabby couldn't get a job, but he was a tricky fellow, and
even if he was always hungry, it wasn't often he couldn't find something
to eat, and something good, at that.

Now, Mr. Rabby knew that Massa Sam couldn't read. So one day he
picked up a piece of paper from Massa Tom's office and scribbled some
lies on it and took it out to Massa Sam. Rabby said, "Massa Sam, Massa
Tom sent this to you, sir." Massa Sam looked at it and asked what it
meant. Rabby took it and said, "Tie Rabby at six in the morning to a
post in that thick patch of cocoa peas; and then let him loose at six
o'clock in the evening." So Massa Sam thought it strange but went
ahead, and Rabby had some good eating that day.

Later, Massa Sam went to Massa Tom and told him he could send
Rabby every day like that if he wanted to, but those were their best
shipping peas, and Rabby was destroying them all. Of course, Massa
Tom said, "I never sent him! If he comes again, fasten him up good, and
I'll come down there and kill him."

The next morning, along comes Rabby, whistling his tune. So Massa
Sam had his rope all prepared for Rabby, and he lashed him up good.
Rabby said, "Massa Sam, you've tied me harder than yesterday." Massa
Sam said, "That's all right, you'll just have to get by like that." Well,
Rabby ate and ate and ate, and then he put some more peas in his bag.
He could see something was going wrong, so he cried out, "Oh, Massa
Sam, I have a terrible pain in my belly. Would you let me loose, please?"
Massa Sam said, "You know the letter says I can't let you go until six
o'clock in the evening. That's Massa Tom's rule."

When six o'clock came, Massa Sam got his horse and left. Rabby
cried, "Oh, Massa Sam, it's six o'clock and you haven't let me loose this
evening." Massa Sam said, "Stay there until I come back. I'm going to
let you eat some more cocoa peas tomorrow, anyhow." So Rabby dried up

his tears and just kept eating and putting peas in his bag through the night.

Now, along came Mr. Elephant. Rabby started to cry out so that everyone that was passing could hear. "Oh, oh, they have me tied up here until I marry the king's daughter, and I just can't do that. She's too rich for my blood." So Mr. Elephant said, "Rabby, what is the matter?" Rabby said, "Man, they have me tied up here until I get good and sleek, so I can marry the king's daughter, and the food is just too rich for my blood." Mr. Elephant said, "Well, let me loosen up that rope, and you can tie me up. I'll marry the king's daughter!"

After Rabby tied Mr. Elephant, he went up in a big tree there. He saw them bringing down a whole wagon full of boilers to scald Rabby to death. Now, when they got to where Rabby was supposed to be, they said, "This is a bigger man than Rabby. This is Buh Elephant." Mr. Elephant said, "Where is the king's daughter I am going to marry? They must be going to cook up a big feast." Well, they got those boilers real hot and they scalded poor Mr. Elephant. He said, "But I'm supposed to marry the king's daughter, not get scalded," and he started to rear and kick until he broke away.

So he ran right under that tree where Rabby was sitting. Rabby said, "What's that you're saying?" Rabby hollered, "You see the man here that you were scalding." Mr. Elephant thought Rabby was talking to Massa Sam and his men. "You see that man you were scalding? Well, he went over there to the west, so you can cut him off if you run now." Mr. Elephant started to run. Rabby hollered again, "Now he's going east. Look out now, get ready. He's coming your way." Now Mr. Elephant was scared and he started running every which way, and he ran so much he ran himself to death, and Rabby got away.

If you think my story isn't true
Just ask the captain of the longboat crew!

—*Bahamas*

63

THE RACE BETWEEN TOAD
AND DONKEY

One day, Master King decided to have a race and he would give a big prize to whoever won. Both Toad and Donkey decided to enter, but Toad got Donkey angry with all his boasting about how he'd win.

Now, the race was to be for twenty miles. So when Donkey looked at Toad he wondered out loud how any animal so small and powerless could hope to keep up with him. "I have very long legs, you know, as well as long ears and tail. Just measure our legs, and you'll see why you can't possibly hope to win this race." But Toad was stubborn—and he was smart, too—and he said that he was going to win the race. That just got Donkey more vexed.

So Donkey told the king that he was ready to start, but the king said that he had to make the rules first. At each mile every racer had to sing out to indicate he had gotten that far—for the king wanted to know what was happening in the race, you know.

Now Toad is a smart little fellow, and he said to the king that he needed a little time to take care of business, so would he let him have a day or two. And the king said to the two of them, "You must come here first thing tomorrow." Donkey objected, for he knew that Toad was a very trickifying creature, but the king wouldn't listen.

Now the toad had twenty children, and they all looked exactly alike. And while Donkey was sleeping, Toad took his twenty children along the racing ground, and at every milepost Toad left one of them. He told them that they must listen for Mr. Donkey, and whenever they heard him cry out, they should do so too. And Toad hid one of his children there behind each of those mileposts.

So the race began the next day. Donkey looked around, and he was so sure in his heart that he was going to beat Toad that he sucked his teeth, *Tche,* to show everyone there how little he thought of Toad. "That little bit of a fellow Toad can't keep up with me. I'll even have a little time to eat some grass along the way. *Tche.*"

So he just went a little way down the road and he stopped and ate some grass. He poked his head through the fence where he saw some good-looking sweet-potato tops and had a taste of some gungo peas. He took more than an hour to get to the first milepost. And as he got there, he bawled out: "Ha, ha, I'm better than Toad." And the first child heard this, and he called, like all toads do,

Jin-ko-ro-ro, Jin-kok-kok-kok.

The sound really surprised Donkey, who of course thought he had gotten there first. Then he thought, "I delayed too long eating that grass. I must run quicker this next mile." So he set off with greater speed, this time stopping only for a minute to drink some water along the way. And as he got to the next post, he bawled out:

Ha! Ha! Ha! I'm better than Toad.

And then the second child called out:

Jin-ko-ro-ro, Jin-kok-kok-kok.

And Donkey said, "Lord, Toad can really move, for sure. Never mind, there are a lot more miles." So he started, and when he reached the third milepost, he bawled:

Ha! Ha! Ha! I'm better than Toad.

And the third child sang:

Jin-ko-ro-ro, Jin-kok-kok-kok.

Now the jackass got very angry when he heard Toad answer him, and he started to smash the toad, but Toad, being a little fellow, hid himself in the grass.

Donkey was then determined to get to the next milepost before Toad, and he took his tail and he switched it like a horsewhip and he began to gallop. And he got to the fourth milepost and he bawled:

Ha! Ha! Ha! I'm better than Toad.

And out came the answer from the fourth child.

When he heard that, he stood up right there and began to tremble, and he said, "My goodness, what am I going to do? I'm going to have to run so fast I really kick that hard, hard dirt." And he galloped off faster than he ever had before, until he reached the fifth milepost. And now he was very tired, and out of breath. He just barely had enough wind to bawl:

Ha! Ha! Ha! I'm better than Toad.

And then he heard:

Jin-ko-ro-ro, Jin-kok-kok-kok.

This time he was really angry, and he raced on harder than ever. But at each milepost he bawled out the same thing, and at each he heard the same answer. And Donkey got so sad in his mind that he just gave up after a while, sad because he knew he had lost that race.

So through Toad's smartness, Donkey can never be a racer again.

Jack Mandora me no choose one.

—Jamaica

196

64
CRAWLING INTO THE ELEPHANT'S BELLY

Oone time, all the animals were look-
ing around for food, but there was none to be had. Anansi and his family
were starving too, and he didn't know what he could do about it. One
day, he saw this old elephant come out of the king's park and he got an
idea. That night, he climbed the wall to the palace where all the elephants
were kept. He crept up to one of them while it was asleep and went in
there behind his tail and crawled way up into his belly. And when he
got there he just chopped off a little piece of meat, and he sneaked back
out and carried the meat home.

Anansi went back night after night, crawling into the belly of one of
the elephants, and each morning, just before daybreak, he sneaked
back home.

Now, Anansi's friend Yawarri the Anteater saw that Anansi was getting fat and here he was as hungry as ever. He tried to get Anansi to
tell him where he was getting his food every morning; but Anansi put
him off the scent by telling him one lie after another.

Yawarri was so hungry that he got sick too. He told his friend Mon-

key about how he felt and how hard it was to watch Anansi growing fat while he and his family were starving. When Monkey heard all this, he told Yawarri to keep a watch near Anansi's house at night, and to follow him to see where he was going to get his food. Yawarri took this advice. He watched Anansi's house, and when Anansi came out he followed his footsteps until they got to the king's palace. Anansi didn't know Yawarri was there. He went to climb the wall of the king's park; then Yawarri called out to him and told him that if he didn't promise to take him in as a partner he would yell out that someone was sneaking into the king's yard and stealing things.

So Anansi promised, and took Yawarri with him that night. Anansi told him how he did this every night. While the king's elephants slept in the park, he went through the asshole and into the stomach of one of them, cut off a small piece of meat, and came back out without waking the elephants. And he made sure that he never tried this trick on the same elephant, so that none of them would ever know what he was doing.

When Anansi and Yawarri had gone ino the yard a little way, they came up to two elephants, and each went into the bowels of one of them. Anansi, after cutting his usual little piece of meat, came out of his elephant. But Yawarri was a selfish kind of animal, anyhow, and he had been hungry for such a long time that he stayed in there eating a long time. Anansi waited a long time for him, and finally yelled out: "Bru Yawarri! Bru Yawarri! Come out, or the day will soon be here!" Yawarri put his head out, and told Anansi: "Oh, Bru! What fat meat there is in here! I can't come out yet. You go on and send back my wife and children to help me take home what I cut." So Yawarri stayed in there, eating and eating until he was full—and just then the elephant dropped over dead because Yawarri had eaten so much of his belly.

Now, the king was vexed, seeing that one of his best elephants was dead. So he ordered the belly split open to see why he had died. The elephant keepers came back and told the king that when they cut inside the elephant's belly they heard this strange noise. The king sent them back to find out what was making this noise, and there they found Yawarri, still cutting off pieces of meat and eating them.

Now the king was really angry. He told his men to kill Yawarri and to keep a better watch from now on. Now, Anansi had carried the message to Yawarri's wife and children, and they got excited, since they were very hungry too. When they climbed over the wall that night, the elephant keepers were there waiting and shot the whole family.

So that's what comes of being too greedy.

—*Guyana*

198

65
A STRANGE WAY TO SLEEP

Every evening when Compere Rabbit returned from his work he passed through a yard where there was a large turkey sleeping on a perch; and like other turkeys, he had his head under his wing when he slept. Every evening Compere Rabbit stopped to look at Turkey, and he asked himself what he had done with his head.

Finally, one evening, he was so curious that he couldn't help himself. He stopped underneath the perch and said, "Good evening, Mr. Turkey." "Good evening," said Turkey, without raising its head. "Pardon me for asking, but do you have a head, Mr. Turkey?" "Of course I have a head," Turkey said. Compere Rabbit asked, "Then where is it?" "My head is here," the turkey answered, still speaking from under his wing.

Compere Rabbit looked and looked, but he still couldn't see Mr. Turkey's head. As he saw that Turkey didn't want to talk to him or show him where his head was, he went to his house and said to his wife: "Do you know that when they go to sleep that turkeys take off their heads? They can sleep better that way. Well, I think I'm going to do the same thing, because it is less trouble to sleep without a head. You don't really need a head when you sleep that way, if you want to speak, because Turkey spoke to me just as easy as can be."

Before his wife had time to tell him anything, he took an ax and cut off his head. His wife tried to stick it back on again, but try as she might, she couldn't get it to stay on.

—Louisiana

66

GOOBERS GONE, RABBIT GONE

Brer Rabbit saw Brer Bear one day setting out with his donkey and dump cart to dig up some goober nuts, those peanuts that taste so good. Brer Rabbit said to himself, me and Missus Rabbit and all those little rabbits sure are hungry for goobers. So he went home and found a red kerchief and he tied it around his neck and he ran and lay down in the road where Brer Bear would be coming by with the cart, carrying his sack filled up with those goobers.

Bye and bye, Brer Bear came along and the donkey shied, almost upsetting the cart. Brer Bear got out and said, "Well, if it isn't Brer Rabbit as dead as a doornail with his throat cut. Now that will make good rabbit stew for me and Missus Bear." So he picked up Brer Rabbit and threw him into the cart and went on. As soon as his back was turned, Brer Rabbit threw out the bag of goobers and he jumped out himself and ran on home. On the way he met Brer Fox, and Brer Fox said: "Where did you get that bag of goobers?" And Brer Rabbit told him.

As soon as Brer Bear come in sight of his house, way behind those dark pines, he hollered out to his old woman: "Hello there. Come here, Missus Bear. Goobers here; rabbits there!" Missus Bear, she ran out of the cabin, she was that hungry herself. She ran around the dump cart and looked in. There was just a few goobers rattling around in the bottom of the cart.

She said, "Goobers gone, rabbit gone, bag gone!" Brer Bear turned around and looked. He scratched his head and said: "That rabbit has left me without anything."

Next day, he hitched up the donkey to the dump cart and started to the patch to haul more goobers home. His old wife told him: "Watch out now, don't drop anything on the big road with this load." This time, Brer Fox figured he'd just use Brer Rabbit's trick and get his winter's provisions by speculating with Brer Bear's load, labor, and land.

Brer Fox got a red string for himself this time. He tied it around his neck. He went to the big road, to the same place where Brer Rabbit had been lying down yesterday. Brer Fox, he lay down right in the same place. He kept as still. Right away, here came Brer Bear with another great heaping load of goobers.

The donkey shied again at the same place. Brer Bear got off the cart, looked at Brer Fox, and said: "What's happening here? Maybe that same thief that stole my goobers yesterday is back again. You got the same red kerchief around your throat. Maybe you are dead, too." He felt Brer Fox, and he said: "You're heavy, too; I'll take you to my old wife and have her make good stew of you."

With that, Brer Fox thought he was going to get a good chance to get his fill of those goobers.

Brer Bear lifted Brer Fox by his hind legs, and said:

> *Maybe you are dead, or maybe no,*
> *But I will make you dead fer sho'!*

And with that he swung Brer Fox around and around and banged his head against the wheel of the cart.

That just about killed Brer Fox. It was all he could do to jerk his hind legs loose from Brer Bear and run home through the dark pines. He had a banged-up head for a long time from that lick. You know, the same cunning trick just isn't apt to work twice.

—*Alabama*

67

ASSAULTING ALL THE SENSES

One day, one of the animals brought back a coconut, but Anansi came and stole it. While he was carrying it away, a tiger saw him and asked: "What are you eating?" Anansi said to Tiger he was eating a piece of his stones (testicles). Then Tiger said to him, "What, Anansi? How does it happen that your stones are so sweet?" He said, "Well, Daddy Tiger, how sweet yours must be that are so much bigger and fatter than mine." So Tiger asked him how he could break his stones off so that he could taste them. "Daddy, come to the corner, for a blacksmith is there and surely, with his hammer and anvil, he'll be able to break your stones." So they went there, and Anansi told Tiger to lay down. Just as he lay down, Anansi struck him with a hammer and broke his stones. Tiger died instantly. So he cut him to pieces, cooked him, and ate him up.

The next day, he met up with Tiger's brother. Now Anansi was drinking a gourd full of honey, and Tiger, smelling something good, and seeing Anansi drinking with such a happy look on his face, said, "Well, what are you drinking there?" Anansi said, "I am drinking a young monkey's piss." The tiger said, "Well, let me have a taste since you are smacking your lips so." Then the tiger said, "I never knew that monkey piss was so sweet! How can I get some more?" Anansi said to him to go down to the creek and he will see lots of monkeys there, and he should have no trouble catching one.

So Tiger did as Anansi suggested and caught a little one, who was very scared for his life. Tiger said, "Don't worry, little one, I'm not going to kill you, but you must piss for me." The monkey was amazed but he went ahead and pissed right on Tiger's hand; but when Tiger tasted it, it didn't seem as sweet as what Anansi had given him. So he said, "Boy, piss some more; if not, I'm going to kill you!" The monkey urinated until blood came out, but it never came out sweet.

Now Anansi came along and asked, "Tiger, didn't the monkey piss for you yet?" Tiger said, "Well, it didn't taste as sweet as what you were drinking yesterday." Anansi said, "Well, maybe you didn't tell him what you wanted in the right way. I'll talk to him." So Anansi said to the monkey, "You must run, and I will duck, as soon as you can."

Tiger said, "What are you telling him?" "I am telling him how to make the right piss for you. But the problem is, you are holding him too tight. Let him a little looser." Well, as Tiger loosened his grip, the monkey ran, and Anansi ducked right under the water.

—*Surinam*

68
BRER RABBIT'S RIDDLE

Now, everyone knew that Brer Rabbit was quite a musician, because he was always singing or patting or doing some other kind of dance to get himself out of trouble. In fact, there wasn't any tune that Brer Rabbit couldn't pat. And when there is someone else there to do the patting, Brer Rabbit can jump into the middle of the floor and just naturally shake the eyelids off of all the others. And it wasn't none of this bowing and scraping and slipping and sliding we're talking about, with four hands around the way folks do these days. It was this up-and-down kind of dancing where they leap up in the air to cut the pigeon-wing.

The time came when old Brer Rabbit began to put this and that together and the notion struck him that he better be home looking after the interests of his family, instead of frolicking all around the settlement. He thought about this in his mind until, bye and bye, he got determined to earn his own livelihood. So he up and cleared off a piece of ground and planted himself a potato patch.

Brer Fox, he saw all this going on, and he suspected to himself that Brer Rabbit's rashness had been subdued because he was scared. Brer Fox made up his mind that he was going to pay Brer Rabbit back for all his selfishness. He started in, and from that time forward he aggravated Brer Rabbit about his potato patch. One night he left the draw bars down, another night he flung off the top rails of the fence, and the next night he tore down a whole panel of fence, and he kept on this way until Brer Rabbit didn't know what to do.

All this time, Brer Fox kept on fooling with the potato patch, and when he saw that Brer Rabbit wasn't getting upset, Brer Fox thought that he had scared him and that the time had come to gobble him up without leave or license.

So he called Brer Rabbit, and he asked him if he would take a walk. Brer Rabbit, he asked where they were going. Brer Fox said, right out yonder. Brer Rabbit, he asked where is right out yonder? Brer Fox said he knew where there were some mighty fine peaches and he wanted Brer Rabbit to go along and climb the tree and fling them down. Brer Rabbit said he wouldn't mind especially if it was what Brer Fox wanted.

They set out, and after a while they came to the peach orchard, and Brer Rabbit picked out a good tree, and up he climbed. Brer Fox, he sat at the root of the tree, because he thought that when Brer Rabbit came down he had to come down backward and then that would be the time to nab him. But Brer Rabbit saw what Brer Fox was doing before he climbed up. When he picked the peaches, Brer Fox said, "Fling them down here, Brer Rabbit—fling them right down here so I can catch them." Brer Rabbit hollered back, "If I fling them down there where you are, Brer Fox, and you miss them, they'll get squashed, so I'll just sort of pitch them out yonder in the grass where they won't get busted."

Then he took and flung the peaches out in the grass, and while Brer Fox went after them, Brer Rabbit, he climbed down out of the tree, and hustled himself until he got some elbow room. When he got off a little ways he hollered back to Brer Fox that he'd got a riddle he wanted him to solve. Brer Fox, he asked what is that. Brer Rabbit, he gave it out to Brer Fox like a man saying a speech:

> *The big bird rob and the little bird sing,*
> *The big bee zoom and the little bee sting,*
> *The little man lead and the big horse follows,*
> *Can you tell what's good for a head in a hollow?*

Old Brer Fox scratched his head and thought and thought and scratched his head, but the more he thought, the worse he got mixed up with the riddle, and after a while he told Brer Rabbit that he dunno how in the name of goodness to unriddle that riddle.

"Come and go along with me," said old Brer Rabbit, "and I promise you I'll show you how to solve that riddle. It's one of those kinds of riddles," said old man Rabbit, "which before you understand it, you have to eat a bit of honey. And I have my eye on a place where we can get some honey!" Brer Fox asked where it was, and Brer Rabbit said there in old Brer Bear's cotton patch, he had bumped into a whole lot of beehives. Brer Fox doesn't have much of a sweet tooth, but he wanted to figure out that riddle.

They set out, and it wasn't long before they came to old Brer Bear's beehives. Old Brer Rabbit, he gave them a rap with his walking cane, just like folks thump watermelons to see if they are ripe. He tapped and he rapped, and bye and bye, he came to one of them that sounded full. And then he went around behind it, and he said: "I'll just sort of tilt it up, Brer Fox, and you can put your head under there and get some of the drippings."

Brer Rabbit tilted it up, and Brer Fox jammed his head underneath the hive. He no sooner stuck his head underneath that beehive than Brer Rabbit turned it loose, and down it came—*kerswosh!*—right on Brer Fox's neck, and there he was. Brer Fox, he kicked; he squealed; he jumped; he squalled; he danced; he pranced; he begged; he prayed; yet there he was, and Brer Rabbit got away off, and turning around to look back, he saw Brer Fox just wiggling and squirming, and right then and there Brer Rabbit gave one old-time whoop and just started running home.

When he got there, the first man he saw was Brer Fox's granddaddy, who folks all call Grandsire Gray Fox. When Brer Rabbit saw him, he said, "How are you, Grandsire Gray Fox?" "I still am not too well, thanks, Brer Rabbit," said Grandsire Gray Fox. "Have you seen any sign of my grandson this morning?"

With that, Brer Rabbit laughed and said that he and Brer Fox had been a-rambling around with one another having more fun. "We've been rigging up riddles and asking them to each other," Brer Rabbit said. "Brer Fox is sitting off somewhere in the bushes right now, trying to figure one out that I gave him. I'll just tell it to you," said Brer Rabbit, "and if you solve it, I'll take you right to where your grandson is, and you can't get there any too soon." Then old Grandsire Gray Fox asked what it is, and Brer Rabbit, he sang out,

> *The big bird rob and the little bird sing;*
> *The big bee zoom and the little bee sting,*
> *The little man lead and the big horse follows,*
> *Can you tell what's good for a head in a hollow?*

Grandsire Gray Fox took a pinch of snuff and coughed easy to himself and thought and thought, but he couldn't make it out. And Brer Rabbit laughed and sang:

The beehive is mighty big to make a fox collar,
Can you tell what's good for a head in a hollow?

After a long time, Grandsire Gray Fox sort of caught a glimpse of what Brer Rabbit was trying to tell him and told Brer Rabbit good day, and shuffled on to hunt up his grandson. And he did find him. Brer Bear heard the racket that Brer Fox was kicking up, and he went down to see what the matter was. As soon as he saw how the land lay, he took a notion that Brer Fox had been robbing the beehive. And he got a handful of chicory and he warmed his jacket and then he turned them loose. It wasn't long before all the neighbors got word that Brer Fox had been robbing Brer Bear's beehives.

—Georgia

69
THE HORNED ANIMALS' PARTY

—

All the horned animals decided to have a party. No one but those with horns were invited to that party. Dog and Pussy heard about it and really wanted to go, so they got busy, killed a goat, and took his horns. Bro' Dog was to use the horns for half the night, then he was supposed to come out and tie them on Bro' Pussy. So Dog took the first turn, but after he was in the party he didn't give a thought to Pussy anymore. You know how once you start singing and dancing you don't think of anything else. After the time passed when he was supposed to come out, he was nowhere around. Pussy got near to the door, you know, and started to holler, "Bro' Dog, Bro' Dog!" He went on so about four times. And Bro' Dog gave no heed to him. After this, Bro' Cattle, who was the boss of the party, he came to the door and said, and he was really angry, "Go away there, go away there! There is no Dog in here!" Well, Bro' Pussy got a little angry himself. He came back, this time shouting: "Bro' Dog, Bro' Dog, Bro' Dog!" Then Bro' Dog, he came out himself and hushed Bro' Pussy—or tried to anyhow. He said, "Don't bother that fellow in there now. No Bro' Dog is in here." Now, Bro' Pussy was so mad he really kept up the calling. Finally, Bro' Cattle said, "Maybe Bro' Dog is in here. Let's just see." And they started to search. Bro' Dog himself started, saying, "Let me see whether Bro' Dog is at this party! Let me see if Bro' Dog is in here!" After searching, they discovered Bro' Dog, and they tore off his horns and started to beat him. And he started hollering, and ran out.

When he ran out, you know, he met Pussy. They had an argument, which soon came to a fight. As Bro' Pussy found that he was getting the worst of it, so he scratched Bro' Dog on the corner of his lip.

And if you notice a dog's lip, in the corner it always looks raw. That's why. And that is why a dog and a cat can never agree.

—*Antigua*

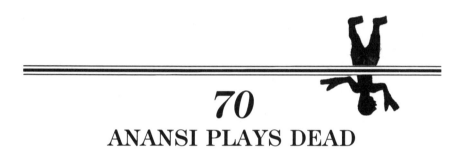

70
ANANSI PLAYS DEAD

Compé Anansi and his wife were starving. So he said, "My wife, saltfish is my favorite food, but there isn't any. If we do a trick, we can get some meat. I could play like I was dead, and you could go out to the road and sing and wail, say, 'My husband's dead,' and so on. Do you think you could do that?" She said, "If I can't do something that easy, then there is no God. So I will do it."

So she went out in the yard. She tied up her jaw and put a band around her waist like she was in mourning, and started bawling, "O my God, my husband's dead. Oy, and now I have to bury him." She cried this, expecting all their neighbors to come by and help with the burial. She went all the way to the edge of the yard, and she sang:

> *My poor Nansi's dead-o*
> *Oh,* ting-wa
> *My poor Nansi's dead-o*
> *Oh,* ting-wa

> *And I have to have him buried*
> *Oh,* ting-wa
> *Let me band my waist and cry-o*
> *Oh,* ting-wa
> *Let me band my jaw and cry-o*
> *Oh,* ting wa.

Compé Hawk came by then. She said, "You see, Compé Hawk, you see Compé Anansi there dead." Compé Anansi was stretched out there like he was dead, with his eyes shut tight. Compé Hawk said, "Well, Compé, you have chosen the better path and heaven waits for you and Thy will be done." After a while he turned his back, and *Whoop!* she killed Compé Hawk. Anansi called his wife, and asked if she had killed Compé Hawk, and she said she had. He said, "My wife, I never knew you were so brave. Now we are going to have something to eat."

Anyhow, he was excited now. He said, "My wife, if we can catch one there, we can catch two." So they went out in the yard again, and she started bawling:

> *My poor Nansi's dead-o*
> *Oh,* ting-wa
> *My poor Nansi's dead-o*
> *Oh,* ting-wa
> *And I have to have him buried*
> *Oh,* ting-wa
> *Let me band my waist and cry-o*
> *Oh,* ting-wa
> *Let me band my jaw and cry-o*
> *Oh,* ting wa.

Well, Compé Bull Cattle passed by. "*Unnhh*, what are you saying?" She said, "My husband's dead." He said, disbelieving this, "You are talking in farts, lady." She said, "He's gone, go on in and see him." When he went in, Compé Bull Cattle said, "Well, man, Compé Anansi has done his time and chosen a better path." Well, Compé Bull Cattle started to look back at Compé Anansi, and *Whoop!* she killed him. He cried, "*Maaah*," and he dropped to the ground, *boop*.

Compé Anansi really was excited now, and said, "My wife, go back again. Start the same bawling again." So she started:

My poor Nansi's dead-o
  Oh, ting-wa
My poor Nansi's dead-o
  Oh, ting-wa
And I have to have him buried
  Oh, ting-wa
Let me band my waist and cry-o
  Oh, ting-wa
Let me band my jaw and cry-o
  Oh, ting wa.

Compé Sheep passed now. He went in, the poor little lamb. Said, *"Maaah,"* and he was dead, *Whoop!* Compé Fowl passed, the same thing happened. All the animals in the world passed by; they killed them the same way.

Compé Ground Dove was there in the tree watching all these doings. Compé Ground Dove reached the yard, and Anansi's wife started bawling out as usual, "God, Compé, I need help here. Compé Anansi's dead, dead, dead." He said, "Dead, dead, dead?" He said, "Dead? And you have the place shut up so. You should not keep the dead in a place like this. Open up the windows. Open up the blinds." He flew around, opening up everything. He said, "Compé, you're really dead?" She said, "Yes, he's dead." Compé Ground Dove said, "Well, I've always heard that dead people have to break a fart." So Compé Anansi heard that and let go with a *boop.* He said, "Yes, yes, yes, you can always hear a dead man fart. When a man is dead he is done with this world." So he let out another *boop* and Compé Ground Dove hopped up and down laughing, making fun of Compé Anansi lying there farting.

And that's why you see there are fools in this world today, some wiser than some, up to today. And that is the end of the story.
— *St. Vincent*

71
ANANSI CLIMBS THE WALL

$\mathbf{B}$ack there a long time ago, Nansi
and Brer Death decided to plant a provision field together. But Nansi and
Death had a lot of quarrels. Nansi was always around smiling, playing
around, making lots of nonsense. He would sit under the bamboo tree and
make like he was some overseer. Anything but working in that field of
provisions. So, of course, his yams and beans didn't grow. But Brer
Death, he carried his hoe all day, and while he was hoeing he was smacking his lips thinking about all the yams and beans he was going to eat.

Nansi, he started thinking too about all the yams and beans growing
in the field. So he told his wife, Tookooma, that he was going to sneak
over to the provision field with his basket to get a taste. He told her to
stay at the gate with a basket, so that when he came back with a basket
of yams, she could hand him one for the beans. Tookooma said, ''Duppies
[ghosts] are going to catch you, husband.'' Nansi sucked his teeth:
''Chuck! Duppies don't bother me. Tonight I'm a white man and the
duppies won't go after me.''

Now, Brer Death thought that his provisions were getting to look
awfully nice, so he started to stand watch over the field at night, with
his cutlass in his hand. Bye and bye, he heard a sound and snuck over and
sure enough he saw Nansi with a basket, right there in the middle of
his field. He said, ''Howdy, Brer Nansi. What's happening with you?''
And Nansi said, ''Howdy, Brer Death, I'm just feeling so-so.'' ''What
brings you into my provision field at this time of night?'' ''I like to
watch your yams grow, Brer Death.'' ''Your mouth is running away with
you, Nansi. Why are you carrying a basket, then?'' ''I'm going to hunt
for crayfish, Brer Death.''

So he could see that Nansi was there to steal his yams, so he flew at
him with his cutlass, and Nansi started running toward home. He called
way down the road: ''Open the back door, shut the front door, Tookooma;
Death is coming after me.'' And Tookooma didn't hear him too well, and
asked, ''Well, did you fill the basket?'' Nansi, who was closer now, said,
''You fool, you; open the back door, shut the front door.'' She still
couldn't hear him well. ''What did you say, my husband, did you bring
the basket?'' ''Oh, you fool, you! Open the back door, shut the front
door. Death is coming after me!''

Nansi ran in the front door, and Death almost caught him and hit him with his cutlass. Nansi ran out the back and into an old shed, and ran up the wall like a big black spider, and he hid himself in a cranny so that Brer Death couldn't find him. And that's why you always find Nansi and all his webs sitting up in the rafters of old sheds and places like that.

—Jamaica

72
DANCING TO THE RIVER

Once there were hard times in a certain town. Nobody could get nothing to eat. The birds flew all about looking for food, but they couldn't find anything. So then, one day, the word went about that one gentleman's corn patch had plenty of corn. It was way far away, but the corn was supposed to be good and ripe.

As the news went around, the pigeons all flew there to look it over. Mudfish was down in the water, and from waking time through breakfast time, he heard the birds' wings: *pa, pa, pa, pa, pa, pa*. He was feeling sorry for himself. He swam to the shore, and when the pigeons flew down to the riverside to get a drink of water, he asked them, "Bru, which way do you go when you look for food?" Pigeon boasted, saying, "Ha! Bru! The white man has a field which is full of corn which is ripe and full. We're going to go there today." Mudfish said, "Bru, why don't you carry me with you when you fly over there?" The pigeon laughed. "Sure, Mudfish! You just better stay where you are, man. What are you going to do in a cornfield?" But Mudfish kept it up. He stayed there right by the shore, so that Pigeon, when he came down to drink, heard him begging again and again, "Bru, take me to that cornfield, please. Won't you take me there?" Pigeon reminded him that a mudfish out of water can't move.

But there was one good-natured pigeon who came there to drink. When Mudfish said to him, "Bru Pigeon, please carry me with you now!" He said, "Bru, what do you want to do in a cornfield?" Mudfish said, "I love corn to eat too, you know?" Pigeon said, "How are you going to get there?" He said, "Bru, I will just lie down there on your back if you will take me." He said, "Bru, supposing you fall down?" He said, "Bru, I'll hold on." Ho said, "Bru Mudfish, I don't want to carry you." He said, "Bru, please carry me!"

Well, the good-natured pigeon finally agreed, and off they went. When they reached the cornfield, he put Mudfish on the ground. Then the pigeon began to eat corn in the field and Mudfish was down below him picking up what he dropped and he was eating away too.

Suddenly they heard that the watchman was coming. The pigeons just fluttered their wings and went away, *pa, pa, pa, pa*. Now Mudfish cried, "Pigeon, pick me up please!" But Pigeon was scared and said, "Bru, we can't wait for you. I told you that you shouldn't come with us, but your deaf ears wouldn't listen. You just had to come here." Now Mudfish really felt sorry for himself, thinking that the watchman was certain to catch him.

When Watchman came, he saw Mudfish and said, "What are you doing here? How did you get out of the water and come here?" He said, "Bru, the pigeons brought me with them when they came here." Watchman took him up and put him there in his bag, saying, "I will carry you to the white man, and you can tell him what you were doing here."

So the watchman walked along, and he began to sing. Mudfish said to himself, "This watchman just loves to sing." So he asked, and the watchman said, "Sure, man, I love to sing, yes." Mudfish said, "Bru Watchman, if you want to hear a man sing, you should hear me." Watchman said, "Is that so?" Mudfish said, "Yes, but I can't sing without water. Put me in a little puddle of water and I'll sing for you." The watchman was so surprised he decided to try it. And the mudfish, when he got in the water, shook himself, and began to sing:

> *Yerry groomer* corn *pempeny,*
> *Groomer yerry;*
> Pigeon bring me *da groomer yerry.*

And the watchman was amazed, and he started to dance. He said, "Mudfish, you surely do sing well." Mudfish said, "Put me in a tub and I will sing even better, Bru." So the watchman put him in a big washing tub. Now Mudfish really began to sing:

Yerry groomer corn *pempeny,*
Groomer yerry;
Pigeon bring me *da groomer yerry.*

The watchman danced and danced until the sweat was dropping from his face. He said, ''Mudfish, you sing sweetly, man.'' Mudfish said, ''If you put me by the riverside where I can smell that river water, you'll really hear me sing.'' He said, ''No, Mudfish! Bye and bye, you'll turn me into a fool!'' Mudfish said, ''No, Bru, you don't have to put my body in the river, just put my tail in there, let it touch the water, and I'll sing for you and make you dance like you're mad.'' Watchman said, ''I will do it, but make sure you don't turn me into a fool.'' He said, ''No, Bru Watchman, just put me down there.'' And he did. Now Mudfish began to really sing; and Watchman began to really dance.

Yerry groomer corn *pempeny,*
Groomer yerry;
Pigeon bring me *da groomer yerry.*

So Mudfish sang there, and he began to dance, too, wriggling his tail. He sang so sweetly that the watchman never looked back at Mudfish. Mudfish wriggled and sang, wriggled and sang, until he got himself back into the water. When he got there he raised up his head and said, ''Bru Watchman, I'll see you later, you hear?'' The watchman jumped after him, but before you could say Jack Sprat, Mudfish was gone!

And that's why you hear people say, ''Never let Mudfish's tail touch water.''

—Jamaica

73

"TROUBLE" COMING DOWN THE ROAD

Now, back in those days, the animals didn't have the problems they have today, especially because they hadn't met Hunter yet. But Anansi saw Hunter coming through the bush one day, and saw how he could shoot things.

So he went back to Rabbit and asked him if he had ever met up with Trouble. Rabbit said he hadn't. Anansi said there were all kinds, and Rabbit asked what kinds they were. Anansi said, "Well, there is middle-of-the-road Trouble, I can tell you that."

So Anansi went up to Hunter and said to him that Rabbit was not afraid of him, so if he was to come to the road tomorrow, Rabbit would be there too, and he could shoot him. Then he went back to Rabbit and told him that tomorrow at six o'clock in the morning he must come to the middle of the road and he would teach him about Trouble.

So the next morning, Rabbit came down to the road, and there was Hunter. He was just about to take a shot at Rabbit when Rabbit darted away.

He came back to Anansi and said he had been on the road at the right time, but this Hunter was there and was going to kill him, so he never did get to see Trouble. So Anansi asked him if he wanted to learn about side-of-the-road Trouble instead, and Rabbit said that would be fine. So Anansi took him along the road until they got to where Tiger lived, with all his young ones. Well, Tiger was off someplace, and Anansi picked up one of the little ones, and as he gave it to Rabbit, he broke one of his hands. The little tiger began to cry, and the others all joined in. So Tiger came running back to see why his children were crying, and Anansi said, "You better watch out, Tiger, because Rabbit did something to hurt that child." Tiger looked at the child and saw his hand was broken. He was very vexed now and he growled, and Rabbit ran away lickety-split, into a hole, with Tiger right behind him. Anansi came trotting behind, and said to Tiger to get a long stick so he could get Rabbit out of the hole. He said he would keep guard.

Tiger went away to look for the stick, and Anansi went over to the hole and said to Rabbit: "Here is some pepper. When Tiger comes back, I'm going to get him to put his eye to the hole and you blow the pepper into it, and you'll be able to get away because he'll be blind then." So Tiger came back with a stick, and Anansi said, "Tiger, you better see if that Rabbit is still in there, because I haven't heard anything from in there since you left." As Tiger put his eye up to the hole, Rabbit blew some pepper into it. Then Tiger ran away. Rabbit came out of the hole, and both Anansi and Rabbit shouted after him, laughing, till their sides hurt.

—Surinam

74
NO CHICKEN TONIGHT

One day, after Brer Fox had been doing all that he could to catch Brer Rabbit and Brer Rabbit had been doing all he could to keep him from doing it, Brer Fox said to himself that he'd pull a good trick on Brer Rabbit. So right away Brer Rabbit came loping up the big road, looking just as plump, as fat, and as sassy as a horse in a barley patch.

"Hold on there, Brer Rabbit," said Brer Fox. "I haven't got time, Brer Fox," said Brer Rabbit. "But I want to have a talk with you about something really important, Brer Rabbit," said Brer Fox. So Brer Rabbit said, "All right, Brer Fox, but you better yell to me from where you are standing because I'm really bothered with fleas this morning and you don't want to get them."

"I saw Brer Bear yesterday," yelled Brer Fox, "and he sort of raked me over the coals because you and me aren't such good friends anymore, so I told him that I'd see you and talk to you about making friends again."

Well, Brer Rabbit scratched one ear with his hind foot and said, "Why don't you drop around tomorrow and have dinner with me. We haven't got a lot of food at our house, but I expect the old woman and the children can scramble around and get up something that will keep back your hunger for a while." "Well, I'm agreeable to that, Brer Rabbit," said Brer Fox. "Then I'll depend on it," said Brer Rabbit.

The next day, Mr. Rabbit and Missus Rabbit got up early before daybreak and raided the garden and got some cabbages and some roasting ears of corn, and some asparagus, and they fixed up a smashing dinner. Bye and bye, one of the little rabbits, playing out in the backyard, came running in hollering, "Oh, Ma! Oh, Ma! I saw Mr. Fox coming!" And then Brer Rabbit took the children by their ears and made them sit down, and they waited quietly there until Mr. Fox arrived. But they kept on waiting because Brer Fox didn't come. After a while, Brer Rabbit went to the door and peeped out, and there sticking out from behind the corner was the tip end of Brer Fox's tail. Then Brer Rabbit shut the door quietly and sat down and put his paws behind his ears and began to sing:

The place where you spill the grease,
Is right there where you're bound to slide,
And where you find a bunch of hair,
You'll surely find the hide.

The next day, Brer Fox sent word with Mr. Mink, to excuse himself, because he had been too sick to come. He asked Brer Rabbit to come and take dinner with him, and Brer Rabbit sent word that would be all right.

So, that evening, Brer Rabbit brushed himself up and sauntered down to Brer Fox's house. When he got there he heard somebody groaning and he looked in the door and there he saw Brer Fox sitting in a rocking chair all wrapped up in flannel and looking mighty weak. Brer Rabbit looked all around, but he didn't see any dinner. The dishpan was sitting on the table, and close by was a carving knife. "It looks like you're going to have chicken for dinner, Brer Fox," said Brer Rabbit. "Yes, Brer Rabbit, they are nice and fresh and tender," said Brer Fox.

Then Brer Rabbit sort of pulled his mustache and said, "You don't have any calamus root, do you, Brer Fox? I've gotten so that I can't eat any chicken without it being seasoned up with calamus root." And with that Brer Rabbit leaped out of the door and dodged among the bushes and sat there watching for Brer Fox; and he didn't have to watch for long, neither, because Brer Fox threw off the flannel and crept out of the house and got in a position to close in on Brer Rabbit when he got back. So in a little while Brer Rabbit hollered out, "Oh, Brer Fox! I'll just put your calamus root out here on this stump. You better come and get it while it's fresh." And with that Brer Rabbit galloped off home. And Brer Fox hasn't ever caught him yet.

—*Georgia*

Part V

THE STRONG
ONES AND
THE CLEVER:
CONTESTS AND
CONFRONTATIONS

INTRODUCTION

In the world of these tales, the boundary is broken down between the village and the bush, and between humans and supernatural creatures. Characters may be animals acting like humans, or humans acting like animals. The stories in this section focus on contests and fights as the contestants, in one way or another, draw on the special powers coming from the nonhuman world.

Some of the most interesting and unusual Afro-American folklore concerns the creatures that inhabit places where humans and the spirit world interact. Because the native healing systems found throughout this area invoke the powers of nature through the use of plant and animal products, a great many personal-experience stories are on record concerning beings with the power to heal and to hurt. Known as *conjuring*, *hoodoo*, and *root work* in the United States and *obeah* in the greater West Indies, these practices are carried on by specialists who seem mysterious primarily because their practices are outlawed in most places. Unlike voodoo (Vodun), Shango, and Santería, which are religious systems with rituals and ceremonies—and which also practice spiritual healing and exorcising—obeah and conjuring are carried out between a client and a worker. These healers commonly live alone, often at the edge of the community, and are depicted as intermediaries between bush spirits (or other forces of nature) and humans.

Although the stories in this section do not derive directly from the realm of the conjuror, they do depict a world in which the distinction between animals and humans is broken down, animals becoming humans and humans calling on the power of animals. In the first story, "Golden Breasts, Diamond Navel, Chain of Gold," pigs with great magical powers of dance bring important practices into play. They become magical helpers to the "poor boy" and bring about his eventual prosperity. In "Trying to Get the Goldstone," the helpers come to the aid of one of their own, the bird Nancy Jane O, in her contest with a frog.

On the other hand, in "Loggerhead," a big bird is a scare figure menacing the community, and must be confronted and killed by Old Witch Boy, demonstrating that this strange hero has supernatural powers equal to any bush figure. Similarly, in "Stackolee," the title character is in league with the Devil and produces mayhem and death wherever he bullies his way. This tale, told in the same verse style and coming from the same urban environment as "The Sinking of the *Titanic*," describes the confrontation of two badmen.

As in "Loggerhead," the conflict in "The Old Bull and the Young One" focuses on the continuity of the group, and by extension, on life itself. But here the confrontation occurs between father and son rather than between bush and village. Indeed, the bush provides a hiding place for the young bull until he can come into his full powers and challenge his father, the bull of the herd.

In "Jack Beats the Devil," as in "Stackolee," we find the widely told story of the confrontation between a human rascal and renegade and the Devil. Jack gambles with the Devil and finally beats him at his own game. This contest involves a disparity of power, in which the apparently weaker character is able to prevail by exercising his wits, a theme which also animates "Three Killed Florrie, Florrie Killed Ten," where the Old Witch Boy is the clever one, and "The Flying Contest," in which little Kunibre triumphs over all of the larger birds.

75
GOLDEN BREASTS,
DIAMOND NAVEL, CHAIN OF GOLD

———

Kri, kra! *Listen to the story!*
Open your ears and hear the story!
There are men! Kri, kra!

A mother had a poor son whose name was Boni-Boni, and he had no cloth to cover his body. She was also raising three pigs—one danced only the dance of the people of the bush, the *apuku*; one danced the waltz; and one danced only the African-style dance brought by the ancestors, the *susa*.

Listen! The story will go on!
The story must go on!

Well, when hard times came, the mother said to her boy, "Well, my boy, I see we have nothing to eat. Go take the pig that dances the dance of the bush people and sell him, so we will have some food."

But the boy had taught that pig to dance himself, and he knew his powers. And he had read in the newspaper that there was this beautiful princess who had three special things on her body. And anyone who could guess what they were, they would be able to marry her. Boni-Boni and the pig that danced *apuku* went away to the village.

Bato!
Sing, sing, my dindyamaka,
Sing, sing, my dindyamaka,
Things will happen, my dindyamaka.

Now, near that village lived a princess, a princess who was known for her beauty. She was handsomer than the sun. The more you looked at her, the more beautiful she appeared. But as the boy was approaching this neighboring kingdom, several soldiers stopped him, and one of them said, "Boy, where do you think you are going? People can't pass here." But the princess was walking in the yard, and saw the boy with the pig. She called him and said she liked the pig. She asked the boy what the pig did. He said, "This pig dances *apuku*." Then she said to the boy, "Well, let me see him dance."

And now the pig began to dance *apuku*, and when everyone else saw this magical dance they ran away. For this dance was one done only by the bush spirits, never by people. And he danced it so well, it was a pleasure to see. And the pig sang as he danced:

Ghosts are in the cemetery,
Where are they?
Ghosts wear white,
Where are they?
Ghosts are in the cemetery,
They are in the burial ground.
Ghosts wear white,
They are in the burial ground.

So the princess asked the boy how much he wanted for the pig. Boni-Boni said, "Ah, my princess, I don't want any money. But if you let me see your breasts, then I will give you the pig." The princess looked at him, and she laughed. She said, "What a silly boy! Are you looking for food, or are you looking for breasts?" But the princess loved the pig, so she showed the boy her breasts. And what were they but two breasts of gold. The boy took out a small book, and he wrote down this wonder.

Now, when the boy went home, the mother was suffering from hunger. So when his mother asked him, "Boni-Boni, where is the pig? Did you sell it already?" the boy had to lie. "No, Mother, the pig, he got away from me. I looked for him everywhere, but I couldn't find him." The mother ran to get a stick, and holding it up, shook it at him: "If you don't bring the pig back, I'm going to break your head." The boy was afraid, so he ran away and hid.

> *Listen to the story!*
> *And listen to the story!*
> *He who takes this story, and repeats it, will turn to marble!*

But the mother was still hungry, so she called out to him again. She said, "Boni-Boni, my son. I beg you, look how I have nothing to eat. Look how we are suffering, and take this pig, this one that dances the waltz, and sell him. But please, please, don't let this one get loose and run away." And so the boy took to the path again and he came once more to the kingdom of the princess.

> Kri, kra! *All men on their* kra, kra!
> *And so, the boy sang this waltz to the pig:*
> Selina fanaida
> *Why do you cry?*
> *You love me for my money,*
> *But you do not love me for myself,*
> *That is why you cry.*
> Bato! *The story must go on!*

Well, my man, when the princess saw this waltzing animal, she said, "Boni-Boni, you must sell me this pig, and I will pay you as much money as you want. Never have I seen a pig dance like a human being like this!" This was not just an ordinary dance, you see, for when the pig danced a waltz you felt the pig's power as far as the street. Boni-

Boni said, "Ah, my princess, I cannot sell him to you," and he began to laugh. The boy said, "My princess, I beg of you one thing, that I don't know if you will agree to it. I want you to let me see your navel. Then I will give you the pig for nothing." And the princess looked at him, and she said, "You are still only a boy. You can't do anything to me, so I will show you." But when the princess bared her stomach, what he saw was a black diamond navel. The boy laughed; and he gave the pig to the princess.

Now the princess had two pigs already, one that danced *apuku* and one that danced an amazing waltz. And all this the boy wrote down in the book.

> *Listen to the story, my man!*
> *Listen to the story!*
> *An Anansi storyteller is here!*

So the boy went to his mother again, and told her, "Mother, you must not be afraid. Good times will come." Now the boy and his mother still had nothing to eat. So he put on his only clothes, a blue coat and a pair of breeches, and a pair of sandals.

So the boy still had the most marvelous pig, one that danced *susa*, the dance of the African ancestors. If the pig struck his foot on the ground, the earth would burst open to see a pig dance so beautifully. Now, while the mother was sleeping, the boy took the pig and went back to the kingdom of the same princess. And there he began to coax the pig to dance with the *susa* song.

> *The rice is falling,*
> *Come pick it, brother,*
> *Things are there.*
> *The rice is falling,*
> *Come pick it, brother.*

When the princess saw this third dance, she was thrilled to silence. When she was able to think and speak, she said to herself that she must have that pig, and she offered Boni-Boni nine hundred guilders for him. But he said, "No, no, you must know, my princess, I can't sell him to you." Then the boy laughed and added, "Princess, I beg you to do one thing for me." She said, "Well, what is that, my boy?" He said, "Princess, I want to see your thighs." And when she agreed he saw the princess's legs had a gold chain wrapped around them, a chain to match her pubic hair. And when she showed him this marvel, he gave the princess the pig.

Now, when the boy went home this time, he had his mother clean for him his pair of blue breeches and a blue coat. So that Sunday the boy went to the priest for confession, and he confessed to the priest that he was in love with the princess. The priest asked him, said, "My boy, I see how you suffer, but how can you ever answer the questions and win the princess?" The boy said, "Pater, do you want me to tell you what the first one is?" The priest was doubtful but the boy insisted.

"Pater, let me tell you a story. The first thing the princess has is two golden breasts." Now the priest was interested in what the boy was saying and took note of these things. He said, "Boni-Boni, what else?" He said, "Pater, I do not know more, hear?" and told him no more.

Well, my man, the story will go on!

Well, the next day they both went to the kingdom of the princess. All the important white men from the area were there to try to answer the questions. Boni-Boni wore his little blue coat and his blue breeches and his sandals; he was a poor boy. When they arrived at the kingdom of the princess to answer the questions, the priest was the first one who went in to answer the questions with the information from the boy. First they asked him, "What is the first thing the princess has?" The priest laughed. He said, "Ha, ha, ha, ha, ha! The first thing? Ah, two golden breasts." Now, the king was a little alarmed that someone there might really know. He asked the priest, "What is the second one?" The priest thought and thought, but he didn't know and could only say nonsense faithfully.

And they called everyone else, but no one even knew one answer. Finally, they called the boy. They said, "You boy, here?" He said, "I will answer the questions till . . . there are questions to spare." He said he would answer more than they thought. The king said, "What is the first thing that the princess has?" He said, "Ah, King, the first thing the princess has? Two golden breasts." The king struck the boy with his foot. "Shut your mouth! You heard the priest say that just now." The boy said, "I told the priest that myself at confession." Now the priest was frightened to death.

The king asked the boy what the second one was. "The second one is a navel with a black diamond in it." The king was standing there frightened and pulling at his hair that such a youngster should answer such a question. "And the third one?" the king said. "What is the third one?"

Boni-Boni said, "The third one, my king, is a golden chain that matches her pubic hair."

All the white men were frightened now, for they saw what powers the boy must have. They lifted the boy from the stool on which he sat. But they still didn't think that the boy was fit to marry a princess. And so they gave the boy five hundred guilders to go and eat. And the king said to them, he said to the boy and the priest, he said, "Tomorrow night, at ten o'clock, I will lock you and the priest and the princess in a room. The princess will be in the middle, the priest on the right hand, and Boni-Boni on the left hand. And at five o'clock in the morning, whomever I see the princess embracing, that one will marry her, and get the entire kingdom."

Bato!
Kri, kra!

So the boy went home happy and said to his mother, "Eat and drink, and be happy. I have already won the battle." When the mother saw the five hundred guilders, she was so happy that she wept, and she embraced the boy. Boni-Boni said, "Mother, don't be afraid now. Take this. Tomorrow I am going to fight a greater fight." So the boy asked his mother for ten of the guilders. He went to the drugstore and got some lavender water and some laxative. And then he went home and took a bath in the lavender water so he would smell sweet for the coming night.

And so he went about nine o'clock at night. The priest was already sitting there like a great man. He was waiting for the hour to come. So at ten o'clock they locked the princess and the priest and Boni-Boni in a room that was beautiful beyond anything Boni-Boni had ever seen. This being the palace, everything was fixed neat and clean beyond words. Well, as they were lying down about eleven o'clock at night the boy began to eat one of the sugar cakes, and the others smelled them and they smelled so good. For the cakes were sweet with sweetness to spare. Now, the princess could smell them, and she yearned for the boy's cakes. But because she didn't want to get close to him, she pretended to be asleep.

Now, the priest smelled the cakes too, and they smelled so sweet. And the boy said, "Pater, if you like a few of the cakes, then take a few and eat." The priest said he thought he might try one, and the boy gave him of it and he ate it. He liked the cake so well that he asked the boy for more. Then the boy gave the priest the cakes with the laxative.

By about one o'clock the priest felt his belly begin to swell and hurt him. He groaned, "Boni-Boni, my boy, I am going to die. You know what? I am going to have to shit in this house. I can't help it." "My God, Pater! They will kill you if you do that."

But the priest couldn't stop, so he went behind the door and he shitted. And now he did not know what to do; he came and lay down again. So the whole room began to smell, until the princess herself woke up from the awful ugly smell.

Now the priest was afraid that he was going to get caught. So he thought to himself that there was only one way of getting rid of the shit —he had to eat it. So the priest went behind the door, ate the shit, and tried to clean things up as best he could.

Well, by that time it was four o'clock in the morning and the princess was getting cold. And so she decided she had to warm herself up, and decided to lie down beside the priest. But when the princess turned that way and began to put her arms around the priest, the smell was just too much for her. So she turned over and went to Boni-Boni's side. She turned again to go to the priest, but she could not stand it. By now it was five o'clock in the morning, and she stayed on Boni-Boni's side.

When they opened the door, they saw how the princess and Boni-Boni were lying next to each other. So they had to let the boy marry the princess and receive the kingdom. And so the priest was ashamed. He could not walk anymore, for feebleness seized him. And the priest went and pulled out his beard. That is why priests do not grow beards anymore. . . .

Now, the story must go on.

And so the boy married, and received the kingdom. And the father, the king, was not pleased that the princess had to marry that boy. Yet they were married.

And so I myself ate at the wedding feast, and they shot me with a cannon, till I sat down here. And so the story comes to an end. And so the boy was singing a wedding song to himself.

> Emilina, todowais;
> Emilina, todowaisende.

> *—Surinam*

76
THE FLYING CONTEST

Now, one time all the birds got to-
gether and decided that they needed a king, because all important creatures had a king. So they went to Lion to have him call a council of
birds, as Lion was king of all the animals.

When the meeting was called, all the birds came together. Kunibre
was the smallest, but he was smart! He thought about the subject, and
finally announced that, despite his size, he would be king. The others
wondered about this, but they didn't really know what to do.

Lion thought about it and asked the birds how they thought it should
be settled. They all talked, and Falcon, who knew he could fly high, hoped
that they would decide by having a contest to see who could fly highest.
But he couldn't suggest this because the other birds would know what
he was up to. Luckily, Nightingale said, "I want to say something, but
I don't know if it will be agreeable to everyone." They all said, "Speak!
Let's hear what you have to say." "I won't suggest that you should
choose by who sings most sweetly, because I know that if I raise a note,
I should win. But let me say that God gave us all one thing and that is
wings. So whoever can fly the highest, he should be made king." Falcon
was pleased when he heard this as it had been on his mind for such a
long time. He jumped up and said, "I think that is the best plan," and
all the others agreed, even Kunibre. What no one knew was that Kunibre
had his own plan in mind.

When they began the contest Kunibre sat right down in the middle of
Falcon's back. Now Kunibre was so small that Falcon didn't even know
he was up there. So they started out, and after a while, when they looked
and saw how high Falcon had flown, they said, "Falcon takes first prize
and he shall be our king." But when he landed, they saw that Kunibre
was there on top. So they had to say, "Well, no, Kunibre was even higher
than Falcon, and he shall be our king."

—*Surinam*

77
LOGGERHEAD

Once upon a time, there was a big bird in the village named Loggerhead. And everybody passing from town going home had to pass this bird:

> Coo-Cayima, Coo-Cayima
> *Loggerhead, Loggerhead*
> Coo-Cayima.

Every day, Loggerhead picked out one person, flew down out of that tree, man, and swallowed him whole. Every day, somebody else who was passing found himself with the same kind of problem.

Old Witch Boy lived alone with his grandmother. He sat in his home, thinking about this bird, and about all kinds of magic with plants and herbs and metals and things. One day, he said, "Granny, I see a little piece of tin on that house over there. I am going to go and get that and make a special knife." When she asked why, he said, "I heard that there is a bird up the road there who, whenever someone passes going home from town, he flies down off a tree and swallows him whole. I want to know how he is so strong and powerful that he can swallow anybody whole." So he got the tin and sharpened it all up and made it into a sharp, sharp knife, and he put a handle on it. When she saw what he was going to do, the old grandmother started to cry. She said, "Oh God, Grandson, you know today, Lord, you're the only family I have left here on earth to look after me. 1 don't have anybody else to look after me but you. If you go up there, you're going to lose your life today." He said, "Granny, don't be frightened for me. I'll go and cool everything for everybody." And he went up the road so, with his little knife.

By the time he reached from here to there, he began to sing this mischievous song they sang about Loggerhead: "Coo-Cayima." And right away, here comes this big bird flying down from where he lived, and he picked up the boy flapping his wings and singing that song:

Coo-Cayima, Coo-Cayima
Loggerhead, Loggerhead
Coo-Cayima.

And he swallowed him right down. And Old Witch Boy took out his little knife and he started to cut a hole in Coo-Cayima's belly, yes, right in the belly, until he cut a hole through and he dropped out on the ground. Then he walked about him with his hand in his pocket, he was a kind of boastful fellow, you know. And he started to call the bird again:

Coo-Cayima, Coo-Cayima
Loggerhead, Loggerhead
Coo-Cayima.

The bird flew down again and picked him up. This was not a little bird that you hear people talk about, you know. You would marvel to see such a large bird that was on this small island then. And when Old Witch Boy had been swallowed and made about three holes up in Coo-Cayima's Loggerhead belly, you know he sang:

Coo-Cayima, Coo-Cayima
Loggerhead, Loggerhead
Coo-Cayima, Coo-Cayima.

And by the time he dropped down again, Loggerhead was dead, and he had made the whole world clean for others. Massa King had made a pledge already that any man that killed that bird would get his daughter, a house, and even a new car. So the Old Witch Boy married a king's daughter immediately.

And there the story ends, right there!

—*St. Vincent*

78

TRYING TO GET THE GOLDSTONE

Once upon a time, there was a bird by the name of Nancy Jane O, and most people said she was the swiftest thing flying through the air. Well, at that time, the king of all the fishes and birds and all the little beasts, like snakes and frogs and worms and terrapins and bugs, and all such as that, was the mole. And he was blind in both eyes, just like all the moles are today.

Now the mole heard that there was way far away a little bit of stone made of gold lying at the bottom of a muddy creek. And if he could get that goldstone and hold it in his mouth, he would be able to see the same as everybody else. He thought and thought, but it appeared that the more he thought, the more he couldn't fix in his mind any way to get it. He traveled so slowly that he had to admit it would be years on top of years before he would get to the creek. So he made up his mind to figure out how he could get someone else to get it for him.

Now, as he was the king and could grant any kind of wish, he sent word everywhere around the countryside that any bird or fish, or any kind of little beast, that could find that stone and bring it to him, he would grant him a wish dearest to their hearts.

Well, man, in a few days the whole world was moving. Some were hopping, and some were crawling, and some were flying, each moving according to his nature.

Well, the birds were in the lead because they were flying so fast, but one day they heard something going *f-l-u-s-h*, *f-l-u-s-h*, and streaked by like lightning. And they all looked way ahead, they did, and they saw Nancy Jane O. Then their hearts began to sink, and they gave up right away because they knew she'd outfly everything on the road.

Someone said, "I'll tell you what we have to do. We'll have to get together and have a feast and get Nancy Jane O to come, and then we'll all club-up together and tie her up."

That really hit everybody's fancy, and they sent a lark on ahead to catch up with Nancy Jane O to ask her to the feast. Well, man, the lark nearly killed himself flying. He flew and he flew and he flew; but it seemed like the faster he went, the farther ahead flew Nancy Jane O.

But being so far ahead of everyone else, and not dreaming that there was any kind of devilment being planned, Nancy Jane O decided to stop and take a little nap. And so the lark, he caught up with her while she was sitting on a sweet-gum limb napping with her head under her wing. The lark spoke up, saying, "Sister Nancy Jane O," he said, "we birds are sure to win the race, and as we have flown so far, why we're going to stop and rest a little and enjoy ourselves at a feast. And Brer Crow, he said that it wouldn't be a proper feast at all unless you could be there. So they sent me to tell you to hold up until they come. They have lots of seeds and bugs and worms, and Brer Crow, he's going to bring the corn."

Nancy Jane O thought to herself that she was fast enough to get ahead of them all again, so she agreed to wait. And bye and bye, here the rest of the birds came flying up. And the next day, they had the feast. And while Nancy Jane O was eating and stuffing herself with worms and seeds, and one or another thing, the bluejay slipped up behind her and tied her fast to a little bush. And all the other birds laughed and flapped their wings, and said, "Good-bye to you, Sis Nancy Jane O, I hope you'll enjoy yourself." And then they rose up and stretched out their wings and flew away.

When poor Nancy Jane O saw the trick they had played on her, she could hardly contain herself, she was so mad. And she pulled and she jerked and stretched trying to get loose, but the string was strong enough and the bush firm enough that she just didn't have enough strength to free herself. So then she sat down and began to cry to herself, and to sing:

> *Please untie, please untie poor Nancy Jane O!*
> *Please untie, please untie poor Nancy Jane O!*

And after a while along came the old bullfrog Pigumawaya. He said to himself, "What's that I hear?" Then he listened, and he heard something going:

> *Please untie, please untie poor Nancy Jane O!*

And he went toward where he heard the sound coming from and found the poor bird lying down tied to a bush.

"Humph," said Pigumawaya, saying, "Isn't this Nancy Jane O, the swiftest-flying bird in the sky?" He said, "What's the matter with you, child? What are you crying about?" And the frog said, "Now look here. I was going to see if I couldn't get that goldstone. It's true I don't stand much chance of getting there before the birds, but then if I ever get there, why I can just jump right in the creek and find the stone while the birds are waiting for the creek to run dry. And now what if I untied you, Nancy Jane O, could you tuck me on your back and carry me to the creek? And then we'd be the sure winners because whenever we got there, I'll find it and we'll carry it back to the king together. And we'll both get our dearest wishes of our hearts. What do you say to that? Speak your mind. If you're able and willing, I'll untie you. If you're not, then good-bye, and I'll be getting along."

Well, Nancy Jane O, she thought and thought in her mind. Bye and bye, she said, "Brer Frog, I think I'll try out your plan. Untie me," she said, "and get on my back and I'll take you to the creek." Then she flapped her wings and started off. It was mighty hard flying with that big bullfrog on her back, but Nancy Jane O was a real flyer, man, you know. And she just took right off and flew and flew, and after a while she came in sight of the other birds. They looked up and saw her coming and they began to holler:

Who untied, who untied poor Nancy Jane O?

And the frog hollered back:

Pig-um-a-wa-ya, Pig-um-a-wa-ya-hooo-hooo!

Then, my friends, you should have seen the race that took place. The other birds did their level best, but Nancy Jane O, in spite of all they could do, she gained on them. And old Pigumawaya, he sat up there and kept urging Nancy Jane O on and on. "Get ahead," he said, pushing her on; "now we're really getting there." And just then Nancy Jane O shot clearly ahead of all the rest. And when the other birds saw that the race was lost, then they all began to holler:

Who untied, who untied poor Nancy Jane O?

And the frog, he turned around and he waved his hand over his head in a circle and hollered back:

Pig-um-a-wa-ya, Pig-um-a-wa-ya-hooo-hooo!

After Nancy Jane O got way ahead of the other birds, she could just go along and go along nice and easy until she got to the stone. She lit on a persimmon bush near the creek, and Pigumawaya slipped off. And he raised up his feet and began to jump around, and, *kerchug!* dove into the water. Then he got back on Nancy Jane O. And, man oh man, she was so proud; she and the frog both, until they flew around and around in joy. And Nancy Jane O began to sing:

Who untied, who untied Nancy Jane O?

And the frog answered back:

Pig-um-a-wa-ya, Pig-um-a-wa-ya-hooo-hooo!

And while they were singing and enjoying themselves, up flew the other birds. And the frog, he felt so big because he had gotten the gold-stone, he stood upon Nancy Jane O's back, and he held up the stone and shook it at the birds and hollered at them:

O pig-um-a-wa-ya, Pig-um-a-wa-ya-hooo-hooo!

And he sang and danced so hard that he felt himself slipping. And that made him clutch on to poor Nancy Jane O, and down they both fell, *kerplash!* right into the creek.

The frog fell right on top of a big rock and busted his head to pieces. And poor Nancy Jane O fell down into the water and drowned.

And that's the end. And the king never did get that stone. And, you know, the mole is still blind.

—Georgia

79
STACKOLEE

Now, you know, everybody heard the joke about Stackolee. Well, they didn't tell you that Stackolee died and Billy died and they went to Hell. Devil said to Billy, ''I seen you every day and I know you was coming. I knowed you was on your way.'' So he told Billy he could have all the fun he wants, just to keep away from his wife.

So Billy was goofing around one day and got hold of the Devil's wife, started working. Got through, he got hold of the Devil's daughter, started to working. Got through, grabbed hold of the Devil's niece, he started working. He was running around Hell trying to catch the Devil's wife. She said, ''Devil, get him down.'' Then three jumpy little bastards jumped out of the wall and said, ''Get that motherfucker before he fucks us all.''

Back in '32 when times was hard
I had a sawed-off shotgun and a crooked deck of cards,
Pin-striped suit, fucked-up hat,
T-model Ford, didn't even have a payment on that.
Had a cute little broad, she throwed me out in the cold.
I asked her why, she said, ''Our love is growing old.''
So I packed all my little rags, took a walk down Rampail Street.
That's where all the bad motherfuckers went down to meet.
I walked through water and I waded through mud,
Come a little hole-in-the-wall, they call the ''Bucket of Blood.''
I walked in and asked the bartender, ''Dig, chief, can I get something
    to eat?''
He threwed me a stale glass of water and flung me a fucked-up piece
    of meat.
I said, ''Raise, motherfucker, do you know who I am?''
He said, ''Frankly, motherfucker, I just don't give a damn.''
I knowed right then that chickenshit was dead.
I throwed a thirty-eight shell through his motherfucking head.
So a broad walked over, she said, ''Pardon me, please.
Can you tell me where the bartender is, please?''

I said, "Sure, whore, behind the bar with his mind at ease."
She looked back and screamed, "No! My son can't be dead."
I said, "You don't think so? Look at the hole in that motherfucker's
    head."
She said, "Who did this terrible crime, may I ask you please?"
I said, "Me, bitch, and my name is Stackolee."
She said, "Oh, I heard of you, Stack, from the tales of old.
Be here when my son Benny Long get back."
I said, "Bitch, I'll be here till the world go to pass.
You tell your son, Benny Long, that I said, 'Kiss my ass.' "
Just then a cute little broad came over, a terrible smile.
She looked me up and down and said, "You look like you ain't had
    none, Daddy, in quite a while."
I said, "Now raise, bitch, don't hand me that shit.
I'm used to pussy quite a bit."
She looked at her watch, it was quarter to eight.
She said, "Come on upstairs, I'ma set you straight."
The bed gave a twist, the springs gave a twistle.
I throwed nine inches of joint to the whore before she could move a
    gristle.
We came back downstairs. They was fucking on the bar, sucking on the
    floor.
Just then you could hear a pin drop, for that bad-ass Benny Long
    walked in the door.
Now he walked over to the bar where his brother lay dead,
And quietly said,
"Who had the nerve to put a hole in my brother's head?"
I jumped up and screamed, "Me, motherfucker, put your mind at ease.
I'm known as a bad motherfucker called Stackolee."
He said, "Oh, I heard of you, Stack, from tales of old.
But you know you done tore your ass when you fucked my hole.
I'ma give you the chance my brother never had. I'ma give you the
    chance to run,
Before I throw open my bad-ass cashmere and pull my bad-ass gun."
Just then some little short motherfucker way over in the corner jumped
    up and hollered, "Somebody call the law."
Benny Long throwed a forty-five shell through the motherfucker's jaw.
His broad walked over, she said, "Benny, please."
He beat that whore down to her motherfucking knees.
Just then everything got black, 'cause out went the lights.
I had that old bad-ass Benny Long in my thirty-eight sights.
When the lights came back on and all the best,

I had sent that old bad motherfucker to internal rest.
Thirteen thirty-eight-bullet holes 'cross his motherfucking chest.
His boys jumped up and said, ''Ain't this a shame.
Here's a man got our boss Benny Long there on the floor dead.
This jive-ass motherfucker's reputation we haven't ever heard.''
They dove in their coats and went down for this shit.
I said, ''Cool it, motherfuckers, let me tell you a bit.
I was born in the backwoods, for my pet my father raised a bear.
I got two sets of jawbone teeth, and an extra layer of hair.
When I was three I sat in a barrel of knives.
A rattlesnake bit me and crawled off and died.
'Cause after I get up and leave, my asshole print leaves 'danger.' ''
                                                    —*Philadelphia*

80
ESCAPING, SLOWLY

A goat was walking along with her two kids looking for some nice sweet grass when it began to rain. It was really coming down, so she ran under a big rock ledge to get some shelter, not knowing that it was Lion's house. When Lion saw the three goats coming, he purred to himself in a voice like thunder.

This frightened the mother and her kids and she said, ''Good evening, Minister.'' And the lion said, ''Good evening.'' She said that she was looking for a minister to baptize these two kids, because she wanted to give them names. Lion said he'd be happy to do that: ''This one's name is Dinner and this one's name is Breakfast Tomorrow and your name is Dinner Tomorrow.''

So now after hearing this roared out by Lion, the goats were really frightened, and the kids' hearts began to leap, *bup bup bup*. Lion asked the mother goat what was the matter with her two kids and she said, ''Well, they always get feeling this way when the room they are in gets so hot.'' So she asked Lion that since they were feeling that way, could they go out and get a little cool air. Lion agreed that they could go out until dinner time, but then they must come back in. So the mother whispered to the two kids to run as hard as they could until dark came.

So when the lion saw that evening was falling, and he didn't see the kids coming back, he started to roar again. She said that she was wondering why they were staying out so long, so she asked Lion if she shouldn't go out and get them before it got too dark. The lion agreed. And as soon as the mother got out, she really took off running.

Women know more about life than men, especially when it comes to the children.

—Jamaica

81
TURNING INTO *NÓUNA*—NOTHING

There was a great hunter called Bási Kodjó. He had hunting dogs that were killing off all the fierce bush cows in the forest, those that look like the tapir but have much more power in every way. Finally, the bush cows held a council meeting. They said, "What can we do to kill this man? Soon there will be none of us left." One of them, a female, spoke. "I'll go to him. I have a plan to lure him back here so we can kill him." And she changed herself into a beautiful woman (for bush cows have that power, you know) to trick Bási Kodjó.

She arrived in his village with a basket on her head, saying that the man who could knock it to the ground would become her husband. She was really beautiful; no one could do it. Finally Bási Kodjó tried, and the basket fell. So this beautiful woman (the bush cow in disguise) became his wife. Every night, when they were in their hammock making love, she would ask Bási Kodjó what his secret was, how it was that he was able to kill so many bush cows without their ever hurting him. Each night she asked, and each night he told her a little more. She was so beautiful.

Often, during the night, the woman would go out behind the house to stare at the row of bush-cow skulls that her husband had nailed against the rear wall as trophies. She would weep and weep, silently, for her dead relatives. When she had finished crying she would return to the house, and Bási Kodjó would ask, "Where have you been?" "I went to urinate," she would say. But every few minutes, she would go back out and just stare at those skulls and weep.

Over and over, each and every night, she asked Bási Kodjó, "Those animal skulls at the back of your house, how in the world were you able to kill all those animals? They're fiercer than any animal alive!"

One night, Bási Kodjó finally told her. "Woman, those animals live in savannahs. I go all the way to the middle of the savannah and there is where I shoot my gun. When they come charging, I toss my gun aside and climb a palm tree and then the animals circle round and furiously chew at the trunk to try and fell it. Meanwhile, back in the village, my mother is stirring the porridge that she feeds my dogs at just the proper moment to get them most excited about going hunting. Then when I see that the palm tree is about to fall, I turn myself into a chameleon, sitting on the trunk, and I call out '*fiiii*,' and this makes the trunk grow even thicker than it was at first. I do this until I know that my dogs have had time to gobble up all the porridge and let that hunting feeling come all over them. Then I let the tree fall. By then the bush cows have realized that I am the chameleon, so I turn into a spot of sand. When they try to eat that up, I use my final disguise and turn myself into a—"

Just then, Bási Kodjó's mother shrieked from her house, "Bási Kodjó! Bási Kodjó! Hurry! Snake! Snake!" Bási Kodjó jumped out of his hammock and ran to kill the snake. When he got to his mother's house she pulled him close and whispered, "There's no snake. But I must warn you. That beautiful woman is not really a woman! Don't tell her the last thing you know how to turn yourself into. Instead, tell her that you become a *nóuna*-nothing."

Bási Kodjó returned to his wife. She said, "That thing you were about to tell me, the very last thing you turn yourself into, when the bush cows come charging at you, what is it?" He said, "I become a *nóuna*-nothing." Now she didn't know what that was, but she was sure that some other bush cow would, so, at last, she was satisfied. They slept.

In the middle of the night, the woman arose very quietly and went to her basket and took out a razor. She prepared to cut Bási Kodjó's throat. Bási Kodjo's gun said, "I will shoot her *kpoo!!*" His cutlass said, "I will cut her *vélévélévélévélé!*" His magical belt (*óbiatatái*) said, "I will tie her *kílikílikílikíli.*" All the posts of the house groaned loudly, "*Hiiiiii.*" Bási Kodjó awoke with a start, saying, "What's going on?"

She answered, "I have no idea. I was asleep." Not a single thing in the house slept during the rest of the night.

At dawn, the beautiful wife asked Bási Kodjó to go off to the forest with her to collect *awara* palm seeds. He told his mother to prepare the porridge for the dogs. And they set off. The woman led him deeper and deeper into the forest until they finally reached the savannah. Bási Kodjó climbed the *awara* tree and began picking fruit. Suddenly, the woman turned back into her natural form, a bush cow, and called out to her relatives. In a moment the savannah was black with bush cows, all coming to eat Bási Kodjó. Quickly, he turned himself into a chameleon. She told them he was now the chameleon. So they began felling the tree. When it finally fell, they couldn't find the chameleon. She said, "Eat that spot of sand. *It* is Bási Kodjó." After a while, they could not find the sand. Bási Kodjó had turned himself into a tiny *awara* palm thorn, and hidden himself by sticking himself into a leaf. She said, "Destroy the *nóuna*-nothing. He's turned himself into a *nóuna*." The bush cows milled around in confusion because, in fact, none of them knew what *nóuna* was (because it meant "nothing").

Meanwhile, Bási Kodjó's hunting dogs, who by then had finished eating their porridge and had been untied, arrived on the scene, and they ripped every last bush cow to shreds. Except for one. Bási Kodjó saw that this last bush cow was pregnant, and he called off the dogs. This bush cow was hiding in a cave near a stream. She called out, "Bási Kodjó, have mercy. You're about to kill your own offspring!" He grabbed her by one side, ripping off the whole leg, and then shoved her back into the cave.

Now you know the importance of *nóuna*—nothing.

—*Surinam*

82
THE OLD BULL
AND THE YOUNG ONE

—

Now, this is a story about a black bull. That bull cattle was so big and powerful that he had all the cows in that herd for his own. And if anyone had any bull calves, he would have them killed.

But one cow, Old Nanny, knew she was going to have a bull calf, so she decided to go into the bush for the birth. And so said, so done, and the bull calf grew and grew. One day, when he had already become quite sizable, he asked his mother, he said, "Where is my daddy; I want to see my daddy." The mother explained his father was a big bull who had all other bulls killed. "If you go to see your daddy," she said, "he will want to kill you too. That way, he's the only bull alive." The bull boy's

name was Superintendent, and he was a pretty-looking fellow, young, and with lots of colors, for his mother was speckled in color.

Well, he was so persistent that his mother said to him, "Before I let you go to see your father, you must be able to take that big stone out there and throw it over your back. Then you will be ready to go and see your father."

Superintendent, being young and frolicsome, he couldn't wait. He ran to the stone with speed, man, and as soon as he reached it, he ran around the rock and pitched it over his back. Well, his mother was worried. So she said, "Yes, you have done that very easily, but you have lost three months' strength in doing it. You must wait at least three months longer before your strength will return enough that you can go and see your father."

So he waited another three months and then started talking about his father again. So this time she took him to a tree, saying, "You must talk to that tree and dig it up and throw it over your back without leaving any sand on your back when you are finished." Superintendent ran up to the tree and threw it over his back, but when he was finished he knew he didn't even have any more strength than just enough to dig it up and throw it with his horns like that. He shook off the sand from his

back, and he shone, standing there in the sun. He was so pretty and his skin was so smooth that none of the sand was left on his back.

Well, all right, he decided then that he was ready. But his mother said, "No, boy, if you go, your father will kill you." He argued, and she said, "All right, you can go, but you must spend six more months building up your strength, because you lost so much of it when you threw the tree over your back." And he agreed.

So Superintendent was eager now. He went into the bush where he found a beautiful field of grass, nothing else but grass. And he began to feed. He fed there for six months. Then he went back to his mother and said to her, "Mommy, I am ready to go and see Daddy." His mother said, "Yes, I believe you are ready." She saw him there so big and shiny in the sun. "But if you die, remember, I am dead too," she said.

So his mother showed Superintendent the way. When they got to a certain place, his mother said, "It's over yonder that your father is living." And he was anxious to find out if he was strong enough to go and meet his father. So he sang out with his strongest voice:

> *A-me Superintendent-eh,*
> *A-me Superintendent-eh;*
> *No other man can stay in the grand champion's ground,*
> *No more Bully Manger.*

Now, Bully Manger was his father's name, and when he heard that, he started to look around wondering who could be brave enough to challenge him like that. When he saw one of his cows was missing from the herd, he said, "My God, Old Nanny has gone, and look now she has brought back a son." So when he looked at this boy now, *he* got mad and he sang out this song:

> *A-me Bully Manger-eh,*
> *A-me Bully Manger-eh;*
> *No other man can stay in the grand champion's ground,*
> *No more Superintendent.*

So Superintendent walked right up to where his father had all the herd, and stopped at the edge of the field. His father called to him, "What do you want now?" When he looked, Old Nanny was at her son's side, and he knew that he was going to have to fight.

In the crowd there was this one beautiful young heifer named Fireling.

So from the time she saw the young shiny, beautiful fellow out there, man she began to fun all around, because she believed that this young chap would be able to kill the father. And she fell in love with Superintendent just standing there in the sun.

So Superintendent marched up to her, for he had never seen any cow like her. As soon as he reached her he started to run, kicking up his heels. And he was feeling so frisky that every time he turned around, his heels went right up. He decided that he was going to kill his father, for otherwise he could never have Fireling.

But his father warned him not to be rude to his elders. The son, taking this as his challenge, said, "We will fight. And if I kill you, I reign, and if you kill me, you reign." His father said, "All right, when would you like to fight?" Old Nanny said, "Tell him twelve o'clock in the day when the sun is high." Young Superintendent said, "I will fight you exactly at twelve o'clock, not later or earlier, twelve o'clock in the day when the sun is in the middle of the sky." Now, remember, Bully Manger was all black, so he couldn't stand the heat of the sun. Superintendent was all different colors, and knew he had his father there. Bully Manger didn't see any shade spot where they could fight so he knew that he would have to kill the boy quickly. They decided that the fight would be the very next day.

The next day, young Superintendent went to his father as soon as he saw him in the field. He sang out:

> *A-me Superintendent-eh,*
> *A-me Superintendent-eh;*
> *No other man can stay in the grand champion's ground,*
> *No more Bully Manger.*

He didn't rush across the field, but forced his father to rush at him. As soon as Bully Manger came out at him, he sang out:

> *A-me Bully Manger-eh,*
> *A-me Bully Manger-eh;*
> *No other man can stay in the grand champion's ground,*
> *No more Superintendent.*

And he just picked up Superintendent on his horns and he threw him up way in the air. And Superintendent, he didn't even stay up there two minutes. When he dropped back he landed on all of his four legs. Superintendent said, "All right, it's my turn now." Bully Manger replied,

"Yes, it's your turn." He was angry and amazed because it looked like he hadn't hurt Superintendent at all; nothing was broken. Superintendent went to him now, and he sang out:

> *A-me Superintendent-eh,*
> *A-me Superintendent-eh;*
> *No other man can stay in the grand champion's ground,*
> *No more Bully Manger.*

And he picked up his father, Bully Manger, and he shot him way up in the air. And while he was up in the air, he and Fireling began to dance and sing together:

> *Fire Girl,*
> *Fireling,*
> *Fire tonight,*
> *Fireling.*

> *Fire Girl,*
> *Fireling,*
> *Fire tonight,*
> *Fireling.*

> *Fire tonight,*
> *Fireling.*
> *Fire tonight,*
> *Fireling.*

Crick!

When old Bully Manger dropped back, he came down with only three legs; one was missing. From the time Fireling saw that, she wanted to run around and to kick up her heels, and Superintendent's mother could see too that her son was going to win.

Well, all right, Bully Manger went up to Superintendent, and sang out again:

> *A-me Bully Manger-eh* [He was angry now, you know.]
> *A-me Bully Manger-eh;*
> *No other man can stay in the grand champion's ground,*
> *No more Superintendent.*

He picked up Superintendent with his horns and threw him way up in the air. Superintendent dropped back, laughing. When he finished laughing, Superintendent sang out:

> *A-me Superintendent-eh,*
> *A-me Superintendent-eh;*
> *No other man can stay in the grand champion's ground,*
> *No more Bully Manger.*

He picked up Bully Manger, shot him up way in the air. While he was up there, he began to sing:

> *Fire girl,*
> *Fireling.*
> *Fire girl,*
> *Fireling.*
>
> *Fire tonight,*
> *Fireling.*
> *Fire girl,*
> *Fireling.*

Crick!

When old Bully Manger dropped back, he dropped back with only two legs this time. Well, all right, Superintendent, he began to feel joyful. Old Bully Manger went at him again:

> *A-me Bully Manger-eh,*
> *A-me Bully Manger-eh;*
> *No other man can stay in the grand champion's ground,*
> *No more Superintendent.*

He picked up Superintendent, threw him up in the air. When he dropped back he was still solid. In fact he was even more shiny and beautiful than ever, because he had hit a little drop of rain while he was up there and it glistened on his back. As soon as he dropped back, Superintendent went at him again and began to sing out:

> *A-me Superintendent-eh,*
> *A-me Superintendent-eh;*
> *No other man can stay in the grand champion's ground,*
> *No more Bully Manger.*

He picked up Bully Manger, threw him up in the air again. And while he was up there he began to sing:

> *Fire girl,*
> *Fireling.*
> *Fire tonight,*
> *Fireling.*

> *Fire girl,*
> *Fireling.*
> *Fire tonight,*
> *Fireling.*

Crick!

When old Bully Manger dropped back this time, he dropped back with only one leg. And all the other cows now began to circle around him, because they knew, even though he tried to rush at them, he couldn't walk on just one leg. And now he dragged himself up to Superintendent again, and he sang the same song, sent him up in the air, and he dropped back this time looking even shinier than before. Because you know, more and more, as soon as everyone looked at him, they saw that he was feeling good and jumping around, looking more flashy, more shiny. He went to his father once more and he sang out:

> *A-me Superintendent-eh,*
> *A-me Superintendent-eh;*
> *No other man can stay in the grand champion's ground,*
> *No more Bully Manger.*

He picked up his father again, sent him way up in the air, and he grabbed hold of Fireling there, this beautiful damsel and he began to sing:

> *Fire girl,*
> *Fireling.*
> *Fire tonight,*
> *Fireling.*

> *Fire girl,*
> *Fireling.*
> *Fire tonight,*
> *Fireling.*

Crick!

When Bully Manger dropped back, he dropped without any head. And all that anyone could see was slime all over his body. And Superintendent reigns up until today.

You will notice that if you have black cattle, they always look worse than those speckled-colored ones, because they can't stand too much hot sun.

—*St. Vincent*

83
FASTING FOR THE HAND
OF THE QUEEN'S DAUGHTER

Bru Pigeon and Bru Owl both fell in love with the queen's daughter. Though they had been friends, they had a big fight over who would win her hand, and they decided that they would have a contest. So they went to the king and told him their problem, and he said that they must have a contest over who could stay hungry the longest from Monday to Friday.

So they went into the bush; the pigeon sat in a berry and the owl in a dry tree. When Monday came, Bru Pigeon started in singing:

> *This day is Monday morning,*
> Tama tama tam.

And Bru Owl answered:

> Whoo-oo tama tama tam.

Meanwhile, Bru Pigeon, when no one could see him at night, sneaked down from the branch he was perched on and ate a few berries and in the morning he drank from the dew that fell on the branch. Since Owl didn't have anything growing like this in his tree, he couldn't even think of pulling such a trick. And there were no mice and other such vermin scampering around on those branches either, the things he likes to eat most.

So Tuesday morning came, and Bru Pigeon started singing his boasting song again just as loudly:

> *This day is Tuesday morning,*
> Tama tama tam.

And Bru Owl answered:

> Whoo-oo tama tama tam.

Now Wednesday and then Thursday and Friday mornings came around, and still Bru Pigeon kept singing the same verses. Now Bru Owl was really getting hungry. Bru Pigeon was eating berries all this time and drinking the water from the morning dew.

When Friday came, Bru Pigeon started in to sing again:

> *This day is Friday morning,*
> Tama tama tam.

But by now Bru Owl had gotten weaker and weaker. He could hardly answer. So when Saturday came and Bru Pigeon started in on his song, he didn't hear any voice in reply at all.

When Bru Pigeon heard no boast coming back at him, he flew over to the tree where Bru Owl was and found Bru Owl was stiff dead. Bru Pigeon took Bru Owl on his shoulder and carried him to the king, and lay Bru Owl down at the King's feet. And by that he won the hand of the queen and king's daughter.

They live in peace, they die in peace, they were buried in a pot of candle grease.

—Bahamas

84
WEAK IN THE DAY
AND STRONG AT NIGHT

Ti Calf's mother had died, so he was an unprotected orphan. Bouki was crossing the fields one day, and he saw Ti Calf grazing all by himself, and Bouki's mouth watered just thinking about the meal he could make of Ti Calf. So he said, "Ti Calf, I haven't seen you for a long time. Where do you live these days?" But Ti Calf knew about Bouki and his tricks. So he said, "I sleep over there on top of the hill." So Bouki promised to bring him a present of some meat the next day.

That night, Bouki told his family he would bring home Ti Calf to eat. He took a sack and crept to the top of the hill. But he couldn't find Ti Calf anywhere because Ti Calf knew what was going on and went to sleep that night in the woods. Bouki searched all night without finding him. When he went home his children said, "Where is Ti Calf?" Bouki just slapped them and told them to keep quiet.

The next day, Bouki saw Ti Calf grazing, and he went over to him in a friendly manner and he asked him, "Ti Calf, where were you last night? I dropped by with the present I promised and I couldn't find you at home." Ti Calf said, "Oh, last night I found a soft place to sleep in the woods, so that's where I sleep now."

That night, Bouki searched in the woods, but he still couldn't find Ti Calf, because he had moved on down by the spring. The next day, he said to Ti Calf, "Oh, Ti Calf, I came by the woods last night to bring you something but I couldn't find you at home. Where were you?" And the calf replied, "Last night I found a nice place to stay by the spring. That's where I'm going to sleep from now on."

So, the next night, Bouki took his sack and searched by the spring, but he didn't find Ti Calf. He began to get really angry. When he saw Ti Calf the next day, he said, "Ti Calf, why have you been telling me lies? Where do you really live?" Ti Calf said to him, "Uncle Bouki, I really live in that cave there in the mountain."

Now, Calf knew that the cave really belonged to Tiger. So that night, when Bouki took his sack and went up to the cave, he called, "Are you there?" The tiger replied, "OF COURSE I'M HERE." So Bouki crept into the dark cave, grabbed hold of the tiger, and tired to put him in the sack. But the tiger knocked Bouki down. He tore his clothes off, bit chunks out of his arms and legs, and mauled him. Bouki ran home. His children wanted to know where Ti Calf was. Bouki said, "Boy, that Ti Calf is a devil! He is so small and weak in the daytime, but at night he's as ferocious as a tiger. So if you happen to meet him anywhere, you better show him the greatest respect!"

—*Haiti*

85
JACK BEATS THE DEVIL

Well, I went up on that meat-skin,
And I come down on that bone
And I grabbed that piece of cornbread
And I made that biscuit moan.

Once, there was a very rich man who had two sons. One was named Jim and the other they called Jack. One night, he called the boys to him and told them, "I don't want you sitting around waiting for me to die to get what I'm going to give you. Here's five hundred dollars apiece. That's your share of the property. Take the money and make men out of yourselves. Put yourselves on the ladder."

Jim took his money and bought a big farm and a pair of mules and settled down. Jack took his money and went down the road, skinning and winning. He won from so many men that he had tripled his money. Then he met a man who said, "Come on, let's skin some money on the wood," he said, and he laid down a hundred dollars.

Jack looked at the hundred dollars and put down five hundred and said, "Man, I'm not here just to dig small potatoes. You're playin' with your head out the window. You're fat around the heart. Bet some money!"

The man covered Jack's money and they went to skinning. Jack was dealing when he thought he saw the other man on the turn, so he said, "Five hundred more, my ten spot is the best." The other man covered him, and Jack slapped down another five hundred and said, "Five hundred more, you lose this time." The other man never said a word. He just put down his five hundred more.

Jack got to singing:

> When your cards get a-lucky, oh pardner
> You ought a be in a rolling game.

He flipped the card, and bless God, it was the ten spot! Jack had lost himself instead of the other man. Now he was on the spot. He said, "Well, I've lost my money, so the game is through." The other man said, "We can still play. I'll bet you all the money on the table against your life."

Jack agreed to play because he figured he could outshoot and outcut any man on the road, and if the man tried to kill him, he'd get killed himself. So they shuffled again, and Jack pulled a card out of the deck, and it was a three. Then the man got up and he was twelve foot tall, and Jack was so scared he didn't know what to do. The man looked down on him and told him, "The Devil is my name, and I live across the deep blue sea. I could kill you right now, but I'll give you one more chance. If you can get to my house before the sun sets and rises again, I won't kill you. But if you don't, I'll be compelled to take your life." Then he vanished.

Jack went on down the road till he met an old man. He said, "What's the matter, Jack? Why are you looking so down?" "I played skin with the Devil for my life, and he won and told me if I can't make it to his house by the time the sun sets and rises again he's going to take my life, and he lives way across that ocean."

The old man said, "You sure are in a bad fix, Jack. There's only one thing that can cross the ocean in that time." Jack asked him what it was, and he said, "It's a bald eagle. She comes down to the edge of the ocean every morning and dips herself in the sea and picks off all the dead feathers. When she's dipped herself three times, she rocks herself and spreads her wings and mounts up into the sky and goes straight across the deep blue sea. So if you could be there when she gets through dipping and picking herself and she begins to mount into the sky, if you jump straddle her back, you just might make it. But get yourself a big yearling, and every time she hollers, you give her a piece of that yearling or she'll eat you."

Jack got the yearling and was waiting for that eagle to come. He was watching her from behind the bushes and saw her when she came out of the water and picked off the dead feathers and rocked, ready to spread her wings and fly off. He jumped on the eagle's back with his yearling, and the eagle was outflying the sun. After a while, she turned her head from side to side and her blazing eyes lit up, first the north then the south, and she hollered, "*Ah-h-h. Ah, ah!* One quarter of the way across the ocean! I don't see anything but blue water. *Uh!*"

Jack was so scared that instead of giving the eagle a quarter of the meat, he gave her the whole bull. After a while, she said, "*Ah-h-h, ah, ah!* One half way across the ocean! I don't see anything but blue water!"

Jack didn't have any more meat so he tore off one of his legs and gave it to her. She swallowed that and flew on. She hollered again, "*Ah-h-h. Ah, ah!* Almost all the way across the ocean! I don't see anything but blue water! *Uh!*" Jack tore off one arm and gave it to her and she ate that. And pretty soon she landed and Jack jumped off and the eagle flew on to her nest.

Jack didn't know which way the Devil lived, so he asked. "That first big white house around the bend in the road," they told him. Jack walked to the Devil's house and knocked on the door. "Who's that?" "One of the Devil's friends. One without an arm and without a leg."

The Devil told his wife, "Look behind the door and hand that man an arm and a leg." She gave Jack the arm and leg and Jack put them on.

The Devil said, "I see you got here in time for breakfast. But I got a job for you before you eat. I got a hundred acres of new ground that hasn't ever had bush cut on it. I want you to go out there and cut down all the trees and bushes, grub up all the roots and pile them and burn them before dinner time. If you don't, I'll have to take your life."

Just about that time, the Devil's children came out to look at Jack and he saw that the Devil had one real pretty daughter. But Jack was too worried to think about any girls. So he took the tools and went on out to the woodlot and went to work.

By the time he chopped down one tree he was tired, and he knew it would take him ten years to clear that ground right, so Jack set down and started to cry. About that time, the Devil's pretty daughter came with his breakfast. "What is the matter, Jack?" "Your father has given me a job he knew I couldn't get done with, and he's going to take my life and I don't wanna die." "Eat your breakfast, Jack, and put your head in my lap and go to sleep."

Jack did as she told him, and went to sleep. And when he woke up every tree was down, every bush—and the roots dug up and burned. It looked as if there never had been a blade of grass there.

The Devil came out to see how Jack was doing and saw that a hundred acres were cleaned off so nice. He said, "Uh, huh, I see you're a wise man, almost as wise as me. Now, I got another job for you. I got a well, a hundred feet deep, and I want you to dip it dry. I want it so dry that I can see dust from it and then I want you to bring me what you find at the bottom."

Jack took the bucket and went to the well and went to work, but he saw that the water was coming in faster than he could draw it out. So he sat down and began to cry again.

When the Devil's daughter came along with Jack's dinner, she saw Jack sitting down crying. "What's the matter, Jack? Don't cry like that unless you want to make me cry too."

"Your father has put me to doing something he knows I can't do, and if I don't get through, he is going to take my life." "Eat your dinner, Jack, and put your head in my lap and go to sleep."

Jack did as she told him to do, and when he woke up the well was so dry that red dust was just boiling out of it like smoke. The girl handed him a ring and told him, "Give my father this ring. That's what he wanted to see. It's my mother's ring, and she lost it in the well the other day."

When the Devil came to see what Jack was doing, Jack gave him the ring and the Devil looked and saw all that dust blowing out of the well. He said, "I see that you're a very smart man. Almost as wise as me. All right, I have just one more job for you, and if you do that I'll spare your life and let you marry my daughter as well. You take these two geese and go up that coconut palm and pick them, and bring me the geese when you get them picked and bring me every feather that comes off of them. If you lose one, I'll have to take your life."

Jack took the two geese and climbed the coconut tree and tried to pick the geese. But he was more than a hundred feet off the ground, and every time he'd pull a feather from one of the birds, the wind would blow it away. So Jack began to cry again. By that time, Beatrice Devil came to him with his supper. "What is the matter, Jack?" "Your father is determined to kill me. He knows I can't pick geese on top of a palm tree and save the feathers." "Eat your supper, Jack, and lay down in my lap."

When Jack woke up both the geese were picked and the girl even had all the feathers; she had caught the ones out of the air that had gotten away from Jack. The Devil said, "Well, now you've done everything I told you to, you can have my daughter. You take that old house down the road apiece; that's where me and her mother got our start."

So Jack and the Devil's daughter got married and went to keeping house. In the middle of the night, Beatrice woke up and shook Jack:

"Jack! Jack! Wake up! My father's coming here to kill you. Get up and hide in the barn. He has two horses that can jump a thousand miles at every jump. One is named Hallowed-be-thy-name and the other, Thy-kingdom-come. Go hitch them to that buckboard and head them this way and we'll escape."

Jack ran out to the barn and harnessed the horses and headed toward the house where his wife was. When he got to the door, she jumped in and hollered, "Let's go, Jack. Father's coming after us."

When the Devil got to the house to kill Jack and discovered Jack was gone, he ran to the barn to hitch up his fastest horses. When he saw that they were gone, he hitched up his jumping bull that could jump five hundred miles at every jump, and he took off down the road. The Devil was really driving that bull, whipping him, and the froth was coming from his mouth and the fire from his nostrils. With every jump he'd holler, "Oh, Hallowed-be-thy-name! Thy-kingdom-come!" And every time the horses would hear him call, they would fall to their knees and the bull would gain on them.

The girl said, "Jack, he's about to catch us! Get out and drag your feet backward nine steps, throw some sand over your shoulders, and let's go!" Jack did that, and the horses got up and off they went! But every time they heard their master's voice, they'd stop till the girl told Jack to drag his feet backward nine times, and he did it, and they ran away so fast from the Devil that the horses couldn't hear them anymore and they got away.

So they got to this crossroad and decided to hide to see if they could fool the Devil once and for all. The Devil passed a man and he said, "Have you seen a man in a buckboard with a pretty girl with coal black hair and red eyes behind two fast horses?" The man said, "No, I think they must have made it to the mountain, and if they have gone to the mountain you won't be able to catch up with them." But you know, Jack and his wife were right there listening to the Devil. When the daughter saw her father coming, she turned herself and the horses into goats and they were cropping grass. Jack was so tough she couldn't turn him into anything; so she saw a hollow log and she told him to hide inside it.

Now when the Devil looked all around, he saw that log and something just told him to go look in it. He went over and picked the log up and saw there was someone inside. So he said, "Ah, ha! I got you!" Jack was so scared he began to pray to the Lord. He said, "Oh Lord, have mercy." You know there's nothing the Devil hates more than to hear the name of the Lord, so he threw down that log and said, "Damn it! If I had known that God was in that log, I never would have picked it up."

So he got back on his bull and picked up the reins and hollered to the bull, "Turn, bull, turn! Turn clean around. Turn bull, turn! Turn clean around!" The jumping bull turned so fast that he fell and broke his own neck and threw the Devil out on his head and killed him.

So that's why they say Jack beat the Devil.

—Florida

86
THREE KILLED FLORRIE, FLORRIE KILLED TEN

Now, this is a story about Old Witch Boy and his mother. She sent her son to the shop at the crossroads to get some provisions, and at the junction was a signboard with a sign on it saying that the king's beautiful daughter would marry whoever can give her a riddle she can't answer. After he bought a pound of flour he ran home and told his mother about what the sign said. His mother said, "A dumb fellow like you, dirty and stupid, how are you going to give the king's daughter a riddle she can't unriddle? So how are you going to get the king's daughter to marry you?" He said, "Mommy, take this flour, please, and bake me three loaves so that I can travel to the king's house and ask his daughter a riddle." So the mother fried him up three bread loaves, but she put poison in them because she was so vexed with her son.

Now, Old Witch Boy had a dog named Florrie and he took him along on his travels. After a while, the boy had to relieve himself, so he went into the bush and he set down the bag with his three cakes. So while he is off in the bush, Florrie stuck his head in the bag and ate all three. And when the Old Witch Boy came back, Florrie was lying down feeling sick. He whistled for him but found he couldn't come, he was dead of the poison. Already the buzzards had begun to eat him, and ten of them were dead from the poison as well. So he said to himself, "Mother made three, three killed Florrie, Florrie killed ten. That's a riddle that I can ask the king's daughter."

Right! Traveling on again, on and on, he reached a huge river, solid water like a lake. Along came a body of a cow that someone had killed and only eaten half. The other half was bloated and floating there, so he jumped on its back and it went bobbing, bobbing, bobbing across the river until it reached the other side. Now he said to himself:

> *Mother made three*
> *Three killed Florrie*
> *Florrie killed ten.*
> *The dead carry over the living.*

So he went on, going, going until he came to an old church at about nighttime. The Old Witch Boy didn't know where he was going to eat or sleep. He caught some birds. He had matches, but nothing to make a fire to cook the birds. He went into the church and found some old Bibles, so he used leaves from one of them to start the fire, and he roasted the birds. So now he said to himself, O.K.:

Mother made three
Three killed Florrie
Florrie killed ten.
The dead carry the living.
The word of God roasted meat for me to eat.

Finally, he reached the king's home. And there were all those suitors: doctors, lawyers, ministers, all of them asking their riddles. Now this Old Witch Boy's real name was Cricket. He stepped up to meet all of them, all of the big men who had come to court the king's beautiful daughter. And he looked terrible, with ragged clothes and his foot all festered up with chiggers. Each asked a riddle, and as they asked them, the king's daughter gave the answer without any trouble. She was sitting behind a screen so no one could see her face to face.

All right, so Cricket's time came now. He said:

Mother made three
Three killed Florrie
Florrie killed ten.
The dead carried the living.
The word of God roasted meat for me to eat.

Right! The king's daughter sat down, and now she had to really think! "What is this now? What can the meaning be?" So she called all of her advisers to her, then—the doctor, the lawyer, the jurymen, every wise soul—but she can't figure out the answer. Finally, she said, "Daddy, tell that man to come back with his answer, because I can't unriddle it for him at all." Well, the king saw that Old Witch Boy had won his daughter so he had his feet washed and cleaned, and new clothes brought. And they had him come into her room.

But all the advisers were upset because they didn't want the king's beautiful daughter to be married to this Old Witch Boy, so they decided to give him another test. They caught a cricket and put it in a glass and covered it over, and then told the Old Witch Boy that if he could tell them what was in the glass, then he wouldn't kill him; otherwise he was a dead man. The Old Witch Boy said, "Poor me, poor Cricket." And, of course, that was what they had in that glass, so he was saved.

Now the story ends and the wire bends.

—*St. Vincent*

Part VI

GETTING
AROUND OLD
MASTER
(MOST OF
THE TIME)

INTRODUCTION

Inevitably, the experiences of slavery and the social marginalization that arose in the plantation world came to be recorded in the stories blacks told about the interactions between themselves and whites. Although these stories resemble those in the earlier sections in the way in which they establish dramatic interest through the opposition of characters in terms of differences in power and wit, they deserve special consideration for the insights they give us regarding the black response to exclusion and exploitation.

The interest of these stories extends beyond a simple community response to a large-scale social process, for they are related not only to genre tales brought from the Old World but to particular family stories as well, reminiscences and anecdotes about how specific members of the family developed ways of getting by during the hardest of the hard times. Though I have not included any of these personal narratives in this section, it is crucial to note the growing body of such lore that has become available recently, most notably in Kathryn Morgan's *Children of Strangers*.[1] Such works amplify the message of the narratives recorded by the Federal Writers' Project during the 1930s that many individual slaves had developed techniques of encountering and even beating whites at their own game.

Humorous and often subversive, these stories commonly report an especially brazen or subtle act in the face of Old Master's authority, or they record the ways in which dispossessed and often hungry people reacted to the presence of food all around them. Like Velma McCloud's great-grandfather, who, as a slave, had become an expert in stealing pigs because his master, Planter Hammond, would give him no meat. Finally, the day of reckoning came. The slave received an investigative visit from Hammond at the very moment he was making the pork stew on which his local reputation rested. When Hammond insisted on tasting the "possum stew" that was cooking there, Great-Grandpa responded by exclaiming how "the possum . . . was about done to a turn!" "Must be all that good spittin' we done," he muttered under his breath. "The *what!*" "Spittin.' . . . Us black folks always spits in the possum gravy. . . . Makes the meat good and tender."[2]

This story, simply aggressive on its surface, resonates with deeper cultural meanings when considered in the light of the social etiquette of the society in which it arose. Like most of the Master-John stories included here, what seems like the report of a *capping* conversation, that is, coming up with the perfect comeback in a contest of wits, is filled with ironic implications both in plot construction and message: the master who does not hesitate to wander into his slave's quarters to taste the food there (whether or not he was checking on the disposition of his pig population), the technique the great-grandfather uses of "loud talking" (that is, seeming to mutter, but in loud enough tones that he is sure to be overheard), the seeming acceptance of the white stereotype of blacks as dirty in their personal habits. All these stories repeat traditional means of getting around Old Master.

A number of stories included here make use of black stereotypes of whites. Not least of these is the idea that blacks had that whites would bet on anything, a trait not without its basis in fact, at least in the Old South, as historians have demonstrated.[3] We can see such stereotypes in "They Both Had Dead Horses" and "Competition for Laziness." This desire to wager became especially strong when the planter could confirm *his* stereotype of slaves and create a contest based on one of the imputed traits. Perhaps the most egregious example was the plantation "bully," the slave used in fights to represent the pride of the plantation, neighborhood, or riverfront towns. (The verse-narrative "Stackolee," given in the previous section, ultimately derives from this practice.) Most of the stories in this section turn on such contests—of strength or of wit.

It is precisely in this area of storytelling that some of the deepest ironies of the plantation system may be seen. For instance, one of the most virulent white stereotypes of blacks was the imputation of stupidity to the slaves, especially with regard to their supposed inability to employ language effectively. Yet, on the evidence of these stories, not only were the slaves as capable of "capping" as their descendants, but specific examples of this ability were built into the anecdotes told competitively between the planters!

As Charles C. Jones, one of the early collectors of black lore, concluded in one of his stories: "The buckra [white] had to laugh at how clever his newest slave was," forgiving him for his transgressions because of his ability to cap effectively. The clever remark that Jones was reporting at the time was, in fact, one of the earliest references we have to the Master-John type of story. In it, the slave is confronted by his master with not having done his assigned job. The slave responds with the well-known riddle: "If there were three pigeons in the tree and I shot one, how many were left?" When the master responds, "Two," the slave laughs and says, "If you shot and killed one of those pigeons, the other two are bound to fly away, aren't they, and then none would be left."[4] Just such uses of riddles for equalizing a power situation are found throughout this section, including "Making the Eyes Run."

The contemporary folklore of Afro-Americans continues to reflect social tensions of this sort, and to record equally ingenious black responses to indignity and inequality. There are many jokes, for instance, in which white man and black man are explicitly pitted against each other, with various humorous results.[5] Most of these stories are drawn from the enormous vault of interethnic jokes—that is, the same fund as "Polack" and other jokes justly called "truly repulsive." One finds in them the same strategies of dramatizing oppositions, as well as many of the same turns of phrase, as in the earlier stories, but they now appear as punch lines.

At the end of this section are a few examples of recent and openly hostile black–white stories that demonstrate both the themes' continuity and the change of tone that has occurred in the last few decades. Chief among these examples are the verse-narratives referred to by many black Americans as *toasts*; "The Sinking of the *Titanic*" is one such story. The tale involves a series of conversations between Shine, the putative black stoker on board the ill-fated luxury liner, and various white characters. Shine is portrayed as a great swimmer; thus he has no fear when the iceberg is hit, and many appeals are made to him for help by the captain, his wife, and his daughter. There is also a boasting interchange between the whale and Shine. This toast is one of the most openly anti-white stories in the black "street" repertoire.

The first time I heard this story was in the late 1950s when I was living in a ghetto neighborhood in South Philadelphia. At that time, the tape recorder was not in common use, and the fact that I had a recorder caused some of the young men in the vicinity to come by; in that decade, the most common street-corner activity was *a capella* quartet singing, and groups dreamed of getting recording contracts or performing on radio or television, so they wanted to hear how they sounded.

I taught a few people how to operate the recorder so that they could record at times when I wasn't home. One day, one of the neighbors asked me if I had heard any toasts. "Such as what?" I responded. He said, "Like 'Stackolee' or 'Shine.'" And he proceeded to tease me with about ten lines of the "*Titanic*" verse featuring Shine. When I showed interest in hearing the whole thing, he laughed and said he would see what he could do.

Sometime later, a group came over and recorded many of the toasts for me in the form of a radio show, with the rhymed introductions that were fashionable among black disc jockeys of the period, and with some blues-singing material—including the version of "*Titanic*" that I reprint here. Since then, the story of Shine has been collected in many places, for it provided a convenient voice of protest during the 1960s.

NOTES

1. Kathryn L. Morgan, *Children of Strangers: The Stories of a Black Family* (Philadelphia: Temple University Press, 1980).

2. Velma McCloud, "Laughter in Chains," reprinted in Albert Spalding, *Encyclopedia of Black Folklore and Humor* (Middle Village, N.Y.: Jonathan David, 1972), 35–37.

3. See, for example, T. H. Breen, "Horses and Gentlemen: The Cultural Significance of Gambling among the Gentry of Virginia," in *Puritans and Adventurers: Challenge and Persistence in Early America* (New York: Oxford University Press, 1980), 148–63.

4. Charles C. Jones, *Negro Myths from the Georgia Coast* (Boston: Houghton Mifflin, 1888), 130–31.

5. A number are printed in my *Positively Black* (Englewood Cliffs, N.J.: Prentice-Hall, 1970); and in Daryl Dance, *Shuckin' and Jivin'* (Bloomington: Indiana University Press, 1978).

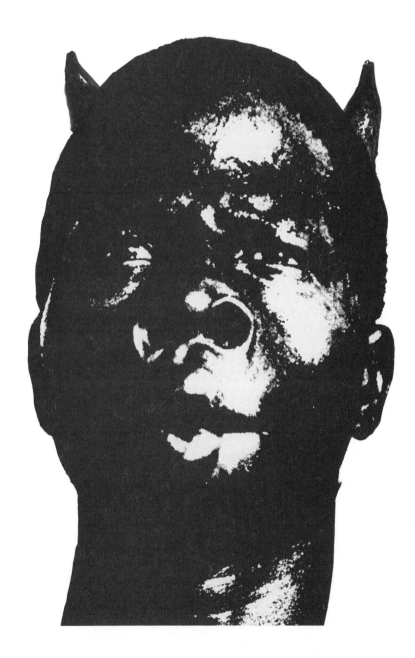

87
THEY BOTH HAD DEAD HORSES

The rooster chews tobacco and the hen dips snuff;
The old biddy can't do nothing but he can strut his stuff.

Ol' John, you know, he was a conjure man. So he could usually tell what Ol' Massa was going to do or say, and let me tell you, that helped him out a lot. In fact, it let him really get up over Ol' Massa one time. You see, Ol' Massa had these two horses. Now, Ol' John had been working for him all these years and so had these horses. And they were all getting long in the teeth, especially this one old nag. So Ol' Massa

decided he would take care of things by giving that old one to John to take care of. And you'd have to say that Ol' John was proud to have that horse for his own, because now he could ride it around without making Ol' Massa mad at him. But still he had to work that old nag next to the other horse when they were out in the field.

Now, things changed a little bit, because when Ol' John got to working the horses, he just couldn't resist hauling off and beating the one that still belonged to Ol' Massa. Of course, he never would hit his own. So then some white folks told Ol' Massa, and he got mad and told Ol' John that if he ever heard of him laying a whip to his horse again, and not his own, that he was just going to take Ol' John's horse and kill it dead as a doornail, and that would be the end of that. But Ol' John really knew Ol' Massa after all these years, and he knew what a fool he could be when it came to money and betting. So he said, "Massa, now if you kill my horse, I'm going to turn around and make more money out of it than you have." Ol' Massa just kind of snorted.

One day, Ol' John hit Ol' Massa's horse again, and, of course, everyone heard about it. So he came on down where Ol' John was hauling roots and stumps and other trash and he took out his big old knife and cut Ol' John's horse's throat. Ol' John jumped down off his wagon and quickly skinned his horse, tied up the hide up on a stick, threw it across his shoulder, and just walked away. He was a sight, I want to tell you!

Now, remember, Ol' John was a conjure man, and everybody around there knew about it. So he met up with this one white man who saw him walking along the road with the skin on the stick over his shoulder, looking a sight, and the man asked him, "What is that you have over your shoulder, Ol' John?" "It's what I use to look into what's going on all over the place." "You mean you can use that old skin to see things?" "That old skin and my stick," he said. "Well, make it tell you something I need to know, and I'll give you a sack of money and this horse and saddle I'm on." John said, "Well, I don't know if it's working today." The man said, "I'll give you five head of cattle beside if you tell me something important." (He was really testing him, you know.) Well, Ol' John put the hide on the ground and he took the stick and he hit the horsehide one lick, and then he held his head down to it like he was listening to something, and then he turned to the white man and said, "Well, I'll tell you one thing; there's a man in your bedroom right now sweet-talking your wife, and I guess that's pretty important to you." The man ran right to his house to see, and that's what he found, I guess, because here he came back shaking his head. He said, "Ol' John, you sure can see things with that old horsehide."

Now a big crowd had gathered around, so this next man said, "John,

I've been having some trouble too. Do you think that old horsehide could help me out?'' Ol' John went and put the stick back inside the hide and lifted it on his shoulder and said, ''Well, you know, he was an old horse and just that one beating made him pretty tired out.'' The white man said, ''I'll give you six head of sheep and four horses and four sacks of money if you get the hide to tell you something I need to know.'' So Ol' John pulled out his stick and hit the hide and held his head next to it as if he was listening again. He said, ''Unh, unh, there's a man in your kitchen opening your stove and eating your wife's good biscuits right now.'' So the man ran to his house. He came back out and told Ol' John that his old horsehide fortune-telling sure was right again. So he gave him all those things he promised.

Now, Ol' John knew how Ol' Massa was going to feel about him getting all the things. But he just couldn't resist riding on past Ol' Massa's house with all his sacks of money and cattle and sheep there alongside of him, just whooping and cracking his whip as loud as he could. ''Yee, whoopee, yee!'' *Crack!* Massa ran out of his door and asked, ''Now, John, where did you get all that stuff?'' Ol' John said, ''I told you if you killed my horse I'd get one back and a lot more beside. And now I've got as much money and cattle as you have, and more.''

Ol' Massa just couldn't stand the thought of John getting more than he had, so he found out how John had done it. So he took that other horse and he killed it, skinned it, put it on a stick over his shoulder, and went to town. Everybody kind of snickered at him and one man said, ''Hold on there. I'll give you two bits for the skin of that horse to make chair bottoms.'' Ol' Massa told him that he must be crazy, that the hide was worth much more than that. He walked on some more, trying to get people to buy his horsehide, but all he could get were more offers to buy it to make chair seats. Everyone just laughed at him trying to sell it, so finally he had to throw it away and buy himself a new horse.

Now that Ol' John was rich, he couldn't resist showing it off. He didn't have to work any more but since he had been fooling with horses all his life, he liked to go riding around showing off everything that he had. Sometimes he would get out of the buggy and take some kids or Ol' Granny around with him. And whenever he would do this, when people asked where he got all his money and stuff, he would tell them about outdoing Ol' Massa. Now, Ol' Massa heard him at this one day, and he got really mad. He said to John, ''You better watch out, because if you bring your old granny by me, I'm going to kill her.'' Well, John just said, ''If you touch my granny I'll just turn around and beat you even worse at making money, you know.''

So, one day, along comes Ol' John out riding his buggy with Granny by his side, and he couldn't resist going on by Ol' Massa's. So Ol' Massa came roaring out there and right in front of everybody he cut Granny's throat, and there wasn't anything John could do about it with all those white folks around.

Ol' John buried his grandmother and went back and got out his old horsehide and stick, put them on his shoulder, and carried them up to town again. By this time he had quite a reputation, you know, and so it didn't take too much reminding for people to remember that he could see things with that old horsehide and stick. They just lined up to get him to see things for them. One man told him, "Why, John, make it talk some for me and I'll give you six goats, six sheep, a horse, and a saddle to ride him with." So Ol' John made it talk and the man was pleased so he gave Ol' John even more than he promised him, and Ol' John went back past Massa's house with all his new stuff so Massa could see him there.

Ol' Massa ran out and said, "Oh, John, where did you get all that?" John said, "I told you that if you killed Granny I would just have to beat you more at making money." Well, you know that is something a white fellow can't stand is to be made a fool, and he went a little crazy again. And he went back in and killed his own grandmother so he could make all that money too.

So Massa went up town hollering, "Grandmother for sale, Grandmother for sale!" Now nobody would even say a thing to him, thinking the man must really be crazy now. So after a while he went on back home and went over to John's and told him: "You made me kill my own grandmother and my own good horse, and I'm going to throw you in the river." So what could John do? He said, "Well, if you throw me in the river, I have to beat you even more at making money." "No you won't either," Massa told him. "You've made your last money and pulled your last trick now." He put Ol' John in a sack and carried him down to the river. But he forgot his weights so he went back home to get some.

While he was gone, one of these treefrogs came by, and John, the conjure man, said to him, "Mr. Hoptoad, if you open this sack and let me out I'll give you a dollar." Toad let him out right then, so Ol' John got a big old softshell turtle and put it into the sack along with a couple of bricks. Then Ol' Massa got his weights and came and tied them to the sack and threw it in the river.

Now, while Ol' Massa was down by the river fooling with the sack, Ol' John got out his horsehide again, went up to town, and started his conjuring again. Along came this rich man who had heard all about how Ol' John could tell things. So he told him to make that hide talk. Ol' John hit that old hide and said to the rich man, "There's a man in your smokehouse right now stealing meat from you, and another one is in your money safe and you know what *he's* taking." Now that man ran into his house and that's what he found. And when he came out he said, "Well, you sure can see things with that hide." And he gave him all kinds of things!

So now Ol' John had the most beautiful horse in town and stuff, and he went riding by Ol' Massa's house bold as brass, with big bags of money tied on each side of the saddle. Ol' Massa just had to know how John had escaped, and gotten all the horses and money too. "I told you that if you threw me in the river I'd make even more money than you could. That's what happens when you throw Ol' John into the water, you see?" So Ol' Massa got himself a bag and had John tie him up and carry him to the river and throw him in with all his weights tied on. As he threw him in, Ol' John said, "Good-bye, Massa, I sure hope you find what you're looking for."

—*Florida*

88

YOU TALK TOO MUCH, ANYHOW

Once, during the time of slavery, the pond was somewhat low. A negro happened to walk down there and found this turtle down there about the size of the bottom of a big tin tub, lying on the bank. So the negro said to the turtle, "Good morning, Mr. Turtle." The turtle at first didn't say anything, but finally said, "Good morning, Mr. Man." The negro said, "My, Mr. Turtle, I didn't know you could talk." Turtle said, "What I say about you niggers is you talk too much." So the negro goes back to his house and tells Old Massa about the turtle. He said, "Massa, don't you know, I was down at the creek this morning, and there was a great big turtle on the bank, and he could talk." Massa said, "Get away from here, you're just lying." The negro said he was telling the truth, but Master told him he lied like a dog. But the negro said, "No sir, he can really talk."

So the master said he would go down to see this turtle, but if he didn't talk he was going to beat the slave half to death. Both of them went back down to the creek and they found the turtle lying on the bank. The negro walked right up to the turtle and said, ''Good morning, Mr. Turtle.'' Turtle didn't say anything, so the negro repeated, ''I say, good morning, Mr. Turtle.'' Turtle still didn't say anything. This time the negro got scared. He said, ''Please sir, Mr. Turtle, please say good morning,'' but Turtle wouldn't talk.

The Master took the negro back to the house and beat him half to death. After he got his beating, he went on back to the creek. He saw the turtle again and said to him, ''Why didn't you say good morning? You knew I was going to get a beating if you didn't talk.'' Turtle said, ''Well, that's what I say about you negroes, you talk too much anyhow.''

—Alabama

89
MAKING THE EYES RUN

O_{nce} upon a time, a king and queen were getting married and had a big wedding fest. They invited all the big shots and the poor people; but the big shots ate with plates and silver and when they were finished they threw their food on the ground for the poor people, who were black. While he was eating, one of the poor men started thinking that this way of eating was dirty, nastiness. So he went around to the big shots while they were celebrating with riddles and stories—all that kind of nonsense—and he listened to them doing Anansi story and stuff, and he figured out that he could do that as well as any rich man.

This man just jumped right in there and told them: ''Riddle, riddle,'' showing that he knew how to play that nonsense as well as anybody. And they replied, ''Shall be,'' so that he could go on with the riddle. But there was such a crowd there, they didn't even know that it was this black man that was making this riddle. So he got up and said,

"Something round and black and runs water. What is that?" There was laughter and there was some screaming because some people thought that was a dirty riddle. A lot of them even got up and walked away from the table saying that they didn't want to talk about it, it was such nastiness. So the black man said, "Do you give up?" And the few that were still there said, "Yes." And he said, "Well, that is my eyes. They are round and black and run water sometimes."

Then some of the rich folks who had gone away came back in, and the others told them the answer the man had given. So they were feeling funny about that. So he said to them that he would give them another good riddle, and he asked them: "What is long, sometimes black, sometimes white, and sometimes red? When you hold it, it runs water?" And they thought and thought because they didn't want to be tricked again. Finally, one said, "That is the eyes again." And he said, "No, that is not the eyes." So they said, "Well what is it, then? We give up." And he said, "It is just what you thought it was before—your pip!"

—*Tobago*

90
MAKING A WAGON
FROM A WHEELBARROW

———

One year, the boll weevils got into the cotton crop on Colonel Clemons's plantation and destroyed most of it. This made times very hard for the colonel, and since he did not make any money, he did not provide enough food and clothing for the hands. So naturally they stole anything they could get away with.

Never a week passed that some of the hands were not arrested and carried to jail.

One day, the sheriff came out to Colonel Clemons's farm and arrested John. With him were two white hands he had arrested on a neighboring plantation. John and the two white hands were all charged with stealing, and they were to be tried on the same day at the same hour.

When John and the two white men were brought in to the courtroom and arraigned for trial, John got very nervous and started trembling. This was the first time in his life that he had not been able to think of an excuse. He knew, however, that they were going to try the white men first; so he decided to listen to their answers and imitate them when his turn came.

The first case called was that of one of the white hands who was accused of stealing a horse.

"Guilty, or not guilty?" said the judge.

"Not guilty," replied the man; "I've owned that horse ever since he was a colt." The case was dismissed.

Then the judge called the second white man to the stand. He was accused of stealing a cow. "Guilty, or not guilty?" asked the judge.

"Not guilty," replied the defendant. "I've owned that cow ever since she was a calf." The case was dismissed.

Then John was called to the stand. He was accused of stealing a wagon.

"Guilty, or not guilty?" demanded the judge.

"Not guilty," replied John. "I've owned that wagon ever since it was a wheelbarrow."

—Texas

91

THE ONE-LEGGED TURKEY

There was a gentleman who was so stingy he kept only one servant. That servant, John, was cook, butler, and everything, including farmyard keeper. One day, the gentleman called on his servant, John, to cook a certain turkey he had been keeping his eye on for a special occasion.

So John cooked the turkey, but it smelled so good that he took a risk and ate one of the legs. Then, when he served the turkey, he put that side down. The gentleman came in, tired and hungry, and ate and ate and ate. When he turned the turkey over he discovered that the leg was missing, so he called to John. "John, what's become of the turkey's other leg?" John said, "That turkey only had one leg, sir!" Just then he looked through a window and saw one of the turkeys standing with one leg under its wing. The master said, "Shit!" and the turkey moved, clucking. The master said, "There you are, John, see the turkey has two legs." John said, "But, Master, did you say shit! to the one in the dish, sir?" The master said, "No," and John replied, "Well, if you had yelled 'shit' at it, it would have put out the other leg too."

—*St. Lucia*

92
JOHN OUTRUNS THE LORD

You know, before surrender Old Massa had a slave named John, and John always prayed every night before he went to bed. His prayer was for God to come get him and take him to Heaven right away. He didn't even want to take time to die. He wanted the Lord to come and get him just like he was—boots, socks, and all. He'd get down on his knees and say: "O Lord, it's once more and again your humble servant, knee-bent and body-bowed, my heart beneath my knees and my knees in some lonesome valley, crying for mercy while mercy can be found. O Lord, I'm asking you in the humblest way I know how to be so pleased as to come in your fiery chariot and take me to your Heaven and its immortal glory. Come, Lord, you know I have such a hard time. Old Massa works me so hard, and doesn't give me time to rest. So come, Lord, with peace in one hand and pardon in the other, and take me away from this sin-sorrowing world. I'm tired and I want to go home."

One night, Old Massa passed John's shack and heard him begging the Lord to come get him in his fiery chariot and take him away; so he made up his mind to find out if John meant it. He went on up to the big house and got himself a bed sheet and came on back. He threw the sheet over his head and knocked on the door.

John quit praying and asked: "Who's that?" Old Massa said: "It's me, John, the Lord, coming with my fiery chariot to take you away from this sin-sick world." Right under the bed John found he had some business. He told his wife: "Tell him I'm not here, Liza."

At first Liza didn't say anything at all, but the Lord kept right on calling John: "Come on, John, and go to Heaven with me where you won't have to plow any more furrows and hoe any more corn. Come on, John." Liza said, "John isn't here, Lord. You have to come back another time."

The Lord said, "Well then, Liza, you'll do." Liza whispered and said, "John, come out from underneath that bed and go on with the Lord. You've been begging him to come get you. Now go on with him."

John was back under the bed not saying a mumbling word. The Lord is out on the doorstep, and he kept on calling.

Liza said, "John, I thought you were so anxious to get to Heaven. Come out and go on with God." John said, "Didn't you hear him say, 'You'll do'? Why don't you go with him?"

"I'm not going anywhere. You're the one who's been whooping and hollering for him to come get you, and if you don't come out from under that bed, I'm going to tell God you're here."

Old Massa, still pretending he was God, said, "Come on, Liza, you'll do." Liza said, "O Lord, John is right here underneath the bed." "Come on, John, and go to Heaven with me to immortal glory." John crept out from under the bed and went to the door and cracked it; and when he saw all that white standing on the doorstep, he jumped back. He said, "O Lord, I can't go to Heaven with you in your fiery chariot in these old dirty britches; give me time to put on my Sunday pants."

"All right, John, put on your Sunday pants."

John fumbled around a long time changing his shirt, and then he went back to the door, but Old Massa was still on the doorstep. John had nothing else to change into so he opened the door a little piece and said, "O Lord, I'm ready to go to Heaven with you in your fiery chariot, but the radiance of your countenance is so bright, I can't come out with you right there. Stand back just a little way please." Old Massa stepped back a little.

John looked out again and said, "O Lord, you know that poor humble me is less than the dust beneath your shoe soles. And the radiance of your countenance is so bright I can't come out by you. Please, please, Lord, in your tender mercy, stand back a little bit farther." Old Massa stepped back a little bit more.

John looked out again and he said, "O Lord, Heaven is so high and we're so low; you're so great and I'm so weak; and your strength is too much for us poor suffering sinners. So once more and again your humble servant is knee-bent and body-bowed asking you one more favor before I step into your fiery chariot to go to Heaven with you and wash in your glory—be so pleased in your tender mercy as to stand back just a bit farther.''

Old Massa stepped back a step or two more, and out that door John came like a streak of lightning. He ran all across the pumpkin patch, through the cotton, over the pasture. John ran and here comes Old Massa right behind him. By the time they hit the cornfield John was way ahead of Old Massa.

Back in the shack one of the children was crying and she asked Liza, ''Mama, you reckon God's going to catch Papa and carry him to Heaven with him?''

''Shut your mouth, talking that foolishness!'' Liza answered the child. ''You know the Lord can't outrun your pappy—specially when he's barefooted at that.''

—*Florida*

93
A FLYING FOOL

This colored man died and went up there to meet his Maker. But when he got to the gates, St. Peter said that God wasn't home or having any visitors—by which he meant no negroes allowed. Well, this old boy, he had been a good man all his life and his preacher had told him that Heaven would be his place, so he didn't exactly know what to do. So he just kind of hung around the gates, until one time St. Peter just had to go and take a pee. So while Pete was gone, this old boy slipped through, stole himself a pair of wings, and he really took off. Sailed around the trees, in and out of those golden houses and all, swooped down and buzzed some of those heavenly singers and all, and had himself a good old time. Meanwhile, of course, St. Pete came back and found out what had happened and called out the heavenly police force to go get him. Well, this guy was just getting the feel of wearing wings, and he really took off, zoomed off. They had some little time bringing him down, him flying all over Heaven fast as he could go. Finally, they got him cornered and he racked up on one of those trees, and I tell you, he looked like a mess with broken wings and all. So they took him and threw him out the gates. Now here comes one of his friends, who asked him, "What happened, man?" He said, "Oh, man, when I got here they wouldn't let me in to the white man's Heaven, but I grabbed me some wings and I had me a fly." He said, "Oh yeah?" Man said, "Yeah, they may not let any colored folks in, but while I was there I was a flying fool."

—Texas

94
HORSES STAY OUTSIDE

A black man went to Heaven by land and knocked on the door. St. Peter came out and said, "Who is that?" Black Man said, "This is me." St. Peter said, "You riding or walking?" Black Man said, "I'm walking." St. Peter said, "Well, you can't get in here unless you're riding." Black Man left; came on back down the road about five miles, met up with a white man. He said, "Mr. White Man, where are you going?" White Man said, "I'm going to Heaven." Black Man said, "You can't get in there walking. I just left there." Then he had an idea. Black Man said, "I'll tell you a way we'll get in there." Black Man said, "Let me be your horse and you get a-straddle me and I'll go riding and carry you up to Heaven; and you knock on the gate, and when St. Peter asks you who you are, you tell him it's you, and he will say, 'Both of you come on in.' " White Man said, "All right, get down." The white man straddled the black man; Black Man went running back up to Heaven with him on his back. Rode him right up to the door. The white man knocked on the door. St. Peter said, "Who is there?" White Man said, "This is me." St. Peter asked,

95

THE SINKING OF THE *TITANIC*

It was a hell of day in the merry month of May
When the great *Titanic* was sailing away.
The captain and his daughter was there too,
And old black Shine, he didn't need no crew.
Shine was downstairs eating his peas
When the motherfucking water come up to his knees.
He said, "Captain, Captain, I was downstairs eating my peas
When the water come up to my knees."
He said, "Shine, Shine, set your black ass down.
I got ninety-nine pumps to pump the water down."
Shine went downstairs looking through space.
That's when the water came up to his waist.
He said, "Captain, Captain, I was downstairs looking through space,
That's when the water came up to my waist."
He said, "Shine, Shine set your black ass down.
I got ninety-nine pumps to pump the water down."
Shine went downstairs, he ate a piece of bread.
That's when the water came above his head.
He said, "Captain, Captain, I was downstairs eating my bread
And the motherfucking water came above my head."
He said, "Shine, Shine, set your black ass down.
I got ninety-nine pumps to pump the water down."
Shine took off his shirt, took a dive. He took one stroke
And the water pushed him like it pushed a motorboat.
The Captain said, "Shine, Shine, save poor me.
I'll give you more money than any black man see."

Shine said, ''Money is good on land or sea.
Take off your shirt and swim like me.''
That's when the Captain's daughter came on deck;
Hands on her pussy, and drawers 'round her neck.
Says, ''Shine, Shine, save poor me.
Give you more pussy than any black man see.''
Shine said, ''Pussy ain't nothing but meat on the bone,
You may fuck it or suck it or leave it alone.
I like cheese but I ain't no rat.
I like pussy, but not like that.''
And Shine swum on.
He said, ''I hope you meet up with a whale.''
Old Shine, he swim mighty fine.
Shine met up with a whale.
The whale said, ''Shine, Shine, you swim mighty fine,
But if you miss one stroke, your black ass is mine.''
Shine said, ''You may be king of the ocean, king of the sea,
But you got to be a swimming motherfucker to outswim me.''
And Shine swum on.
Now when the news got to the port, the great *Titanic* had sunk,
You won't believe this, but old Shine was on the corner, damn near drunk.

—*Philadelphia*

96
COMPETITION FOR LAZINESS

O nce, there were three white slave-owners sitting around discussing how lazy their slaves were. Each had one slave they said was the laziest man alive, so they decided to make a bet. So the first took them to his place and pointed to this man out in the fields sleeping. He said, ''Man, couldn't nobody's slave be any lazier than mine, 'cause mine is so lazy he lays in the field all day and lets flies swarm all over him and snakes crawl on him and still he won't move.''

So they went to the house of the next man and he pointed out this slave, and said, "Your slave isn't anything. You see that one, I saw him the other day in the cotton field and a cow came by and just shit and pissed all in his face and he didn't move." Now John really was the laziest, but he was all the time putting it over on Marster. But this was one time Marster didn't mind, 'cause when they went over to that place, John knew they were coming and what for and he just lay there on the ground moaning. Marster said, "Y'all ain't heard nothing yet. You see John there; well, yesterday I heard moans and groans coming from the barn and I went out to see what was wrong. There the man was, lying in the corner moaning and groaning. You know what was wrong? He was lying on his nuts and was too lazy to move." That was what John told him, and that's why Marster won that bet.

—Texas

97

JOHN OUTWITS MR. BERKELEY

This story begins with a very covetous man, Mr. Berkeley, who was a very rich and a very selfish man, too. Everything he saw, he wanted. One day, he met an old woman who had a fine cow she was taking to market. He knew it was worth about a hundred dollars, but he said to the woman, "You don't want to take that cow all the way to the market. I will give you five dollars for it right here." Not knowing much about the value of anything, the old woman thought that five dollars was a lot of money, so Mr. Berkeley got the cow.

When she got home, she told her only son, whose name was John, what she had done, and he said, "Damn! Mommy, Mr. Berkeley really paid you nothing close to what that cow was worth. But I'm going to make Mr. Berkeley really do a flying dance for what he has done to us." So he made a plan. His mother had a nice bucket in the house filled with some good-looking sugar. John went and got some cow manure and other shit and put it into the bottom of a pan, and then covered that over with the sugar. He carried it down that same road that his mother was taking the cow earlier, knowing that was where Mr. Berkeley passed all of the time.

When Mr. Berkeley saw John and all that nice sugar, he asked him, "John, what do you have on your shoulder there?" John said, "Sugar, Mr. Berkeley, some nice sugar to sell at the market." Mr. Berkeley came over to him and said, "Well, that's pretty good-looking sugar. Why don't you sell it to me instead of carrying it all the way to the market?" John said, "Well, I want five hundred dollars for it." Well, Mr. Berkeley, when he saw something that he really liked, he just had to have it. So he paid him the five hundred dollars for the panful.

He carried it on home and invited all his friends to come and have tea with him so they could taste this wonderful sugar that he had found. They came and thought the sugar was just wonderful in their tea. After using the sugar for a few days, though, Mr. Berkeley dipped in his spoon and it came up smelling awful! He said, "Good God, I'm going to beat that John when I catch up with him." And he took off for John's house right away.

Well, John had thought out the whole plan. He had taken a large copper boiling pot that they use for making sugar, filled it with yams and potatoes and other provisions from the garden. He balanced the whole thing on three stones and built a large fire under the pot, and began to boil the whole thing down. But there was one spot where the fire was so hot it showed through the covering of ashes, which he covered over with fresh dirt.

As soon as Mr. Berkeley got there, he called out to John, and John answered, "I'm in here, Mr. Berkeley." And before Mr. Berkeley could say anything, John said, "Mr. Berkeley, Mr. Berkeley, come and see this pot that cooks food by itself." He hit the kettle as hard as he could with a whip, and he said, "Mr. Berkeley, just listen to that." Sure enough, the kettle was boiling. He hit it again, and the kettle seemed to boil even harder. Mr. Berkeley didn't have to hear the third crack of the whip when he said, "You have to sell me that pot that cooks food by just lashing it." John said, "Well, I have to have five hundred dollars for the pot and another five hundred for the special whip." So Mr. Berkeley gave it to him, five hundred for the pot and five hundred for the whip.

So he took it to this large field, put the pot on these stones, and brought lots of food to put into it. Then he invited all his friends to a great big cook-up, to show them how he was going to boil food without any fire. So all the friends came bright and early, before they had eaten their food at home, even, expecting to have a big feast at Mr. Berkeley's. Well, when they got there, they saw Mr. Berkeley taking this whip and hitting the pot, *Whop!* He gave it a hard lash but nothing happened. He hit it a second time, but the food stayed just as cold as when he put it in. He gave the pot a hundred lashes, and still the water stayed as cold as before. He was disappointed and getting mad now. And all his friends left, hungry and laughing at the same time.

Now, John went on to the next part of his plan. He killed a goat and took out its heart and had his mother put it inside of her dress, right on top of where her own heart was. He told her to play dead when he touched it with a knife. As soon as he saw Mr. Berkeley coming to him, as vexed as he could be, he took out a knife and he stabbed his mother right in the goat's heart, and she fell over. Now Mr. Berkeley supposed that he had seen John stab his mother, because his mother fell over as if she was dead. Mr. Berkeley said, "John, you have killed your mother." He was scared, you know, with the knife in John's hand and the blood all around. John said, "Oh, Mr. Berkeley, Mama will raise herself up once more, you'll see." So he took up this shell and he blew on it *pouu—uu*. His mother stirred a little. He blew it again *pouu—uu*; his mother opened her eyes. The third time he blew she sat up, and the fourth time she got up and started to walk around.

Mr. Berkeley was astonished. He asked, "John, what do you want for a knife that cuts like that?" John said, "Well I have to have five hundred dollars." So he gave John the money, and five hundred more for the shell.

Now he went home, got all his servants, his wife and his children, and put them all in a row. Again he invited all his friends over to see how he was going to kill all these people and then bring them back to life again. He took the knife and stabbed his wife and she fell dead. He took all the servants and killed them, and the rest of his family. They were all dead on the ground in front of him, so he blew on the shell, *pouu—uu*, and nothing happened. He blew again and again, from morning to night, but nobody came back to life. He looked around and said, "All right, I am going to kill John with just one stab, too, for God's sake."

This time, John had no other tricks, so Mr. Berkeley tied him up, wanting to shame John like John had shamed him in front of all his friends. He brought him up to the bay side, to the rum shop there, and started to have a drink with all his friends while they laughed at John, all tied up there. But another man, whose name was Wolf, passed by there. He saw John crying, and said to him, "Friend John, how did you get yourself in this fix?" John said, "I have discovered this huge gold field under the water on Mr. Berkeley's property, and you know how he is, being so selfish, so he has tied me up until he can get all that gold and split it up between us." Wolf said, "But it seems so cruel that you should be tied." And John said, "It is, it is, but you know Mr. Berkeley. He must have his gold. Maybe, if I told you where the gold is, you would want to have my half of it." Wolf said, "Would you do that?" And John said, "Yes, because he is making so much fun of me in front of his friends." So Wolf unloosened the ropes, and they exchanged clothes, and John tied him up just as tightly as he had been tied. So John went away and left Wolf there in his place; and when Mr. Berkeley came out of the rum shop later, he just picked up Wolf without looking and carried him out to his boat and went out on the open sea and shoved Wolf over and drowned him.

About three months later, Mr. Berkeley saw John coming toward him in the carriage he had taken when he changed places with Mr. Wolf. He said, "Is that you, John?" and John said, "Oh yes, Mr. Berkeley." He asked, "Well, how did you come back to life and get such a fine carriage?" John said, "Well, you remember when you threw me into the sea? Well, I fell right into a gold field itself!" Mr. Berkeley said to John, "You have to show me where this gold field is. Will you do that for me?" John said, "Yes, but you must give me something in return." Mr. Berkeley said he would give him anything he wanted. John said, "But you know it is deep in the ocean, and you must put weights on your body so you can get down to it." So John tied Mr. Berkeley as tightly as Mr. Berkeley had tied him, put some stones on his body and put him in the boat, went out on the open sea, and shoved him over. That's the gold mine Mr. Berkeley wanted, but now John had all the things that Mr. Berkeley had, and John was alive, too.

That's the reason why an envious and covetous man always loses when he tries to get too much.

—Trinidad

98
BLACK JACK AND WHITE JACK

There were two ladies, one colored
and one white, who came from foreign parts. The colored lady was supposed to be the maid of the white lady. So they came to live in this
strange land, where they didn't know anybody. On the first day that
they were there, they went out for a walk. And they took with them a
bottle of water each. They walked a mile. When the water was finished,
they turned back. The second day, they went for another walk, and they
took two bottles of water with them. This time they went two miles. That
water was finished, too, so they turned back. They went the third day
and they took three bottles of water. They went three miles, and when the
water was all gone they turned back again. Now on the fourth day they
took four bottles of water, and they went four miles, and the water was
all gone again. But they didn't turn back this time. They went on for
four more miles. They got thirsty, of course, and then they saw two
ponds. One was running white water, and one was running black water.
The white woman drank from the white pond, and the black woman
drank from the black pond. Then they returned home, and both fell very
sick. They called in the doctor, and the doctor said they were both pregnant. And they remained sick for the whole nine months. The time came
for the babies to be delivered. The white woman had a white son, and
the black woman had a black son. The white one called her son White
Jack. The black woman called her son Black Jack. Well, they grew up
together like brothers. They looked alike, except one was dark, the other
light.

After they had grown up to be young men, Black Jack said one day,
"Would you like to go out hunting?" And White Jack said that he
would go along with him. Black Jack brought the knife, which he always
carried with him. And they went out to hunt. They caught three different kinds of animals each—a lion, a unicorn, and a bear. They tamed
them so that the animals would do anything they asked them to do.

One day, while they were walking in the woods, they came to a crossroad, where there was a large tree. Black Jack stuck his knife into that
tree and said, "White Jack, if you come back and see that knife has
dropped and is all rusty, then you'll know I'm dead." So they took their

departure, each on one of the roads. They each had their three animals along.

Black Jack heard of a king that had a daughter. And every year a lion came there to destroy that girl. Any man who could kill that monster could have the girl to be his wife. So Black Jack made his way to the king's palace. He made arrangements that he would volunteer to kill the monster. The next day, the king sent his daughter in a coach out to the woods where this lion was, for this is what he had to do every year. And Black Jack was there, lying in ambush. When the monster came out after the girl, Black Jack said to one of his beasts, "Hold on, my lion, my unicorn, and my bear!" And his three beasts tore up this monster, and they killed him. Now Black Jack didn't want the king to know it was he who had killed the lion. So he asked the girl not to tell the father it was he, for he had some plan in his mind.

So, while they were going back, the coachman told the girl to say to the father it was he that killed the lion. He threatened to kill her if she did not. So the girl told the father that it was the coachman that killed the lion. And the king agreed to have the girl marry the coachman.

On the next day, Black Jack was passing by the palace, and the girl was looking out from the veranda. She saw Black Jack, and she said to the King, "Ah, Papa, Papa! That was the man who really saved me from the lion." And the king called him in. And they hanged the coachman for telling a lie. Two days after that, Black Jack married the girl.

The day after they were married, they were both on the veranda looking out, and Black Jack saw a cottage far away. Black Jack asked his wife, "What place is that over there? I would like to go there." "Many have gone there, and haven't returned; for there is an old woman who lives there who eats people," his wife told tim.

Black Jack replied, "I am not afraid. I will go." His wife could not persuade him not to go. After he went, she felt like she didn't have a husband, because she knew he would lose his life there.

Black Jack, with his lion, his unicorn, and his bear, walked about four miles till they reached a river. He met an old man with a boat in that river. He said to the old man, "Old Man, take me over this river, will you please?"

The old man said, "No sir! There is an old woman over there that eats people." Black Jack said, "Old Man, take me over the river, and I will give you a guinea." He said, "No sir, for many have gone and haven't returned."

Then Black Jack said, "Hold on, my lion, my unicorn, and my bear!" And his beasts took him over the river. He came to a gate, and he rapped on this gate. The name of this gate was Open-unto-me. Just then the old lady came along. She said to the gate, "Open-unto-me," and she and Black Jack went on in. But he left his three beasts outside. When he went in, the old woman said to herself, "Um, a pretty human this one is." Then she took him all through the house, you know. And when she got him to one certain room, she struck him dead with her magic, and she threw his body in a room with the many other bodies of the people she had killed before.

On that same day, White Jack returned from his journey and came to the tree. And he saw the knife on the ground and rusted. And he said to himself, "My brother, Black Jack, is dead. Wherever his body is, I must find him." So he set out in search of him. He walked all day till he came to the king's palace. He stopped and asked for a drink of water. Now the two Jacks, Black Jack and White Jack, looked so alike that this girl took him for her husband. And the father also. So White Jack slept with the girl that night. The next day, they were both on the same veranda looking out, and he asked her, "What place is that over yonder?" She told him, "You asked me that before. There is an old woman over there who eats people!" Then he said to the girl, "I want to go, and I will go." And he set off with his three beasts.

When he reached the river, he saw the same old man with the boat. He said, "Old Man, take me over this river, would you please?" He said, "No sir! I saw one man pass here like you, and he didn't come back."

White Jack said, "Old Man, if you take me over the river, I will give you ten guineas." He said, "No sir! There is an old woman over there who eats people."

White Jack said to his beasts, "Hold on, my lion, my unicorn, and my bear!" And his beasts took him over the river. When he got over the river, he saw the three beasts of Black Jack mourning. He was mad now. He rapped on the gate. The old woman said, "Open-unto-me!" and the gates opened and he went in. The old woman said, "Um, um, a pretty man to eat." With White Jack were the three beasts of Black Jack and his own beasts. When the old woman said "a pretty man to eat," he said, "The Devil and Hell, a man to eat! Go find my brother, Black Jack!" The old woman got scared, you know. She asked him to come into the rooms. He went, and took the beasts with him. When he reached that certain room, he would not go in. He started to threaten the old woman. She got so scared, and took up some of a bottled medicine to bring people back to life, and went to where Black Jack was, and used it on him till he came to life. As he got to life, White Jack said, "Hold on, my lion, my unicorn, and my bear!" And they tore the old woman to pieces.

They left the place. While they were on the way back, Black Jack did not tell White Jack that he was married to the king's daughter. So when they came near the king's palace, White Jack said he slept there last night with the daughter of the king. And Black Jack started to tell him it was his wife. But he was so mad that he hauled off and killed White Jack, because he had slept with his wife. Then he saw what he had done, killing this man who was like his brother and who had just saved his life. They had brought away with them the medicine which the old woman used. So Black Jack had it, and in his sorrow he brought back White Jack to life. Black Jack went home to his wife, and White Jack married to the king's next daughter.

And I was to the weddin', and I got a glass a wine and a kick.

—Antigua

99
PHILANEWYORK

———

One time, after Master and John had worked together for a long time, they got along real easy. So it happened that Master had to leave for a while, and he wanted to test out if John could run the plantation while he was away. So he told John that he was going north to New York and could John take care of things, when in fact Master just went a little ways up the road.

So after John thought that he had left, John called all his friends around and said, "Come on over and have a good time here. Master has gone off to Philanewyork and he won't be back until next Javember." So all the people on the plantation came up to the big house; they danced and sang and ate everything and just had a grand old time. Master heard about this, of course, and he blacked himself up and came to the party, and nobody there recognized him. John started into singing:

Turn your partner 'round and 'round,
And bring her back home again to me.

Then, after he was dancing around for a while, he grabbed somebody and started spinning him, and he looked awfully familiar. So while he was leading the dancing he sang:

> *Oh, Master, is that you?*
> *Oh, Master, is that you?*

Then he just kept on calling the dance:

> *Swing your partner 'round and 'round,*
> *And bring her back home again to me.*

Master, he was sweating by now, and he had to wipe his face. So John just kind of said to himself without thinking, ''Hmm, Ol' Master's wiped sweat off his face.'' And he kept on singing and dancing:

> *Swing your partner 'round and 'round,*
> *And bring her back home again to me.*

Now, the next time the circle went around, he could see Old Master's face as clear as can be. Now it came to him what he was seeing. John said, ''Oh, Master, is that you?'' and he kept singing that over and over. Next thing you knew, John was in the next county, and he didn't stop there either.

—Mississippi

100
THE BARN IS BURNING

During slavery time, there was a rich old master in Brunswick County that owned more than three hundred slaves. Among them was one very smart slave named Tom. What I mean by smart is that he was a smooth operator—he knew what was happening. He came to be so smart because he would crawl under the master's house every night and listen to the master tell his wife what kind of work he was going to have the slaves do the next day. When the master would come out of the house the next morning and begin to tell the slaves what kind of work he wanted them to do that day, Old Tom would say, "Wait just a minute, Master. I know exactly what you're going to have us do." So the master would stop talking and let Old Tom tell the slaves what he had in mind for them to do that day. Old Tom could always tell the slaves exactly what the master wanted them to do, too; and the master was very surprised, because he didn't know how Old Tom was getting his information.

Old Tom wanted to prove to his master that he was the smartest slave on the plantation, because the smartest slave always got the easiest work —and Old Tom was tired of working so hard. Sometimes the masters let their smart slaves sleep in a bed in the big house, too; so Old Tom had been dreaming about how, one day maybe, he would get to sleep in a real bed instead of on an old quilt on his cabin floor. And it wasn't long before his dreams came to be true, because the next week after Old Tom had started prophesying what work the slaves were supposed to do that day, Old Master told his wife that he thought he was going to bring Old Tom to live in the house with them. And he did, and he gave him a room to sleep in with a big old bed and everything. Old Tom was so tickled he didn't know what to do with himself—just think, living in the same house with Old Master.

One winter night, when the master and his wife were seated around the fire, the master called Old Tom in to test his smartness. He pointed to the fire and said, "Tom, what is that?" "That's a fire, Old Master," said Tom. "No, it isn't either," replied Old Master. "That's a flame of evaporation."

Just then a cat passed in front of the fire, and Old Master said, "Tom,

do you know what that was that just passed by in front of the fireplace?"
"That's a cat, sir," replied Tom. Then Old Master said, "No, it's not
either. That's a high-ball-a-sooner."

Old Tom was getting tired of answering questions by this time, so he
went over to the window and started looking out. The old master walked
over to the window where Tom was and said, "Tom, what is that you're
looking at through the window?" "I'm looking at a haystack," said
Tom. Then Old Master said, "That's not a haystack, that's a high
tower."

Then Old Tom sat down in a chair and started getting ready to go to
his room up in the attic to go to bed for the night. He didn't want to
get the carpet all spotted up with dirt in the living room, so he started
unbuckling his shoes and taking them off. When the old man looked and
saw Tom taking off his shoes, he said, "What are those, Tom?" And
Tom said, "Those are my shoes." "No, they aren't either," said Old
Master. "Those are your tramp-tramps."

Then the old master pointed through the archway to where a bed
could be seen in his bedroom, and said, "What's that I'm pointing to in
there, Tom?" "That's a bed," said Old Tom. "No, it's not either," said
Old Master. "That's a flowery bed of ease, and I'm going right now and
get in it because we've all got a hard day's work coming up tomorrow."

So the old master and the old missus went into their bedroom and
went to bed. Then Old Tom went on up to the attic room where they
had him sleeping and he got in his big old bed. But just then the cat
ran through the fire in the fireplace and caught on fire and started raising a howl. So Tom jumped out of bed and looked, and saw the cat run
out to the haystack and set it on fire. Old Tom was there at the window,
and when he saw the cat on fire and the haystack on fire, he started
yelling as loud as he could, "Master, Master, you better get up out of
your flowery bed of ease and put on your tramp-tramps because your
high-ball-a-sooner has run through your flame of evaporation and set
your high tower on fire." Old Master didn't move a peg—he just chuckled
to his wife and said, "Listen to that high-class slave up there using all
that Latin."

Then once more Old Tom yelled out, "Master, Master, I said that you
better get up out of your flowery bed of ease, and put on your tramp-
tramps, because your high-ball-a-sooner has run through your flame of
evaporation and set your high tower on fire."

But Old Master just chuckled to his wife again, and said, "That sure
is a smart slave, that Tom, isn't he? Just listen to him talking all that
Latin up there again."

Old Tom went on yelling like this about five more times. But when he saw that Old Master wasn't getting out of bed, he yelled, ''Master, you better get up out of that bed and put on your shoes and go out there and put out that haystack fire that your cat started, or else your whole damn farm's going to burn up!'' I guess that got Old Master up pretty quick!

—North Carolina

Part VII

IN THE END, NONSENSE

INTRODUCTION

Tricksters have no monopoly on non-sense; jocular stories abound, including ones that could almost be called entertainment ''routines'' because they are so fixed in form and topsy-turvy in subject. Many of them are told not only at tale-telling sessions but emerge in stage events of the variety shows and the ''fancy talk'' oratorical contests mentioned earlier.

Few of these entertainments actually tell a story. Instead, they are the kinds of clownish routines, told in the first person, that the wits of the community seem to feel free to break into on any social situation drifting toward nonsense. They are all controlled by a kind of formulaic repetition; in fact, in some of them, the repetition provides the humor. Sometimes the routines focus on the strange sounds that animals make, as in ''Animal Talk,'' and underscore the ability of the performer to display his range of talents in building such sound effects in a story.

I have placed them at the end of the book because they strongly resemble the kinds of little jokes found not only at the conclusion of tales but also in the final remarks of orations on topics as serious as the Gospel story at Christmas or the coming of the news of freedom on Emancipation Day. For, as one speechmaker from St. Vincent put it when he finished the major portion of a grandiloquent speech on Emancipation Day, ''Shall I continue?'' The audience shouted, ''Yes!'' of course, to which he replied:

> No, I will not, for if I continue these beautiful ladies will fall upon me like the falls of Niagara. No, if I go on I will break down the stage, leaving no place left for the more common orators who are to follow me. Under such circumstances, I will not, I cannot continue. But I will take my congratulations from you all, for I am an orator of orators, the cock with the brightest comb!

101
BIG-GUT, BIG-HEAD, STRINGY-LEG

There were three boys went out hunting—Bro' Big-Gut, Bro' Big-Head, Bro' Stringy-Leg. They traveled and traveled and traveled until they came to one hole with a banana tree in it, with one big ripe bunch of bananas on it. They wanted these bananas. And Bro' Big-Head said to Bro' Big-Gut, "You go up and get it, and bring it down and let me eat." And Bro' Big-Gut said, "No, man, you go up. My gut is too big." So Bro' Big-Head said to Bro' Stringy-Leg, "You go up." And Bro' Stringy-Leg said, "No, man, I can't go. My leg's so small it may break. You go up." Bro' Big-Head said, "No, you go! my head's too big. If I go, when I go, my head will burst, and I will kill myself."

So they all teased each other. Bro' Big-Head went up first. Just as he was going to put his hand on the bananas, his head swung back and he fell down and he mashed up himself fine, fine. And Bro' Gig-Gut laughed till his gut burst. Bro' Stringy-Leg ran so (to carry the news), his leg popped.

—*Bahamas*

102
A CHAIN OF WON'TS

Sometime back, I went to the market and I picked up a ha'penny. All I could buy with it was a little stick. I asked the stick to beat my goat. It said, "I won't beat the goat; it hasn't done me any harm.'' So I said to my cutlass, ''Cut the stick, because the stick won't beat the goat.'' ''No, I won't cut the stick, because it hasn't done me any harm.'' Then I begged the fire, ''Fire, burn the cutlass.'' Fire said, ''No, because the blade hasn't done me any harm.'' So I cried, ''Water, put out the fire, please, because the fire won't burn the cutlass.'' Water said, ''No, I won't because the fire hasn't done anything to me.'' So I passed a bull, and said, ''Bull, drink that water because it won't put out the fire.'' But Bull said, ''No, because the water hasn't done me any harm.'' So I ran to the butcher and said, ''Butcher, cut up that bull,'' and he said, ''No, because he hasn't harmed me in any way.'' So I saw a rope, and I told it to hang the butcher. ''I won't hang the butcher for he hasn't done anything to me.'' So I ran to the grease, there, and said, ''Grease, grease that rope.'' ''I won't grease the rope because it's done nothing to me.'' I met a cat: ''Cat,'' I said, ''eat that grease.'' ''I won't eat that grease because it has not harmed me in any way.'' So I ran to my dog and said, ''Dog, catch that cat.'' ''How can I catch that cat when it has done nothing to me?'' Now I got very vexed. ''Dog, catch that damned cat, for cat won't eat grease, grease won't grease rope, rope won't hang butcher, butcher won't cut bull, bull won't drink water, water won't drown fire, fire won't burn cutlass, cutlass won't cut stick, stick won't beat kid, and I'm not going to get home before midnight the way things are going.''

—*Montserrat*

103
ANIMAL TALK

———

One said to another, ''Tell the other one, other one, other one!'' till the word scattered over the whole world.

Cock said, ''If it's tru*uue*, yes!''

Horse stamped his foot on the earth, ''What's in my stomach, let it stay in there.''

Jackass said, "The world isn't equal!" (for if the world was level he would have to wear a cropper on his tail).

Cow said (slowly and drawlingly), *"Mas-sa wor-r-r-k ne-v-er don-n-ne!"*

Mule said (quickly and with energy), "It will done! it will done! it will done! Massa work will done!"

Crab said, "Mustn't trust shadows after dark!"

Ground Dove said, "My ears! my ears! my ears!" (that is, he won't listen to what his parents tell him).

Hopping Dick got up on a sharp stump and White Belly got up on a tall tree and made a bet, one bet who can stay the longest without eating. Hopping Dick said, "*Chem chem* cherry o!"

White Belly said,

> Coo coo coo, *me hearie you!*
> Coo coo coo, *me hearie you!*

Hopping Dick went down to the ground and picked up a worm. White Belly stayed up in the tree all that time. White Belly fell down dead.

—*Jamaica*

104
A COMIC CONVERSATION

Massa came down the road on his mule.
His boy said, "Howdy, Massa!"
Massa said, "Thank you boy. Dinner ready?"
"Yes, sir."
Clup, clop, clup, clop, clup, clop, clup, clop.
"Dinner ready, dinner ready?"
"Yes, sir; yes, sir."
Clup, clop, clup, clop, clup, clop, clup, clop.

"Dinner ready, dinner ready?"
"Yes, sir; yes, sir."
[Pause.]
"Howdy, Massa!"
"Thank you boy. Dinner ready?"
"Yes, sir."
Clup, clop, clup, clop, clup, clop, clup, clop.
"Dinner ready, dinner ready?"
"Yes, sir; yes, sir."
Clup, clop, clup, clop, clup, clop, clup, clop.
"Dinner ready, dinner ready?"
"Yes, sir; yes, sir."

—*Jamaica*

105
A SMOKING STORY

Cavalier took a ride across the desert on a Camel, just because he was in love with somebody called Fatima. Philip was blasting off to Morris. Now Raleigh decided since he had made a Lucky Strike he was going down to Chesterfield's. He had a whole pocketful of Old Gold. And so, last but not least, he decided to go on a Holiday.

—*Philadelphia*

106
THE THINGS THAT TALKED

One time, a man planted some nuts. He said to himself that he wasn't going to reap them until the "hard time" came around—that's October. But a famine came before then, so he took up his hoe, his basket, and his dog, and he went to the field to pick the nuts. When he got to the field, the hoe said, "I'm not going to dig anything!" The basket said, "I'm not going to carry anything." The dog laughed. So the man took up his hoe to hit his dog. The hoe stick said, "Watch out, or you'll make the dog bite me."

The man left his field and ran. And as he was running, he met up with a man carrying a bundle of wood on his head. And he told the man what had just happened. The man said, "And you are running away just because of that?" And the bundle of wood said, "What do you mean, are you running just because of that?"

—*Nevis*

107
ENDINGS

———

I had on a paper suit, so it looked like it was going to rain, so I couldn't-a stayed to see it end. (Wouldn't-a had nothing to wear home, you see.)

Had on a pair of old shoes and no heels and I stepped on a slippery plank and got to sliding, and I couldn't stop to see the end.

—Michigan

APPENDIX:
SOURCES, ANNOTATIONS,
AND INDEX OF TALES

As I indicated in the Preface, the provenance of these stories is a fascinating part of the record of Africans in the New World. I have therefore written rather long annotations for some of the stories that have interesting histories. After giving the source of each story, with a reference to one of the bibliographical entries, I survey the scholarship on that tale, using the following abbreviations:

Aa-Th Antti Aarne and Stith Thompson. *The Types of the Folktale.* Folklore Fellows Communications, no. 184. Helsinki: Finnish Scientific Academy, 1961.

Baer Florence C. Baer. *Sources and Analogues of the Uncle Remus Tales.* Folklore Fellows Communications, no. 228. Helsinki: Finnish Scientific Academy, 1981.

Bascom William Bascom. "African Folktales in America." A series of articles appearing in *Research in African Literature* 8–14 (1976–82).

Dorson Richard M. Dorson. *American Negro Folktales.* Greenwich, Conn.: Fawcett, 1976.

Dundes "African and Afro-American Tales." In Daniel J. Crowley, ed., *African Folklore in the New World,* 181–99. Austin: University of Texas Press, 1977.

Flowers Helen H. Flowers. *A Classification of Folktales of the West Indies by Types and Motifs.* New York: Arno Press, 1980.

JAF *Journal of American Folklore.*

Klipple May Augusta Klipple. "African Folktales in Foreign Analogues." Ph.D. dissertation, Indiana University, 1938.

Motif Stith Thompson. *Motif-Index of Folk Literature.* Bloomington: Indiana University Press, 1955–58.

RAL *Research in African Literatures.*

All other references are to articles and books given in the Bibliography. In each annotation the place of collection is given in italics, followed by the last name of the author-collector, then the page number on which the original text appears. The tales are arranged alphabetically according to the titles I have given them in the text, and the page on which they appear in this volume is given in parentheses after that title.

To a nonfolklorist, the numbers that denote tale types and motifs may be incomprehensible, so let me briefly explain their uses. These reference tools have made the comparative study of folktales possible but they have severe limitations that can cause a good deal of frustration to anyone wishing to run down the distributional history of a specific tale. The difficulties reflect as much the elusive character of oral tales as the inconsistent minds of the scholars who worked out the plan of these compendia. The tale-type index begun by Antti Aarne and revised by Stith Thompson assigns numbers and short descriptions to all tales that these scholars encountered in which the same sequence of episodes has been found in a number of geographical areas. Because the work grew out of annotations for the Grimm tales, it is considerably biased toward European reportings. The same is true of Thompson's *Motif-Index* (from which all my motif numbers are taken). Thompson attempted to redress the shortcomings of the early edition of this work by encouraging his graduate students to write dissertations on the body of lore from outside the Indo-European world; one result is the Flowers volume. These students made extraordinary efforts to assign existing Aarne-Thompson motif numbers to their data; only for the most recalcitrant materials were new numbers suggested. Nevertheless, the students each had an idiosyncratic reading of the master's words: so, for example, what Flowers assigns to one motif and its number, another student, such as May Klipple, places under a different number. Working with these documents has meant being issued hunting licenses!

That this has frustrated scholars who wish to study culture flow (from Africa or Europe) is abundantly recorded in the Baer, Bascom, and Dundes documents. Nonetheless, again and again, the numbering system has provided an accurate and intuitively insightful place to begin. The problem is complicated by Dorson's almost blind adherence to the Thompson descriptions to annotate his extensive collection of American Negro tales. It is from this base that he argues the essentially European or New World "origins" of North American black tales. Crowley usefully surveys this controversy in the introduction to *African Folklore in the New World*, as do Bascom and Baer in the introductions to their works.

As noted in the Preface, I have edited the stories. Generally, I have followed the wording of the original, changing only those passages that seemed most difficult or rendered in an archaic way. Of the stories I recorded myself, most were taken down in one or another form of Creole—some closer, some farther away from standard American English. I have attempted to maintain the narrative flow and the stylistic cadences of the narrator while taking out all the orthographic tricks that have been used to render black English as it is heard by the transcriber. My objective, of course, has been to make the texts more immediately understandable to readers. I have made no attempt to introduce stylistic homogeneity to the texts, but have translated as fully as I could the narrative "voice" of the original into the American vernacular. The more Creole the original, the more I have felt the need to translate. Thus, some stories depart from the recorded text more than others. This is especially so with texts recorded in the West Indies, the originals of which I plan to publish in a scholarly monograph.

Anansi Climbs the Wall (p. 210). *Jamaica*; Trowbridge, 286–87. Thompson A2261.2, "Spider Transformed for Greediness Now Occupies Dark Corners."

Flowers (373), has only two stories under this number, neither of which is a version of this story. On the other hand, under A2433.5.3, "Haunts of Spiders" (382), she has this story and no other. There are numerous other stories in which Death figures as a character in Afro-America.

Anansi Plays Dead (p. 207). *St. Vincent*; recorded by Abrahams. This is one of the most widely collected stories in Afro-America. Aa-Th 66B, Motif 607.3, "Sham Dead-Man Deceived into Making a Gesture." Found widely in Africa, though its provenance is widespread elsewhere, it is also found among American Indians. See Baer, 38–39; Dundes, 48.

Animal Talk (p. 301). *Jamaica*; Beckwith, 178. This has a passing reference to "the fasting contest," given here as "Fasting for the Hand of the Queen's Daughter," and treated by Bascom in RAL.

Assaulting All the Senses (p. 202). *Surinam*; Herskovits and Herskovits, 183–85.

The Barn Is Burning (p. 293). *North Carolina*; Brewer. 61–64. This is an international tale; it is widely found in this form in Great Britain, as reported by Kenneth Jackson and Edward Wilson in "The Barn Is Burning," *Folk-Lore* 47 (1947); 190–202. Dorson, 115, notes that though Aa-Th tale type 1833E has been suggested for its assignment, the tale is sufficiently distinct to have a number of its own.

Being Greedy Chokes Anansi (p. 122). *Jamaica*; Coleman-Smith, 278. Flowers cites five versions of this story under Motif C496*, "Tabu Using Certain Words" (409–10).

Between the Fiddler and the Dancer (p. 121). *Bahamas*; Parsons, *Andros*, 132–38.

Big-Gut, Big-Head, Stringy-Leg (p. 300). *Bahamas*; Parsons, *Andros*, This story is widely found in Europe as well as in the West Indies. Cf. Flowers, B610.1 (394).

Black Jack and White Jack (p. 288). *Antigua*; Johnson, 77–80. This is a version of Aa-Th 303. "The Twins or Blood Brothers," and is unusual only in the black-white references. Otherwise, the tale is well-known in the Old World (both Europe and Africa).

A Boarhog for a Husband (p. 108). *St. Vincent*; Abrahams, *Man-of-Words*, 171–72. This is one of the most common stories in the Antilles involving a marriage of the king's beautiful daughter with some kind of animal. Flowers, under Motif 610 (601?), "Marriage of Person to Beast," gives 29 versions, and a number of others under B611, "Beast Paramour"; B613, "Reptile Paramour"; B621, "Beast as Suitor"; B622, "Reptile as Wooer"; B640.1, "Marriage to Beast by Day and Man by Night"; B651, "Marriage to Beast in Human Form"; G81, "Unwitting Marriage to a Cannibal"; and D655, "Transformation to Receive Food," where there are two other texts in which the animal is a boarhog. Under this last number, she gives many African references, but none to European sources. Baer discusses the pattern in reference to the *Uncle Remus and His Friends* text "Why Brother Bull Grumbles and Growls." She argues that the story is clearly African but with the motive changed, for there the animal is going to eat his new wife. She refers (128) to Alice Werner's discussion of the pattern in Africa in which the notion of the younger brother saving his sister is central to the fiction. (Werner in Jeckyll, 191, 193, 196–97.)

Brer Bear's Grapevine (p. 147). *North Carolina*; Cobbs and Hicks, 14–18.

Brer Rabbit's Riddle (p. 203). *Georgia*; Harris, *Nights*, no. 10. This is an artful combination of an international tale—Aa-Th 49, K1023, "The Bear and the Honey"—and a motif of punishment found often in Africa, as Baer has noted (53). The introduction of the riddle as a way of piquing the fox's interest and leading him into a trap is unusual in this story, but a common Afro-American contest device in tales. See, for instance, "Three Killed Florrie, Florrie Killed Ten," "Making the Eyes Run," and "Never Seen His Equal."

Bringing Men and Women Together (p. 45). *Surinam*; Price and Price, 187–88.

Brother Rabbit Takes a Walk (p. 183). *Georgia*; Harris, *Nights*, no. 53. As Dundes notes, after giving references to a number of related African and U.S. texts, mouth mutilation is part of Trickster's repertoire. This is closely related to the voice-modification techniques, drinking acid or using a hot poker, called on by Trickster. Baer says, judiciously: "Structurally, and from the standpoint of motivation, the tale is related to Aa-Th 110, 'Belling the Cat.' The suggestion of sewing up or otherwise altering a bodily orifice is certainly a popular motif in Africa . . . but without evidence of closer analogues this tale would be most safely categorized as an Afro-American variant of a European tale" (98).

Buh Nansi Scares Buh Lion (p. 72). *Tobago*; recorded by Abrahams.

Buying Two Empty Hands (p. 142). *St. Vincent*; recorded by Abrahams.

A Chain of Won'ts (p. 300). *Montserrat*; Parsons, *Antilles*, 2:305. This "routine" derives from the very widely collected story called in English "The Old Woman and Her Pig," Aa-Th 2030. That these acts are not actually occurring but are part of the goat-owner's wishes and the delivery of the routine in the first person are the idiosyncratic features of this rendering. While Flowers (563–64) gives seven versions, and there are a number of reportings from Africa, the story is too widely found to say anything definitive about its pattern of dissemination.

A Comic Conversation (p. 302). *Jamaica*; Trowbridge, 278.

Competition for Laziness (p. 283). *Texas*; Abrahams, *Positively Black*, 66.

Crawling into the Elephant's Belly (p. 197). *Guyana*; C. D. Dance, 85–87. This strange and gory story is widely reported in the New World; the various renderings are discussed by Bascom in RAL 10 (1979): 323–40, where he argues its

African origins. It invokes one of the most common of all Afro-American episodes, in which a prohibition against eating too much results in the capture and/or death of the Trickster or dupe, a "motif" that often occurs inside a large animal's body. Flowers (227ff.) lists a number of versions of this story under Aa-Th 676, "Open Sesame," because entrance into the animal's belly is achieved through a password. In fact, the story is structurally related to that famous story of the robbers storing their booty inside a mountain, because Aa-Th 676 commonly involves the capture of the imitator because he forgets the password. In many West Indian versions, the imitator is caught both because of cutting the animal's heart and forgetting the password to get out.

The Cunning Cockroach (p. 163). *Antigua*; Johnson, 66–67. Motif A2494.5.18, "Enmity of Fowl and Cockroach," cited in Flowers (385–86). She gives so many stories explaining why chickens eat roaches that it is clearly a favorite subject in the West Indies.

Cutta Cord-La (p. 144). *Georgia*; Harris, *Nights*, 195–99. This is, according to Bascom in RAL 13 (1981) : 187–95, a combination of two distinctly African tales, "Agreement to Kill Mothers" and "Cutta Cord-La." In contrast to Thompson (who has it as Motif R311.3) and Flowers (who has it as K963, with a close analogue as K231.1.1), Baer argues that this story is most appropriately included under Aa-Th 123.

Dancing to the River (p. 211). *Jamaica*; Murray, 24–29. Flowers reports five versions of this story from the West Indies under Motif K622, "Captive Plays Further and Further Away from Watchman and Escapes." I have heard it many times in the West Indies, and this early (1877) text indicates that it has lived in the region for some time. In addition to these reports, Flowers notes the Uncle Remus tale (Harris, *Nights*, no. 3) and the Cape Verdean and African versions, but none from Europe. Baer says that it should be included under Aa-Th 122, "Other Tricks to Escape from Captor," and notes finally that "it is clearly an African Afro-American story."

The Devil's Doing (p. 62). *American South*; Branner, 28–30.

The Doings and Undoings of the Dogoshes (p. 123). *American South*; Branner, 80–82.

Don't Shoot Me, Dyer, Don't Shoot Me (p. 125). *St. Vincent*; recorded by Abrahams. Flowers (437) has a number of versions under F915, "Victim Speaks from the Swallower's Body," and refers only to African cognates. (Only her no. 2 and no. 3 are versions of this story, however.) Under D1619.2, "Eaten Object Speaks from Inside Person's Body," she includes three versions of this tale (426–31). The story is a strange one because in some versions (e.g., Fortier, 120) the animal (here a fish) is the lover of a girl who is sacrificing himself so she can eat him. He gives her orders to catch him up and eat him, as opposed to the prohibitions on such things in this version. In another version, from St. Vincent, that I collected, the bird has the benevolent protection of Compé Sun.

Endings (p. 305). *Michigan*; Dorson, *Negro Tales*, 281.

Escaping, Slowly (p. 240). *Jamaica*; Beckwith, 161–62.

Fasting for the Hand of the Queen's Daughter (p. 251). *Bahamas*; Parsons, *Andros*, 97–98. Again, Bascom has demonstrated that this is an African tale, with no European versions, in "Birds Fasting (Singing) Contest," RAL 9 (1979). Flowers (457) includes this story under the general rubric of H331, "Suitor Contests: Bride Offered as Prize."

The Feast on the Mountain and the Feast under the Water (p. 140). *Surinam*; Herskovits and Herskovits, 287–89.

The Fight over Life (p. 46). *Guadaloupe*; Courlander, 90–91. He gives an African version (585), and says that the story is widely told there. Flowers (368) refers to one Haitian text, under Motif A1335.

The Flying Contest (p. 230). *Surinam*; Herskovits and Herskovits, 193.

A Flying Fool (p. 280). *Texas*; Abrahams, *Positively Black*, 36. This tale is widely collected in the United States; see, for instance, Daryl Dance, *Shuckin' and Jivin'*, 13–14. She notes ten versions printed in other American collections (306).

A Foolish Mother (p. 149). *Providencia*; Washabaugh, 22–23.

Get Back, Get Back (p. 77). *Florida*; Hurston, 48–49. A number of explanatory tales for human coloration differences are found throughout the New World, stories with special power when found as part of the black repertoire. See, for instance, Daryl Dance, *Shuckin' and Jivin'*, 333–34, and the notes she provides there.

Getting Common Sense (p. 52). *Jamaica*; Bennett, 67. This story is widely found in the West Indies and the Guianas. It is given a new motif number by Flowers, H1263+, but she provides no descriptive name and includes a number of related stories concerned with God's decision, after a number of tests, that Trickster is wise enough already and doesn't need any more endowments. Bascom would surely have included this story in the general complex of the African-derived story "Trickster Seeks Endowments." See "Hankering for a Long Tail," below.

The Gifts of Dipper and Cowhide (p. 69). *Alabama*; Fauset, 215–16. From an informant, Cudjo Lewis, "born in Dahome (*sic*), West Africa about 85 years ago" (in 1927?).

The Girl Made of Butter (p. 167). *Bahamas*; Parsons, *Andros*, 125–26.

Golden Breasts, Diamond Navel, Chain of Gold (p. 223). *Surinam*; Herskovits and Herskovits, 401–13. A version of Aa-Th 850, "The Birthmarks of the Princess." Though widely found throughout the Indo-European world (including the Grimm collection), Herskovits notes (401) the especially African character of the locking up on the *ménage à trois*. The dances of the pigs are a special Surinamian note, relating the story to specific religious practices.

Goobers Gone, Rabbit Gone (p. 200). *Alabama*; Carmer, 181–83.

Hankering for a Long Tail (p. 53). *South Carolina*; Stoney and Shelby, 175–92. This is a version of one of the most widespread and interesting African tales, "Trickster Seeks Endowments," studied by Bascom in RAL 9 (1979): 218–55. As Bascom notes, this type readily divides in three in terms of the tasks assigned the figure who has unnatural needs to add a feature to his body (as here) or his abilities. The three tasks are often found together, often as separate stories (as in "Why They Name the Stories for Anansi"), and are: (1) Measuring the Snake; (2) Challenging Birds (Insects) to Fill a Container; (3) Milking a Cow (Deer) Stuck in a Tree.

He Pays for the Provisions (p. 159). *Tobago*; Abrahams, 347.

Hide Anger until Tomorrow (p. 141). *Surinam*; Herskovits and Herskovits, 347.

The Horned Animals' Party (p. 206). *Antigua*; Johnson, 59–60.

Horses Stay Outside (p. 281). *Alabama*; Carmer, 184.

Jack Beats the Devil (p. 255). *Florida*; Hurston, 70–77. This story brings together motifs from a number of fairytales without fitting specifically into one tale type. It begins, for instance, with Motif S22.3, "Youth Sells Himself to an Ogre in Settlement of a Gambling Debt."

The John Crows Lose Their Hair (p. 63). *Jamaica*; Rampini, 124–28. A2317.11, "Why John Crow Has Bald Head." Flowers (375) gives four references, two of them to other Jamaican versions of this story. Similar tales are found in the continental United States, as discussed in Baer (143–44), including a rare "Ann Nancy" version from Georgia. Dorson, 109–10, gives a different tale on this theme, a fight between Fox and Buzzard in which Buzzard sticks his head in a place where Fox can pull out Buzzard's head feathers.

John Outruns the Lord (p. 278). *Florida*; Hurston, 96–99. This story is widely found among black storytellers in the United States; it is commonly given Motif J217.0.1.1, "Trickster Overhears Man Praying for Death to Take Him." Daryl Dance gives a recently collected text in *Shuckin' and Jivin'*, 134, and notes other places it may be found in her notes (346–47), including one African reporting.

John Outwits Mr. Berkeley (p. 284). *Trinidad*; Parsons, *Antilles*, 3:48–58. This story well illustrates the problem of bringing together black tales and European-based motif and tale-type indices. This is an elaboration of the story pattern, widely found in Africa, of an unsuccessful and often fatal imitation by a dupe, assigned Motifs K941.1 and K913, which is part of Aa-Th 1535, "The Rich and Poor Peasant." (It is, in this rendering, put into the frame of a test of wits between a white power figure and a black subordinate.) As in Aa-Th 1535, the fatal imitation is combined with K842, "Fatal Deception," in which Trickster persuades a dupe to take his place being tied up. Aarne and Thompson indicate in their latest edition that, based on Flowers's West Indian tale-type and motif index, there are 20 versions of this tale type collected in the West Indies. Flowers, however, includes no references to Aa-Th 1535, nor to any stories under the Motif number K941 and its relatives. On the other hand, she does have three stories, closely related to the unsuccessful (fatal) imitation stories studied by Paulme in Africa, under K851, "Deceptive Game."

The Knee-High Man Tries to Get Sizable (p. 49). *Alabama*; Carmer, 177–78.

The Latest Song (p. 99). *Jamaica*; Jeckyll, 7–9. This is one of a great many stories found in Afro-America that involve teaching a song that then incriminates the singer. As Bascom argued in *RAL* 12 (1981): 203–12, the self-incrimination usually occurs for a slightly different crime: Trickster's consuming the children of his (larger) friend. For a related story, where the song is sung by the children of the miscreant (Motif K435), see "Poppa Stole the Deacon's Bull."

A License to Steal (p. 192). *Bahamas*; Parsons, *Andros*, 84–85. Under Motif K362, "Theft by Presenting False Order to Guardian," Flowers gives this and seven other versions from the West Indies. Baer (referring to the tale in Harris, *Nights*) assigns the story to Aa-Th 122Z, "Other Tricks to Escape from Captor," on the basis of its provenance in Africa; he says "it is clearly an African/Afro-American tale" (60–61).

The Lion in the Well (p. 185). *Mississippi*; Sale, 44–52. This is a combination of Aa-Th 20, "Animals Eat One Another Up: The Fox Persuades Them to Begin with the Smallest," and Aa-Th 92, "Lion Dives For His Own Reflection" (K1715.1). Baer (132) discusses the wide provenance of the latter tale.

The Little Bird Grows (p. 132). *Haiti*; Comhaire-Sylvain, 242–45. Tales of such large and demanding birds are found throughout the world; stories concerning them are assigned Aa-Th 1960J, "The Great Bird."

Little Boy-Bear Nurses the Alligator Children (p. 164). *Georgia*; Harris, *Nights*, no. 60. This story, which Harris reports from the Sea Islands, is very often found in Africa. See Aa-Th 37, "Fox as Nursemaid for Bear."

Little Eight John (p. 128). *North Carolina*; Aswell, 105.

Loggerhead (p. 232). *St. Vincent*; recorded by Abrahams.

Making the Eyes Run (p. 275). *Tobago*; recorded by Abrahams. This turns on the use of a common riddle as a "catch." The use of the riddling contest in this black versus white form is unusual as far as collections of tales are concerned. But the technique of using a riddle and its answer as an animating force in a story is widespread in Afro-America, and is represented in this book by "Never Seen His Equal," "Brer Rabbit's Riddle," and "Three Killed Florrie, Florrie Killed Ten."

Making the Stone Smoke (p. 97). *St. Vincent*; Abrahams, *Man-of-Words*, 169–70. Bascom argues in RAL 13 (1981) : 196–98, on the basis of four African and five U.S. reportings, with none from anywhere else, that this is an African tale. Though this is the first reported text from the West Indies, it is far from rare there, being one of the more common stories told at wakes.

Making a Wagon from a Wheelbarrow (p. 276). *Texas*; Brewer, 103.

The Man Makes and the Woman Takes (p. 42). *Florida*; Hurston, 49–54. The pattern of getting to the Lord to make your request first is far from unusual in Afro-American tales about the beginning of life; see, for instance, "The Fight over Life," above.

Meeting the King of the World (p. 85). *Florida*; Hurston, 171–74. This is a version of Aa-Th 157, "Learning to Fear Man" (Motif 517). This is a tale found often in the United States (Owens has it in his early article, for instance) and the West Indies, but not found in Africa nearly as often as in Europe. See Baer, 102.

Mr. Bamancoo Gets Dropped (p. 87). *St. Vincent*; recorded by Abrahams.

Mr. Possum Loves Peace (p. 75). *Georgia*; Harris, *Songs*, no. 3. Baer, surveying what has been said of the piece, calls it "quite possibly an indigenous American Negro tale" (31).

My Mother Killed Me, My Father Ate Me (p. 113). *Providencia*; Washabaugh, unpaged. The tale is a version of Aa-Th 780B, "The Speaking Hair"; Flowers groups it with "The Singing Bones" (Aa-Th 780).

Never Seen His Equal (p. 41). *Michigan*; Dorson, *Negro Tales*, 281–82.

No Chicken Tonight (p. 216). *Georgia*; Harris, *Songs*, no. 1. This version of Aa-Th 122, "The Wolf Loses His Prey: Escape by False Plea," is recognized by Baer (28–29) as a paradigmatic African form of fable involving the duping and then a clever escape by Trickster. This rendering calls for a combination of Motifs K757, "Capture by Feigning Illness," and K567, "Escape by Pretending to Perform Errand [do work] for Captor." Of Flowers's stories listed under Aa-Th 122, only the Beckwith Jamaican text "The Goats in the Lion's Den" is a version of this tale.

No Justice on Earth (p. 78). *Surinam*; Herskovits and Herskovits, 419. This is a version of the international tale "Devil Always Blamed," Aa-Th 846. While the ironic cast of the story is characteristic of Afro-American tales, it is almost never reported in Afro-American collections. Though Flowers does not list any versions under this number, it may be found in Beckwith's Jamaican collection (70–71) ; the Herskovitses provide a number of references to African tellings (418–19).

The Old Bull and the Young One (p. 244). *St. Vincent*; Abrahams, *Man-of-Words*, 173–77. This story, found widely throughout the West Indies, is listed as L111.1*, "Fugitive Bull Calf Returns when Grown and Defeats His Father." Details of the loss of the body parts are consistent and are a typically African folktale device, as is the opening segment in which all the men-children (or women-children) are ordered killed.

Old Granny Grinny Granny (p. 151). *Georgia*; Harris, *Nights*, no. 54. Motif G.61.1, "Child Recognizes Relatives' Flesh," describes to some extent the ending of the first part. Both Baer and Bascom relate the story to Aa-Th 1530, "Holding Up the Rock," but Bascom notes that the motivation for the holding (of a tree, in this instance) is quite different in using the ruse as a device of escape. He argues that a separate tale type exists here, one that is characteristically African and Afro-American. See Bascom, RAL 11 (1980) : 479–95.

The One-Legged Turkey (p. 277). *St. Lucia*; Parsons, *Antilles*, 1:156. Flowers (568), assigns this K402.1, "The Goose Without a Leg."

The Owl Never Sleeps at Night (p. 66). *American South*; Branner, 24–25.

Philanewyork (p. 291). *Mississippi*; Fauset, 267.

Pig's Long Nose and Greedy Mouth (p. 50). *American South*; Branner, 36–39.

The Poor Man and the Snake (p. 130). *Georgia*; Jones, 46–50.

Poppa Stole the Deacon's Bull (p. 169). *Philadelphia*; Abrahams, *Deep Down*, 183–85. This is version Aa-Th 1735A, "The Bribed Boy Sings the Wrong Song," K1631 and K435, "Child's Song Incriminates Thief." It is one of many stories told in Afro-American tradition in which a key revelation is made in a song; in this case, the idea is embodied in a joke rather than the more discursive type of tale. For songs of self-incrimination, see "The Latest Song," above.

The Race between Toad and Donkey (p. 194). *Jamaica*; Jeckyll, 39–43. This well-known tale, usually known as the race between the tortoise and the hare, is Aa-Th 1974, "Race Won by Deception; Relative Helpers." It is found world-wide, but is especially popular throughout Africa and Afro-America. All the indices from these areas include a number of versions, and Baer (44–45) following Mofokenge's argument, establishes that the New World black versions came from African sources. For a prototypical African rendition, see Abrahams, *African Folktales*, 75–78, where the race for the hand of the King's daughter is between Falcon and Tortoise, the latter being a man who has been transformed into the animal.

The Rooster Goes Away in a Huff (p. 175). *American South*; Owens, 749–50.

The Signifying Monkey (p. 101). *Philadelphia*; Abrahams, *Deep Down*, Aa-Th 59, "Jackal Carries False Challenges. . . ." Motif K1084, "Liar Brings About Fight between Dupes." Widely collected as both a toast and a story in the United States, this tale might seem to be a New World confection. But the idea of a fight or contest stirred up by Trickster is in fact widely found in Africa, strongly suggesting that this is an importation from that part of the Old World.

316

The stories listed in the Aa-Th tale-type index represent a cognate Indian tradition, but it is sufficiently distinct to suggest that a different tale-type number should be assigned to this story in the future. Henry-Louis Gates has written an important article concerning this and other "signifying monkey" texts (see Bibliography). For a different development of this kind of drummed-up fight, see "The Tug-of-War between Elephant and Whale."

The Singing Bones (p. 105). *Tobago*; recorded by Abrahams. As noted in the Introduction, this is a version of international tale Aa-Th 780. This story, as well as the related "My Mother Killed Me, My Father Ate Me" and "The Telltale Pepper Bush," is included by Flowers (252–55).

The Sinking of the *Titanic* (p. 282). *Philadelphia*; Abrahams, *Deep Down*, 120–29.

A Smoking Story (p. 303). *Philadelphia*; Abrahams, *Deep Down*, 255.

Some Up and Some Down (p. 33). *Texas*; Abrahams, *Positively Black*, 51–52. Aa-Th 32, "The Wolf Descends into the Well in One Bucket and Rescues the Fox in the Other." Motif K651. Baer suggests that this is a European-derived tale, though it has been widely collected among Afro-Americans in the United States.

Spreading Fingers for Friendship (p. 124). *Surinam*; Herskovits and Herskovits, 355.

Stackolee (p. 238). *Philadelphia*; Abrahams, *Deep Down*, 129–42.

A Strange Way to Sleep (p. 199). *Louisiana*; Fortier, 25. Bascom surveys Old and New World versions of this surprisingly widespread story (surprising because of the unusual stupidity of Trickster) in RAL (1979): 57–74.

Tadpole Loses His Tail (p. 65). *American South*; Branner, 31–33.

The Telltale Pepper Bush (p. 94). *St. Vincent*; recorded by Abrahams. Like "My Mother Killed Me, My Father Ate Me," this is a version of Aa-Th 780B, "The Speaking Hair." However, on the basis of the evidence, this story is a localized version of sufficient stability that it should be assigned a new number (780C?), with variants reported not only from the British and French Antilles but from Puerto Rico, the Dominican Republic, and Cuba.

Testing the Good Lord (p. 74). *Mississippi*; Puckett, 559.

They Both Had Dead Horses (p. 270). *Florida*; Hurston, 64–68.

The Things That Talked (p. 304). *Nevis*; Parsons, *Antilles*, 2:350. This story is widely collected with both talking objects and talking animals, and how this talking surprises humans. Parsons not only gives versions from throughout the Antilles but in her notes (3:300) indicates a great many other Afro-American sources. Flowers assigns the stories Motifs D1610, "Magic Speaking Objects," and C811.2, "Tabu: Heeding Magic Yam That Says Not to Pick It," neither of which really suit the story. Dundes (50) is much closer to the mark in placing it as Aa-Th 1705, "Talking Horse and Dog." An individual is frightened by a talking animal (e.g., a horse); when he remarks on this to his dog, he is astonished to get a response. He calls attention to the relationship of the tale to a shaggy-dog story. Dundes remarks, in summary of the animal story, that "it does not occur in Europe, and it apparently does in Africa." (50).

Three Killed Florrie, Florrie Killed Ten (p. 260). *St. Vincent*; recorded by Abrahams. The story invokes the most common neck-saving riddle in the West Indies, about the poisoned animal poisoning others, which leads to further adventures. As a riddle involved in the story of the prisoner who saves his neck by profounding a riddle the king or judge cannot guess, it is called Aa-Th 923, "Out-Riddling the Judge," and is treated in Abrahams, *Between the Living and the Dead*. The story in which it is found here is the international tale Aa-Th 851, "The Princess Who Cannot Solve the Riddle," which is where we find most West Indian versions of the riddle listed in Flowers (265–69). The final question about Cricket comes from yet another widely found tale, Aa-Th 1635, "Dr. Know-All," K1956, "Sham Wise Man."

Tiger Becomes a Riding Horse (p. 91). *Jamaica*; Rampini, 116–19. This tale, Aa-Th 72, "Rabbit Rides Fox A-Courting," and Aa-Th 4, "Carrying the Sham Sick Trickster" is the most commonly heard Anansi story in the anglophonic West Indies. (I was never at a wake where it didn't come up in some form.) This particular version comes from its earliest appearance in print from Afro-America (1877), though its telling in *Letters from Jamaica* is not very different from later reports, except perhaps for its fullness and some of its literary flourishes. Harris himself had no doubt of its African origin in his introduction to *Uncle Remus*. Dundes (188) surveys the evidence, as does Baer (34–35.)

Tricking All the Kings (p. 136). *St. Vincent*; Parsons, *Antilles*, 97–100. This is a wonderfully strung together set of motifs by a master storyteller. The opening section is Aa-Th 175, "The Tar-Baby and the Rabbit" (Motif K741). The shark incident involves another, and the Lion episode yet two more, one of which is Aa-Th 73, "Blinding the Guard."

"Trouble" Coming Down the Road (p. 214). *Surinam*; Herskovits and Herskovits, 293–94. This story has two parts, the second of which (the escape of Rabbit by blowing pepper in Tiger's face) is classified as Aa-Th 73, "Blinding the Guard," a story found in many parts of the world. But, as Baer points out, only African and Afro-American versions call for a blinding by throwing sand, blowing pepper, or spitting tobacco juice. Elsewhere, the captor simply gives up the guarding after a while, drifting away. Dundes summarizes the evidence (48), pointing out that the tale in its many versions is extremely rare in Europe, while found throughout the black world; Baer concurs strongly (94–95). The escape is found in combination with a number of other tales in the black world, in this case Aa-Th 157, "Learning to Fear Man"—though here the word "Hunter" is not specified as a man. See "Meeting the King of the World" for a different rendition of the idea.

The Trouble with Helping Out (p. 173). *Surinam*; Penard and Penard, 248–50. The first part of this story is a version of Aa-Th 155, "The Ungrateful Snake Returned to Captivity." Flowers refers to three African reportings and gives summaries of a number of West Indian tales she says are versions. One draws on the typical African-style solution of having the judge call for a reenactment of the original situation and, as a judgment, returning the ungrateful animal to its original predicament. In this case, the ungrateful snake turns into a helping creature.

Trying to Get the Goldstone (p. 234). *Georgia*; Pyrnelle, 112–18.

The Tug-of-War between Elephant and Whale (p. 89). *Louisiana*; Fortier, 116–20. There seem to be two traditions to this story, both widely found in Africa and Afro-America. The first has Trickster tying the rope to a root or trunk of a tree (which is how we find it in *Uncle Remus*, no. 26); the other has an arranged tug-of-war between the two largest animals. Flowers (495–97) notes 11 West Indian tests under Motif K22, "Deceptive Tug of War," all of them of this second variety. Baer, on the hand, under both Aa-Th 291 and Motif K22, argues the primacy of the first type in the black world (51–52), drawing on the comparative work within Africa by Motokeng (6–122, esp. 33–38, 95, 97–99, 101, 117–18). The story is widespread in Africa and seldom found elsewhere, although Aarne-Thompson refer to two Amazonian sources. The relationship of this story to "The Signifying Monkey" is patent, though this tale involves the carrying back and forth of false challenges and insults (cf. Aa-Th 59*, Motif 1084). On occasion, the tug-of-war begins because Trickster himself challenges first one and then another large animal; see, for instance, Parsons, *Andros*, 74–75. Parsons, *Antilles*, 3:77, provides notes to a great many African sources. Though these should have been assigned the same tale-type and motif numbers by Flowers, she does not so include them. Indeed, the only story she has under K1084, "Liar Brings About Fight between Dupes," is not this story at all. The motif of the trees and stones crying "Shame" is found in a number of other West Indian stories; see, for example, Parsons, *Antilles*, 3:97–98.

Turning into *Nóuna*—Nothing (p. 241). *Surinam*; Price, 13–14.

Weak in the Day and Strong at Night (p. 253). *Haiti*; Courlander, 74.

What Makes Brer Wasp Have a Short Patience (p. 119). *South Carolina*; Stoney and Shelby, 81–84. Motif A2302, "Animal's Body Made Smaller." Flowers (374) has one version of this story, from Jamaica.

Why Hens Are Afraid of Owls (p. 68). *Kentucky*; Harmon, 114.

Why They Name the Stories for Anansi (p. 182). *Tobago*; recorded by Abrahams. This impossible task (Motif *K713.4, "Trickster Ties Snake to Stick in Pretense of Measuring His Length") is often connected with Trickster's desire to be more cunning. As Bascom has shown in RAL 9 (1978): 216, it is very often found, in combination with other tasks, in Africa and Afro-America. He notes that Trickster's task story is "perhaps best known in the Ashanti version

in which Anansi . . . seeks the right to have folktales known as 'Anansi stories.' "
However, as far as I have been able to discover, this design is unique in New
World texts. Baer (82–84) discusses the pattern with regard to the *Uncle Remus*
text; see also Dundes (37–38). Flowers lists the tale as H12631, to which she
gives no title, though something like "Quest for Great Wisdom (Cunning)"
might be appropriate; but none of the versions she cites involves the measure-
ment of the snake. More appropriate would have been H1154, "Task: Capturing
Animals," but Flowers does not include the West Indian versions here. Dundes
has uncovered a number of American Indian texts that he regards as borrowing
from blacks. His dictum on the subject: "Clearly this is an African Afro-
American Tale Type" (38).

The Wind and the Water Fighting (p. 47). *Florida*; Hurston, 166–67.
Herskovits (274), comments on the similarity of technique (especially the per-
sonification of natural forces) with tales he collected in Dahomey, but similar
stories are found in other parts of the Old World as well. See Aa-Th 298, "The
Frostgod and his Son," for example.

The Woman Who Was a Bird (p. 111). *Bahamas*; Parsons, *Andros*, 39–43.

The Word the Devil Made Up (p. 48). *Florida*; Hurston, 204–5.

Words Without End (p. 1). *Tobago*; recorded by Abrahams. This type of
story without an end is given a catchall number, 1199, in the Aarne-Thompson
Index. This version is closest to 1199B, "The Long Song," which involves singing
a never-ending song as a respite from death. Flowers includes no West Indian
stories under this number. Motif K551, "Respite from Death Granted until
Particular Act Is Performed," is embedded in a number of other, more complex
tale types.

You Never Know What Trouble Is until It Finds You (p. 153). *South Caro-
lina*; Stoney and Shelby, 87–97. This is one of the most common Uncle Remus
stories, included not only in Harris's *Nights*, no. 26, but also in Jones and
Dorson. The latter gives one text (79–80) and refers to another he has collected.
Baer (71–72, 77–78), discussing this Uncle Remus story and the related "Mr.
Fox Figures as an Incendiary" (Harris, *Nights*, no. 17), suggests that Motif
K1055, "Dupe Persuaded to Get into Grass . . . Grass Is Set on Fire," which is
usually assigned to these stories is not really appropriate. She suggests *K1055
"Dupe Asleep in Field of Grass Finds 'Trouble' ('Devil') When Grass Is Set on
Fire."

You Talk Too Much, Anyhow (p. 274). *Alabama*; Fauset, 277. Bascom treats
this African tale in his initial article on "African Folktales in America," RAL
(1977): 267–91. He gives 43 versions of the story: 24 from Africa, 19 from the
New World.

BIBLIOGRAPHY

Aarne, Antti, and Stith Thompson, eds. *The Types of the Folktale: A Classification and Bibliography.* Translated and enlarged by Stith Thompson. Folklore Fellows Communications, no. 184. Helsinki: Finnish Scientific Academy, 1961.

Abrahams, Roger D. *African Folktales.* New York: Pantheon Books, 1983.

Abrahams, Roger D. *Between the Living and the Dead: Riddles Which Tell Stories.* Folklore Fellows Communications no. 225. Helsinki: Finnish Scientific Academy, 1980.

Abrahams, Roger D. *Deep Down in the Jungle: Negro Narratives from the Streets of Philadelphia.* Chicago: Aldine, 1970.

Abrahams, Roger D. *The Man-of-Words in the West Indies.* Baltimore: Johns Hopkins University Press, 1983.

Abrahams, Roger D. *Positively Black.* Englewood Cliffs, N.J.: Prentice-Hall, 1970.

Abrahams, Roger D., and John Szwed, eds. *After Africa.* New Haven: Yale University Press, 1983.

Abrahams, Roger D. and John Szwed, eds. *Discovering Afro-America.* Leiden: E. J. Brill, 1975.

Aswell, James, et al. *God Bless the Devil: Liar's Bench Tales.* Chapel Hill: University of North Carolina Press, 1940.

Baer, Florence C. *Sources and Analogues of the Uncle Remus Tales.* Folklore Fellows Communications, no. 228. Helsinki: Finnish Scientific Academy, 1981.

Beckwith, Martha Warren. *Jamaica Anansi Stories.* Memoirs of the American Folklore Society, vol. 17. New York: American Folklore Society, 1924.

Ben-Amos, Dan, ed. *Forms of Folklore in Africa.* Austin: University of Texas Press, 1977. (The articles are reprinted from *Research in African Literatures*; that of Denise Paulme is translated into English.)

Bennett, Louise. *Anansi and Miss Lou.* Kingston: Sangster's Book Stores, 1979.

Branner, John C. *How and Why Stories.* New York: Henry Holt, 1921.

Brasch, Walter M. *Black English and the Mass Media.* Amherst: University of Massachusetts Press, 1981.

Brewer, Mason J. *Worser Days and Better Times.* Chicago: Quadrangle Books, 1965.

Brown, Virginia Pounds, and Laurella Owens. *Toting the Lead Row: Ruby Pickens Tart, Alabama Folklorist.* University: University of Alabama Press, 1981.

Brown, William Wells. *My Southern Home.* Boston: A. G. Brown, 1980.

Carmer, Carl. *Stars Fell on Alabama.* New York: Doubleday, 1934.

Cobbs, Lucy A., and Mary Hicks. *Animal Tales of the Old North State.* New York: E. P. Dutton, 1938.

Coleman-Smith, Pamela. "Two Negro Stories from Jamaica." *Journal of American Folklore* 9 (1896) : 278.

Comhaire-Sylvaine, Suzanne. "Creole Tales from Haiti." *Journal of American Folklore* 50 (1937) : 207–306; 51 (1938) : 219–346.

Courlander, Harold. *Afro-American Folklore.* New York: Crown, 1976.

Crowley, Daniel C. *I Could Talk Old-Story Good.* Berkeley: University of California Press, 1966.

Dance, C. D. *Chapters from a Guianese Log-Book.* Demara, 1881. Pp. 85–90.

Dance, Daryl Cumber. *Shuckin' and Jivin': Folklore from Contemporary Black Americans.* Bloomington: Indiana University Press, 1978.

Dillard, J. L. *Black English: Its History and Usage in the United States.* New York: Random House, 1972.

Dorson, Richard M. *American Negro Folktales.* Greenwich, Conn.: Fawcett, 1967.

Dorson, Richard M. *Negro Tales from Pine Bluff, Arkansas, and Calvin, Michigan.* Bloomington: Indiana University Press, 1958.

Dundes, Alan. "African and Afro-American Tales." In Daniel J. Crowley, ed., *African Folklore in the New World,* 181–99. Austin: University of Texas Press, 1977.

Fauset, Arthur Huff. "Negro Folktales from the South (Alabama, Mississippi, Louisiana)." *Journal of American Folklore* 40 (1927) : 211–78.

Flowers, Helen H. *A Classification of Folktales of the West Indies by Types and Motifs.* New York: Arno Press, 1980.

Fortier, Alcee. *Louisiana Folk-Tales.* Boston and New York: G. E. Steckert, 1895.

Gates, Henry-Louis. "On 'The Blackness of Blackness': A Critique of the Sign and the Signifying Monkey." *Critical Inquiry* 9 (1983) : 685–723.

Harmon, Marion F. *Negro Wit and Humor.* Louisville, Ky.: Harmon, 1914.

Harris, Joel Chandler. *Nights with Uncle Remus.* Boston: Houghton Mifflin, 1881.

Harris, Joel Chandler. *Uncle Remus and His Friends: Old Plantation Stories, Songs and Ballads, with Sketches of Negro Character.* Boston: Houghton Mifflin, 1882.

Harris, Joel Chandler. *Uncle Remus, His Songs and His Sayings.* New York: D. Appleton, 1880.

Herskovits, Melville J. *The Myth of the Negro Past.* New York: Harper's, 1941.

Herskovits, Melville J. and Frances S. Herskovits. *Suriname Folk-Lore.* New York: Columbia University Press, 1936.

Hughes, Langston, and Arna Bontemps. *The Book of Negro Folklore.* New York: Dodd, Mead, 1949.

Hurston, Zora Neale. *Mules and Men.* Philadelphia: Lippincott, 1935.

Jeckyll, Walter. *Jamaican Song and Story.* London: David Nutt, 1907.

Johnson, John H. "Folklore from Antigua, British West Indies." *Journal of American Folklore* 34 (1921) : 40–83.

Jones, Charles Colcock. *Negro Myths from the Georgia Coast, Told in the Vernacular.* Boston: Houghton Mifflin, 1888.

Klipple, May Augusta. "African Folktales with Foreign Analogues." Ph.D. dissertation, Indiana University, 1938.

Laws, G. Malcolm. *American Ballads from British Broadsides*. Philadelphia: American Folklore Society, 1957.

Levine, Lawrence W. *Black Culture and Black Consciousness*. New York: Oxford University Press, 1977.

McCloud, Velma. *Laughter in Chains*. New York: Lenox Press, 1901.

Mofokeng, Sophonia Machabe. "The Development of Leading Figures in Animal Tales in Africa." Ph.D. dissertation, University of Witwatersrand, South Africa, 1954.

Morgan, Kathryn L. *Children of Strangers: The Stories of a Black Family*. Philadelphia: Temple University Press, 1980.

Murray, Henry. *Manners and Customs in the Country a Generation Ago: Tom Kittle's Wake*. Kingston: E. Jordan, 1877.

Ong, Walter, J. *Orality and Literacy*. London and New York: Methuen, 1982.

Owens, William A. "Folklore of the Southern Negroes." *Lippincott's Magazine* 20 (1877) : 748–55.

Parsons, Elsie Clews. *Folk-Lore of the Antilles, French and English*. 3 vols. Memoirs of the American Folk-lore Society, vol. 26. New York: American Folklore Society, 1933, 1936, 1943.

Parsons, Elsie Clews. *Folklore of the Sea Islands, South Carolina*. Memoirs of the American Folk-lore Society, vol. 16. Cambridge, Mass., and New York: American Folk-lore Society, 1923.

Parsons, Elsie Clews. *Folk-Tales of Andros Island, Bahamas*. Lancaster, Pa., and New York: American Folk-lore Society, 1918.

Parsons, Elsie Clews. "Folklore from Aiken, South Carolina." *Journal of American Folklore* 34 (1921) : 1–39.

Parsons, Elsie Clews. "Tales from Guilford County, North Carolina." *Journal of American Folklore* 30 (1917) : 168–200.

Penard, A. P., and T. E. Penard. "Suriname Folk-Tales." *Journal of American Folklore* 30 (1917) : 239–50.

Peterkin, Julia. *Roll Jordan, Roll*. New York: Bobbs-Merrill, 1933.

Price, Richard. *First Time: the Historical Vision of An Afro-American People*. Baltimore: Johns Hopkins University Press, 1983.

Price, Richard, and Sally Price. *Afro-American Arts of the Suriname Rain Forest*. Los Angeles: University of California Press, 1980.

Puckett, Newbell Niles. *Folk Beliefs of Southern Negroes*. Chapel Hill: University of North Carolina Press, 1926.

Pyrnelle, Louise-Clark. *Diddie, Dumps and Tot, or Plantation Child Life*. New York: Harper & Bros., 1898.

Rampini, Charles. *Letters from Jamaica*. Edinburgh, 1873.

Rawick, George. *From Sun-Down to Sun-Up: The Making of the Black Community*. Westport, Conn.: Greenwood Press, 1972.

Sale, John B. *The Tree Named John*. Chapel Hill: University of North Carolina Press, 1929.

Stoney, Samuel Gaillard, and Gertrude Mathews Shelby. *Black Genesis, A Chronicle*. New York: Macmillan, 1930.

Thompson, Stith. *Motif-Index of Folk Literature*. Bloomington: Indiana University Press, 1955–58.

Trowbridge, Ada Wilson. "Negro Customs and Folk-Stories of Jamaica." *Journal of American Folklore* 9 (1896) : 279–87.

Washabaugh, Bill and Cathy. *The Folkways of Old Providence*. Providencia, mimeographed, n.d.

Werner, Alice. "Introduction." In Walter Jeckyll, *Jamaican Song and Story*, ix–xxxvii. London: David Nutt, 1907.

PERMISSIONS ACKNOWLEDGMENTS

We are grateful to the following for permission to reprint or adapt from previously published material. In the case of adaptation, the author may have retitled some of the tales. *JAF* indicates *Journal of American Folklore; MAFS, Memoirs of the American Folklore Society*.

"Animal Talk" and "Escaping, Slowly" from *Jamaica Anansi Stories* by Martha Warren Beckwith, *MAFS*, vol. 17: 178, 161–62 (1924). By permission of the American Folklore Society.

"Assaulting All the Senses," "The Feast on the Mountain and the Feast Under the Water," "The Flying Contest," "Golden Breasts, Diamond Navel, Chain of Gold," "Hide Anger until Tomorrow," "No Justice on Earth," "Spreading Fingers for Friendship," and " 'Trouble' Coming Down the Road," from *Suriname Folk-Lore* by Melville J. Herskovits and Frances S. Herskovits. Columbia University Contributions to Anthropology Series. Copyright 1936 by Columbia University Press. By permission of the publisher.

"The Barn Is Burning" and "Making a Wagon from a Wheelbarrow" from *Worser Days and Better Times* by Mason J. Brewer. Copyright © 1965 by Mason J. Brewer. By permission of Times Books, a division of Random House, Inc.

"Between the Fiddler and the Dancer," "Big-Gut, Big-Head, Stringy-Leg," "The Girl Made of Butter," "A License to Steal," "The Woman Who Was a Bird," and "Fasting for the Hand of the Queen's Daughter" from *Folk-Tales of Andros Island, Bahamas* by Elsie Clews Parsons. *MAFS*, vol. 13: 137–38, 147, 125–26, 84–85, 39–43, 97–98 (1918). By permission of the American Folklore Society.

"Black Jack and White Jack," "The Cunning Cockroach" and "The Horned Animals' Party" from "Folklore from Antigua, British West Indies" by John H. Johnson. *JAF*, vol. 34: 77–80, 66–67, 59–60 (1921). By permission of the American Folklore Society.

"A Boarhog for a Husband," "He Pays for the Provisions," "Making the Stone Smoke," and "The Old Bull and the Young One" from *The Man-of-Words in the West Indies* by Roger D. Abrahams. Copyright © 1983 by Johns Hopkins University Press. By permission of the publisher.

ABOUT THE AUTHOR

Roger D. Abrahams is Professor of Folklore and Folklife at the University of Pennsylvania in Philadelphia. He holds a B.A. from Swarthmore College, an M.A. from Columbia University, and a Ph.D. from the University of Pennsylvania. He is a past president of the American Folklore Society, a former chairman of the English Department at the University of Texas, and a Phi Beta Kappa Visiting Scholar.

Professor Abrahams has done fieldwork in a range of African-American communities, from a ghetto neighborhood in Philadelphia to the Caribbean. He has also studied and written about Anglo-American folk songs and children's lore. He has contributed widely to academic folklore journals as well as to such magazines as *Smithsonian,* and his most recent books include *Singing the Master, After Africa* (with John Szwed), and *African Folktales,* the companion volume to this book.

The Pantheon Fairy Tale and Folklore Library

African Folktales by Roger D. Abrahams   0-394-72117-9

African American Folktales by Roger D. Abrahams   0-375-70539-2

American Indian Myths and Legends by Richard Erdoes
and Alfonso Ortiz   0-394-74018-1

Arab Folktales by Inea Bushnaq   0-394-75179-5

Chinese Fairy Tales and Fantasies by Moss Roberts   0-394-73994-9

The Complete Grimm's Fairy Tales by Jacob
and Wilhelm Grimm   0-394-70930-6

An Encyclopedia of Fairies by Katharine Briggs   0-394-73467-X

Favorite Folktales from Around the World by Jane Yolen   0-394-75188-4

Folktales from India by A. K. Ramanujan   0-679-74832-6

French Folktales by Henri Pourrat   0-679-74833-4

Gods and Heroes by Gustav Schwab   0-394-73402-5

Irish Folktales by Henry Glassie   0-679-77412-2

Japanese Tales by Royall Tyler   0-394-75656-8

Legends and Tales of the American West by
Richard Erdoes   0-375-70266-0

The Norse Myths by Kevin Crossley-Holland   0-394-74846-8

Northern Tales by Howard Norman   0-375-70267-9

Norwegian Folk Tales by Peter Asbjørnsen and Jørgen Moe   0-394-71054-1

The Old Wives' Fairy Tale Book by Angela Carter   0-679-74037-6

Russian Fairy Tales by Aleksandr Afanas'ev   0-394-73090-9

Swedish Folktales and Legends by Lone Thygesen Blecher
and George Blecher   0-679-75841-0

The Victorian Fairy Tale Book by Michael Patrick Hearn   0-679-73258-6